ESSAYS IN POST-KEYNESIAN INFLATION

LIST OF CONTRIBUTORS

Elizabeth E. Bailey, Civil Aeronautics Board
William J. Baumol, New York University and Princeton University
Kenneth E. Boulding, University of Colorado
Martin Bronfenbrenner, Duke University and Federal Reserve
    Bank of San Francisco
E. Ray Canterbery, Florida State University
David C. Colander, Oxford University
James H. Gapinski, Florida State University
Abba P. Lerner, Florida State University
Mancur Olson, University of Maryland
Don Patinkin, The Hebrew University of Jerusalem
Edmund S. Phelps, New York University
Leonard A. Rapping, University of Massachusetts
Charles E. Rockwood, Florida State University
Tibor Scitovsky, University of California, Santa Cruz
Irvin Sobel, Florida State University
Sidney Weintraub, University of Pennsylvania

ESSAYS IN POST–KEYNESIAN INFLATION

Edited by
James H. Gapinski
Charles E. Rockwood

Ballinger Publishing Company • **Cambridge, Massachusetts**
A Subsidiary of Harper & Row, Publishers, Inc.

 This book is printed on recycled paper.

International Standard Book Number: ISBN 0−88410−684−5

Library of Congress Catalog Card Number: 79−22879

Printed in the United States of America

Library of Congress Cataloging in Publication Data

Conference on Inflation, Florida State University, 1979.
  Essays in post-Keynesian inflation.

  Papers presented in honor of A.P. Lerner.
  Includes indexes.
   1. Inflation (Finance)−Addresses, essays, lectures.
2. Lerner, Abba Ptachya, 1903−   −Addresses, essays, lectures.
I. Gapinski, James H. II. Rockwood, Charles Edward, 1932−
III. Lerner, Abba Ptachya, 1903−   IV. Title.
HG229.C58 1979   332.4'1   79−22879
ISBN 0−88410−684−5

To

Abba P. Lerner

With the Deepest Respect and Fondest Admiration of
Your Many Significant
Achievements and Contributions

Including

The Economics of Control
The Economics of Employment
Essays in Economic Analysis
Everybody's Business
Flation
The Economics of Efficiency and Growth
(with Ben Shachar)
MAP The Market Antiinflation Plan
(with David C. Colander)

More than One Hundred Articles

and

The Marshall-Lerner Condition
Lange-Lerner Welfare Conditions
Functional Finance
The Marginal Efficiency Clarification
Distributive Efficiency
The Lerner Plan
High Full and Low Full Employment
Administered Inflation
Expectational Inflation
A Wage Increase Permit Plan
The Market Antiinflation Plan

CONTENTS

List of Figures   xi

List of Tables   xiii

Preface   xv

I.   CAUSES AND EFFECTS OF INFLATION

Chapter 1   3
Home Truths About Inflation
Tibor Scitovsky

Chapter 2   11
Inflation as a Process in Human Learning
Kenneth E. Boulding

Chapter 3   31
The Domestic and International Aspects of
Structural Inflation
Leonard A. Rapping

Chapter 4   55
On Some Microeconomic Issues in Inflation
Theory
William J. Baumol

Chapter 5   79
Inflation, Necessities and Distributive
Efficiency
E. Ray Canterbery

II.   INFLATION: AN INTERNATIONAL PROBLEM

Chapter 6   107
Inflation's International Dimensions
Martin Bronfenbrenner

Chapter 7   125
The Inflationary Experience: Some Lessons
from Israel
Don Patinkin

III.   THOUGHTS ON INFLATION CONTROL

Chapter 8   137
An Evolutionary Approach to Inflation
and Stagflation
Mancur Olson

Chapter 9   161
The Antiinflation Value of Direct Controls
Charles E. Rockwood

Chapter 10   179
Obstacles to Curtailing Inflation
Edmund S. Phelps

IV.   THE MARKET SOLUTION TO INFLATION

Chapter 11   197
Rationality, Expectations and Functional
Finance
David C. Colander

Chapter 12   217
The Market Antiinflation Plan: A Cure
for Stagflation
Abba P. Lerner

Chapter 13   231
A TIP for MAP
Sidney Weintraub

V.   POLICY INGREDIENTS

Chapter 14   251
Political and Economic Partnership in
Regulatory Reform
Elizabeth E. Bailey

VI.   TRIBUTE TO A PIONEER

Chapter 15   265
Abba Lerner on Employment and Inflation:
A Post-Keynesian Perspective
Irvin Sobel

VII.   SYNOPSIS AND SYNTHESIS

Chapter 16   289
Post-Keynesian Inflation: Causes,
Consequences, and Controls
James H. Gapinski and *Charles E. Rockwood*

Name Index   299

Subject Index   303

About the Editors   311

About the Contributors   313

LIST OF FIGURES

2-1   Components of the Gross Capacity Product, 1929-1977   15

2-2   Percentage Change in the Gross National Product Implicit Price Deflator, 1929-1977   16

2-3   Unrealized Product and Major Components of the Gross National Product Expressed as a Percentage of the Gross National Product, 1929-1977   18

2-4   National Income by Type of Income, 1929-1977   20

2-5   Corporate Profits and Net Interest as a Percentage of the National Income, 1929-1977   21

2-6   Federal Purchases of Goods and Services for National Defense, Expressed as a Percentage of the Gross National Product, and Percentage of the Civilian Labor Force Unemployed, 1929-1977   22

2-7   Money Stock M_1 and the Consumer Price Index, 1929-1977   26

2-8   Federal Government Surplus (+) or Deficit (-) and the Consumer Price Index, 1929-1977   27

2-9   Total Public Debt and the Consumer Price Index, 1929-1977   28

5-1   Lexicographical Wants in Two Space   84

5-2   Lexicographical Engel Curves in Three Space   86

5-3	Wage-Employment LOCI, An Industrial Union Labor Market	100
6-1	Balance of Payments Equilibrium	109
6-2	Aggregate Demand and Supply	111
6-3	Inflationary Expansion and the Balance of Payments (Locomotion Theory)	112
6-4	Brookings J-Curve Analysis	114
6-5	Inflation in Supplier Countries (OPEC Case)	116
6-6	Inflation in Customer Countries (Scandinavian Case)	118
6-7	Pressure on the Disinflating Country	120
6-8	Stability and Instability of the Foreign Exchange Rate	122
10-1	The Wage Game I	181
10-2	The Wage Game II	184

LIST OF TABLES

3-1   Inflation Rates for Selected Countries by
Period   33

3-2   Annual Percentage Growth in Real GNP for
Several Countries, 1960–1978   39

3-3   Percentage Growth Rates of Food, Energy
and Other Prices, 1971–1978   42

4-1   Inflation Rates, Unemployment Levels, and
Other Variable Values Corresponding to
Different Values of Government Contributions
to Excess Demand for Labour (x^*) 74

7-1   Percentage Change in the Consumer Price
Index and Real Gross Domestic Product for
Israel, 1954–1978   127

PREFACE

This volume contains a collection of new essays which evolved from a Conference on Inflation held in honor of Abba P. Lerner, March 28-30, 1979 at Florida State University.

Several forces provided the *raison d'etre* for the Conference topic. One was the high inflation of the past and forecasts of its continuation or worsening in the future combined with the unsatisfactory record of unemployment and the emergence of public demand for major policy changes. A second motivation was the appearance of federal economic experiments ranging from the adoption by the Carter Administration of wage-price guidelines to the deregulation of air transportation. A third factor was the advancing state of the theoretical literature in economics dealing with post-Keynesian inflation experiences. No longer do economists appear to be mystified by the simultaneous existence of inflation and unemployment and no longer do they profess an affection for naive solutions such as those espoused by "monetarists" and "fiscalists" of an earlier era. The thinking of economists knowledgeable about the stagflation problem has progressed much beyond this basic level, and that thinking, it was felt, needed to be more effectively collected, evaluated, and brought to the attention of a broad audience. Perhaps most importantly a gathering of leading economists to discuss selected issues on inflation seemed to be an appropriate way to publicly honor Dr. Abba Lerner on the occasion of the 75th year of his birth and the 50th year of his coming to the study of economics. A member of the Florida State University

Economics faculty, Professor Lerner has been a pioneer in the study of inflation and ranks as an internationally respected authority on the subject.

A preliminary program for the Conference was formulated by first identifying inflation topics which stood in the forefront of both scholarly research and policy relevance and which would comprise a logical sequence for exposition. After the principal themes had been decided, a list of economists well-known for their theoretical and policy work on the subject was proposed and matched to those topics.

The principal strengths of this volume are therefore its exclusive and consistent focus on inflation as the central macro-economic problem of the present age and its appeal to widely recognized authorities in the field. The papers address important aspects of the inflation problem, and do so from diverse points of view. However, while this volume should be of interest to the serious student of inflation economics, the level of writing is held to that suitable for an advanced undergraduate. Consequently, the volume could be used as a readings book for an intermediate course in macroeconomics or economic policy.

Staging the Conference and developing this collection of papers proved to be a considerable undertaking, and life during that busy period was made tolerable through the unselfish giving by many individuals. Bernard Sliger, President of Florida State University, allowed ready access to his office for Conference matters and ably officiated at the opening ceremonies. William Laird, Chairman of the Department of Economics, was most tolerant and encouraging despite the continued demands placed upon the Department's all-too-scarce resources by the Conference and the book.

Conference moderators performed admirably. Thanks are extended to Bernard Sliger, George Macesich, Warren Mazek, Joan Haworth, and Matthew Marlin. A special note of appreciation is also extended to Lieutenant Governor Wayne Mixson for addressing the Conference despite his especially crowded schedule.

The graduate students of the Department must be acknowledged for their spirited involvement in Conference matters. Too many participated to permit recognition of each separately, but—at the risk of slighting some—public praise should be accorded Maria Espino, Idelle Marshall, and John Moerlins. They persevered until the seemingly endless tasks were completed.

In the rush of activity one typically turns to secretaries for crucial help, and this rule applied perfectly to the events associated with the Conference. Gennelle Jordan, Martha Causseaux, and Nancy Grimes willingly, even eagerly, assisted with whatever needed attention and met every deadline with time to spare. Nancy Grimes deserves an extra nod for her remarkable resiliency and sense of organizational insight. She went above and beyond without complaint on numerous occasions from the moment when the first speaker was contacted to the moment when the last paper was mailed to the publisher.

Funds for the Conference were provided by the President's Office of Florida State University with supplemental support from the Economics Graduate Student Association. Valuable assistance with planning came from the Center for Professional Development and Public Services, in particular from Mary Pankowski and Robert Brown.

Hunter Barnett typed camera-ready copy for the publisher and must be complimented for her skillful effort. The Ballinger Publishing Company and especially Carol Franco must be lauded for their support of the project, and for the maintenance of a prompt production schedule.

To everyone involved with the Conference or with this volume, we extend our sincerest gratitude.

J.H.G., C.E.R.

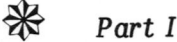 *Part I*

CAUSES AND EFFECTS OF INFLATION

✳ *Chapter 1*

HOME TRUTHS ABOUT INFLATION

*Tibor Scitovsky**

INTRODUCTION

This chapter will focus on some of those home truths about inflation that seem too obvious to mention and so are often overlooked and forgotten. Most of them have to do with the motivation of management and labor in setting prices and negotiating wages [1].

I believe we owe to Abba Lerner the important distinction between demand-pull and cost-push inflation. We know today that if we wanted to classify according to what gives the initial impetus, we would have many more types of inflation, distinguishing for example between nonwage cost-push and wage cost-push. But the crucial thing is the interaction between price and wage increases, the mechanism that keeps the inflation going. It is pretty obvious how that mechanism functions in a time of full employment; the still unsettled question is whether there is such a mechanism also in an underemployed economy. The now ruling orthodoxy holds that there is not. If that were true, then we would have to accept our present five to six percent unemployment as the definition of full employment in our society, or, to use the now fashionable expression, as the natural rate of unemployment. That also would mean that there is no such thing as cost-push inflation, at least not as far as the wage-price spiral mechanism is concerned.

---

*Professor of Economics, University of California at Santa Cruz.

DEMAND–PULL INFLATION

I propose to take the opposite view and to present a simple-
minded model of the interaction of prices and wages, which has
very little to do with the level of employment. To begin with,
however, I should also like to say a few words about demand-pull
inflation, first about the kind where the increase in demand
presses against and is frustrated by the limits to supply set by
the full employment of labor. That is the simplest case, because
the same limited supply of labor that accounts for the rise in
wages also explains the rise in the prices of products. Firms'
marginal costs will rise as a result of the rise in wages; but they
are likely to rise by more if the tightness of the labor market
causes firms to employ less efficient labor or to resort more to
the use of overtime. In other words, not only will marginal cost
curves shift upward; but as demand curves shift to the right,
they cause firms to operate on a higher part of their cost curves.
That would explain a greater rise of prices than of wages and a
consequent shift to profit in the distribution of income. To keep
prices and wages rising, aggregate demand must continue to
exceed total potential supply and therefore also total income. A
sustained excess of spending over income, however, is unlikely to
be maintained without a sustained Governmental budget deficit.
Concerning demand-pull inflation of that kind therefore, I would
agree with the monetarists that increasing the money supply is
essential-although I would add that it has to be done by outside
money creation linked with a budget deficit.

For completeness' sake, let me also mention the other kind of
demand-pull, where the increase in demand presses against limits
imposed on supply by the limited capacity of manufacturing
equipment, and which is hardly inflationary. Marginal cost
curves rise and approach the vertical also in this case, so that
the expansion of demand provides an inducement to raise prices;
but lacking in this case is the upward pressure on wages. While
the marginal worth of products rises with the rise in prices, the
marginal physical product of labor falls, which means that the
marginal revenue product of labor may fall as well as rise on
balance and probably will not change very much either way.
Besides, when, as in this case, capacity limitations are binding,
the firm can hardly employ and bid for more labor. The big
change in this case is the rise in the marginal efficiency of
capital and the encouragement of investment; and that is the
process whereby market forces ensure that manufacturing capa-

city is expanded to keep step with rising demand and the expansion of the labor force. Organized labor may demand wage increases in response to the fall in real wages; but such demands are likely to be granted with a lag, as additional capacity gets readied and adds to job opportunities and the demand for labor. In short, demand-pull against capacity constraints is probably characteristic of those periods of high investment, fast growth, great prosperity, and moderate inflation, which so many countries experienced in the early part of the post war period.

COST-PUSH INFLATION

Let me now come to my main topic: cost-push inflation. All forms and types of inflation are due to some kind of incompatibility: demand-pull inflation to the excess of aggregate demand over the maximum available supply, cost-push inflation to the excess of the sum of income claims over the total income generated. The important and interesting thing about this latter kind of excess is that it can exist independently of what the degree of utilization of the labor force and productive capacity happens to be. After all, income shares can be incompatible whatever their recipients choose to do with their incomes. That is why cost-push inflation can proceed under conditions of depression and unemployment. The only question is how, why, and under what conditions such incompatibility arises.

Factor and Product Market Relationships

The function of markets is not only to transmit information and facilitate the division of labor but also to distribute income; that is, claims to the output produced among the owners of the factors of production. If income distribution were the function exclusively of factor markets, it would be impossible for the income shares to add up to more than 100 percent of the income generated, because the entrepreneur is party to all factor-market transactions and his share in income is the residue, which remains after he has paid income to all the other claimants. The sum, therefore, of the income shares he distributes and retains is bound to be exactly equal to the total income generated.

The possibility that the income shares agreed to in market transactions should add up to more than the total income generated arises only when economies of scale lead to a disparity between the number of buyers and sellers in product markets and that gives producers the power to set the prices of their products.   Their conscious influence over prices splits the distributive function between factor and product markets and so opens up the possibility of incompatible income shares.

If producers set product prices by adding a percentage profit mark-up to marginal costs, which is determined by well-established tradition or stable price elasticities of demand, then their gross profit becomes an irreducible proportion of the Gross National Product.   What is more relevant, of course, is the proportion of net profits to the net product; and that depends not only on the proportion of gross profits to gross product but also on costs and restraints on entry and on the level of capacity utilization, which determines the economies of scale.   When restraints on entry give rise to monopoly and oligopoly profits, the distributive function of product markets is obvious, and so is its coming into conflict with the distributive function of labor markets [2].   Let me now focus on the more general case, leaving it open whether entry is free or restricted; and it will be the simplest to discuss it with the aid of a couple of examples.

To begin with, imagine an economy with only two variable factors of production: labor and an imported input I shall call oil. Assume that initially all firms are in equilibrium in both product and factor markets: they equate marginal costs of production with marginal revenues from sales in product markets and the marginal costs of factors to their marginal revenue products in factor markets.   Then, equilibrium is disrupted by a rise in the price of oil, which shifts the terms of trade against the country, thereby reducing its real income.   The question is how will the economy absorb the shock and distribute the loss in real income between wages and profits.

The rise in the price of oil causes its marginal cost to exceed its marginal revenue product and also causes marginal costs of production to exceed marginal revenues in product markets.   The first reaction of firms will be to restore equilibrium in product markets by raising prices sufficiently to reestablish the equalities between marginal costs and marginal revenues.   The next step, in economies where most of the labor force is unionized, would be equally simple and obvious.   Noting that the rise in product prices lowers real wages, unions would demand and obtain wage increases calculated to restore real wages; and since that would further raise marginal costs, it would start a never-ending wage-price spiral. I said never-ending, because labor's ability to negotiate the maintenance of preexisting real wages and management's ability to maintain undiminished profit mar-

gins create incompatible claims to income in the present case
where total real income is diminished by the worsening of the
terms of trade. Yet, the incompatibility of those claims remains
unnoticed, because they are claimed in different markets.

That argument, however, does not really apply to the United
States, where less than a quarter of the labor force is unionized,
union power is on the decline, and the great majority of firms set
wages unilaterally in a bureaucratic way. Let us look, therefore,
to the theory of production for hints on what is likely to happen.
When firms raise product prices in response to the higher cost of
oil and so equate marginal revenues to the now higher marginal
costs of production, they also diminish but do not eliminate the
excess of the marginal cost of oil over its marginal revenue
product; and they create an excess of the marginal revenue
product of labor over its marginal cost. Those discrepancies in
the two factor markets are opposite in sign and mutually
offsetting, which is what renders disequilibrium in the factor
markets compatible with equilibrium in product markets.

At that state, firms become conscious of the fact that while
oil is too expensive, labor is too cheap—cheaper than its marginal worth. To restore factor-market equilibrium therefore, labor
would have to be substituted for oil until the marginal revenue
product of each became equal to its marginal cost. In practice,
however, the scope for such substitution is largely limited to
investment in new capacity. In established plants, the elasticity
of substitution tends to be close to zero.

That raises the question, what will established firms with
established plants do in such circumstances? When the marginal
revenue product of labor exceeds its cost, that could be an
inducement to employ more labor but hardly to take the initiative in paying higher wages, although it may be an inducement to
respond easily and promptly to outside circumstances that call
for a rise in wages. There are plenty of such circumstances. To
begin with, workers themselves will note that the prices of both
products and cooperating factors have risen; consequently they
will become as aware as management of the fact that labor has
become a cheap, underpriced factor of production. Moreover,
when product prices are raised in *proportion* with the rise in
costs and not just by the *amount* by which costs have risen;
income is redistributed in favor of profits and against wages.
After all, labor's real income falls when product prices rise and
money wages remain unchanged; whereas profits rise in proportion with product prices, which keeps real profits unchanged.

Accordingly, workers are bound to become aware also of the redistribution of income in favor of profits. Other circumstances are the willingness of new plants and firms to employ more labor and pay higher wages, and the rise in wages elsewhere, where they are governed by escalator clauses in wage contracts and by union demands for wage increases. In short, both sides of the labor market become aware of the fact that labor is underpriced, in quite a variety of meanings of that term.

Under those conditions, labor needs no overwhelming bargaining strength to obtain a raise, and management is quite likely to take the initiative in proposing one, accepting a short-run reduction in profits for the sake of reducing quit rates and raising morale. Every wage increase will, of course, raise costs and so call for a further price increase; and full equilibrium will only be restored when wages and product prices have risen in proportion with the initial rise in the prices of imported inputs that started the whole process.

That result is pretty obvious. If initially marginal costs equaled marginal revenues in all product and factor markets, and all production coefficients are fixed, allowing no factor substitution anywhere, then an initial rise in one factor price must be matched by proportionate rises in all other prices to re-establish all-around equilibrium. That is an extreme limiting case, of course, since some substitution is usually possible; but it illustrates the principle. One must further bear in mind that what substitution is possible will put additional pressure on management to raise wages in response to the rise in other prices and costs.

Wage Drift

As a second and very similar example, I would like to remind you of the Scandinavian theory of wage drift [3]. In Scandinavia, with 80 percent of the labor force organized into centrally controlled strong unions, with the tradition of all wage contracts' expiring and being renewed at the same time, there has sprung up a deliberate policy of wage equalization at the occasion of the annual contract renewals. Thereafter during the rest of the year, there is wage drift: the unofficial raising of skilled workers' wages here and there, which largely restores the wage differentials the annual wage contracts eliminate.

That, presumably, is the same process illustrated also by the previous example. The annual wage contracts raise unskilled wages the most; and as product prices respond, skilled workers become the cheap factor, their marginal worth exceeding their marginal cost, which leads to the rise in their wages, union policy to the contrary.

CONCLUSION

All I have done was to spell out in detail how market forces might be expected to operate in an economy where producers have the initiative and play the active role of price maker in both product and labor markets. I asserted at the beginning that the producers' role as price maker is crucial for the inflationary nature of the adjustment process; and I hope that that has become clearer in the course of the argument.

The producers' initiative and control over prices in product markets renders the process of adjustment more indirect, more roundabout, and for that reason also easier. Because they can, or think they can, escape part of the loss of profit they would suffer from a rise in factor prices by shifting it over onto their customers' shoulders, producers do not make a very strong stand against rising prices or demands for higher prices in factor markets. They believe they can be fairly passive, generous, conciliatory. That attitude imparts an inflationary bias to the economy whenever those on the other side of factor markets have the strength and the skill to exploit such attitude. Whether, and under what circumstances, the successful exploitation of that attitude also secures a real economic gain to those exploiting it is an altogether different question, with which we do not have to be concerned here.

NOTES

1. This chapter might be viewed as a supplement to two articles which I recently published on inflation: "Market Power and Inflation," *Economica* 45 (1978): 221-33 and "Asymmetries in Economics," *Scottish Journal of Political Economy*, 25 (1978): 227-37.

2. I dealt with this case in my recently published article "Asymmetries."

3. O. Aukrust, "Inflation in the Open Economy: A Norwegian Model," in *Worldwide Inflation*, eds. L.B. Krause and W.S. Salant (Washington, D.C.: The Brookings Institution, 1977).

Chapter 2

INFLATION AS A PROCESS IN HUMAN LEARNING

Kenneth E. Boulding *

A LESSON UNLEARNED FROM EXPERIENCE

Inflation is a common phenomenon in human history. Almost from the very invention of coinage, there have been "depreciations of the currency." On many occasions monarchs called in an old coinage and replaced it by one with more coins of the same name but with less precious metal in them. With the development of paper money the opportunity for inflation became much larger, and with the development of bank deposit money the opportunities became still larger. Even in the eighteenth century there was John Law in France and the "Continentals" ("not worth a Continental") in the United States. In the twentieth century we have had a number of spectacular hyperinflations like Germany in 1923 or Hungary in 1946. We are having an increasing number of what might be called "persistent inflations" which do not reach the hyperinflation stage but which seem almost impossible to stop, like Brazil for the last 150 years and almost everybody since 1945.

Deflations are less common but they are by no means rare. The drain of specie to India from the Roman Empire and in the early medieval period seems to be an example. In more modern times we had the long deflations and depressions after 1815 and after 1865 and, of course, what may well have been the great

---

*Distinguished Professor of Economics, University of Colorado.

deflation of all times—the Great Depression and deflation from 1929 to 1933.

The human race seems to have learned deplorably little from all this experience of the centuries. One would think after all these ups and downs that governments would have learned how to stabilize within reasonable limits both the price-wage level and the level of employment. Yet they clearly are not doing this today. It looks as if we have learned nothing from the past and as if both inflation and deflation continually take us by surprise. If our skills in handling these problems increase at all, they increase painfully slowly and almost imperceptibly. This is a curious contrast to our skills in many other areas of life, in such things, for instance, as navigation, in increasing the expectation of life, in innumerable processes of agriculture and manufacture, and so on. A very important question, therefore, is why does a learning process take place in some areas and not in others. In the management of conflict, for instance, skills again only improve, if they do at all, at the pace of a snail. It seems remarkably difficult to improve skills in the management of complex social systems.

THE NEED FOR "MAPS"

It is possible that the key to this failure is the absence of adequate "maps" showing the topological relationships, especially through time, of the processes that we are trying to manage. If social learning is to transcend individual experience so that knowledge and skill can cumulate from one generation to the next and become part of the continuous heritage of the human race, then there must be something like maps that can be transmitted from one generation to the next and can summarize the experience of large numbers of people in the past. Geographical maps and charts are a good case in point. Until the development of charts and maps and navigational aids, which enabled the navigator to pinpoint his position on these charts, it was very hard for one generation of seafarers or even landfarers to learn from the experiences of their forebearers. People went on becoming lost and wrecked generation after generation, with these experiences being transmitted only in very vague and unsatisfactory ways from those who handed them to the next generations that needed them. Travelers' tales are a very poor substitute for maps, and even sketch maps are a very poor substitute for accurate surveys. Yet in economic and social life travelers' tales are often all that we have, and the record of the past does not become embodied in the forms that can be transmitted to the present generation.

The development of moderately accurate time series of social and economic data, especially the collection and publication of national income statistics (from 1929 in the United States), has opened up a great possibility of improvement in this regard, which has not, however, up to the present been utilized to any large degree. Part of the reason perhaps is that we have been obsessed by numbers themselves without realizing that numbers are primarily significant insofar as they can be mapped into topological patterns that can be perceived as such by the human mind. We could express all the information contained in a map of the world by a vast pile of numerical computer printouts of latitudes and longitudes. This would convey very little to us. It is only as the numbers are actually mapped into maps themselves that they become meaningful. In what follows I have tried to map certain time structures over the last forty-nine years or so that seem relevant to the perception of the true nature of the problems we are considering. If these can become as much a part of the mental apparatus of our decisionmakers as the road maps which they use to find their way about the country, one suspects that the learning process will be enormously improved. The time maps that follow refer only to the United States, mainly because of the availability of data [1]. The United States is a large society for which foreign trade is only a relatively small proportion of the total economic activity. It has a government which is concerned with these matters, and so it seems an appropriate unit in which to examine the general problem.

MAPS FOR THE UNITED STATES

Overall Measures

We begin, then, with Figure 2-1. It shows some overall measures of the aggregate product of the economy from 1929 on. Line 1 shows what I have called the "gross capacity product," which is roughly what the gross national product at current dollars would have been if those statistically measured as unemployed had been producing at the average level of productivity. This is not an ideal measure of the concept of capacity, but it has the convenience of being very easy to calculate, and other measures do not give very different results. Line 2 is the gross national product in the current dollars of each year. The difference between 1 and 2 is the unrealized product; that is, the product that would have been produced if the unemployed had been producing at the average level.

Line 3 is the gross national product in 1929 dollars. This estimate may be subject to quite serious errors as a result of a change in the commodity mix. It is impossible to say, for instance, what was the price of a color TV set in 1929, as the commodity did not exist, but the price deflator is presumably the best that government statisticians can do. The vertical distance between Line 3 and Line 2 measures the cumulative amount of inflation, as reflected in the GNP deflator. As we see, we have lived in an age of inflation at least since 1940. The scale of the diagram does not show clearly what happened before 1940; that is shown in other diagrams. The last forty years have clearly been an age of inflation. In that period, indeed, in only one year has the price deflator declined.

Line 4 shows the per capita real GNP. The difference between Lines 4 and 3 represents population increase. Line 5 is per capita disposable income. The difference between Line 5 and Line 4 represents what might be called "non-personal pro-duct," measured essentially by government purchases, as government product is unmeasurable. The increase in real per capita economic "riches" lies somewhere between Lines 5 and 4, depending on how much government product we want to allocate to private satisfaction.

Decades of Disturbance and Stability

Figure 2-2 shows the rate of inflation in more detail. This is the percentage change in the implicit price deflator from one year to the next. We see how deflation reached 10 percent per annum in the Great Depression and how inflation reached a level which has rarely been exceeded since in 1934, when unemployment was still 20 percent. This episode has not received the analysis that it deserves. It has something to do with the NRA and the initial impact of the New Deal. It also represents some inflation in the speculative commodity markets. It certainly shows that the inflation-unemployment dilemma is not just a phenomenon of the 1960s and the 1970s. The suppressed inflation during World War II in 1944 and 1945 is noticeable, as is the explosion of 1946, when controls were removed. There was the Korean war inflation of 1951, which oddly enough anticipated the Korean war. This, again, is an episode that needs careful

Figure 2-1.   Components of the Gross Capacity Product, 1929-1977.

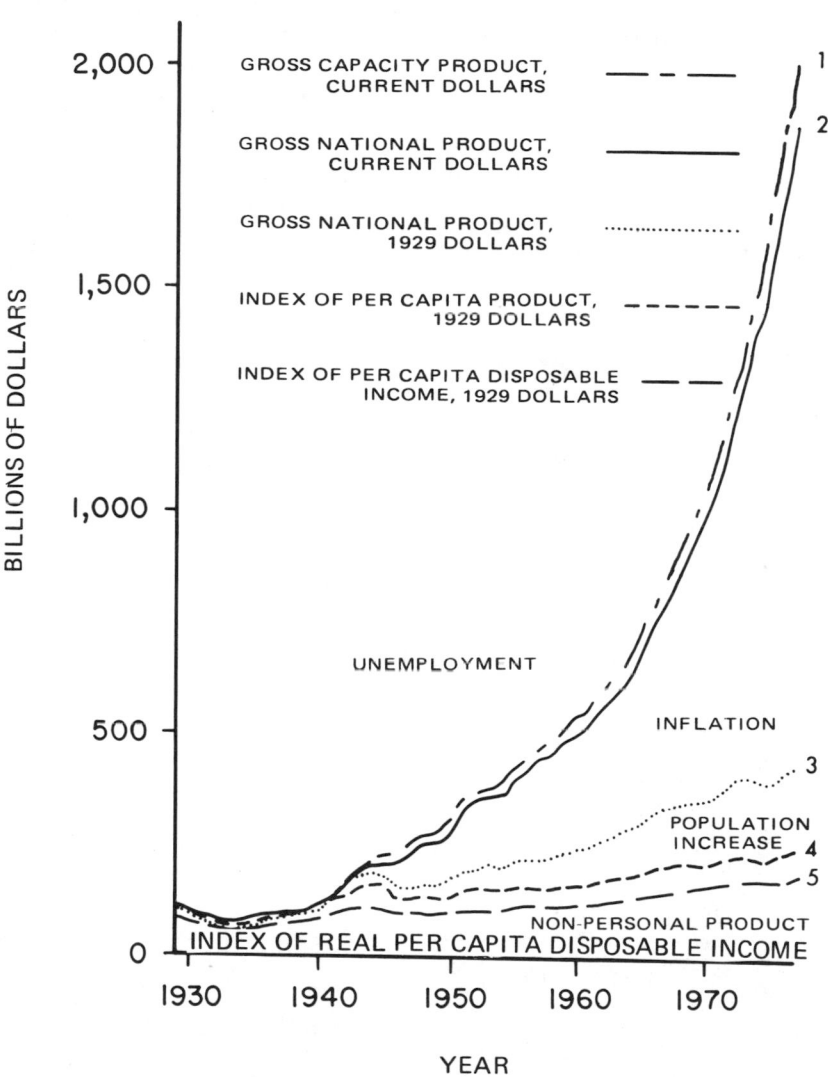

study.   We see steady but low rates of inflation from 1952 through the early 1960s, with accelerating inflation from about 1965 on.   This is very disconcerting.   It is clear, however, that there is a great difference between the period from 1929 to about 1950 or 1952 and the period after this.   The first was characterized by very violent year-to-year fluctuations and was a period of great overall instability.   The second period was one of relative stability, with a modest rate of inflation, even though there are alarming symptoms of accelerating inflation in the 1970s.

Figure 2-2.   Percentage Change in the Gross National Product Implicit Price Deflator, 1929-1977.

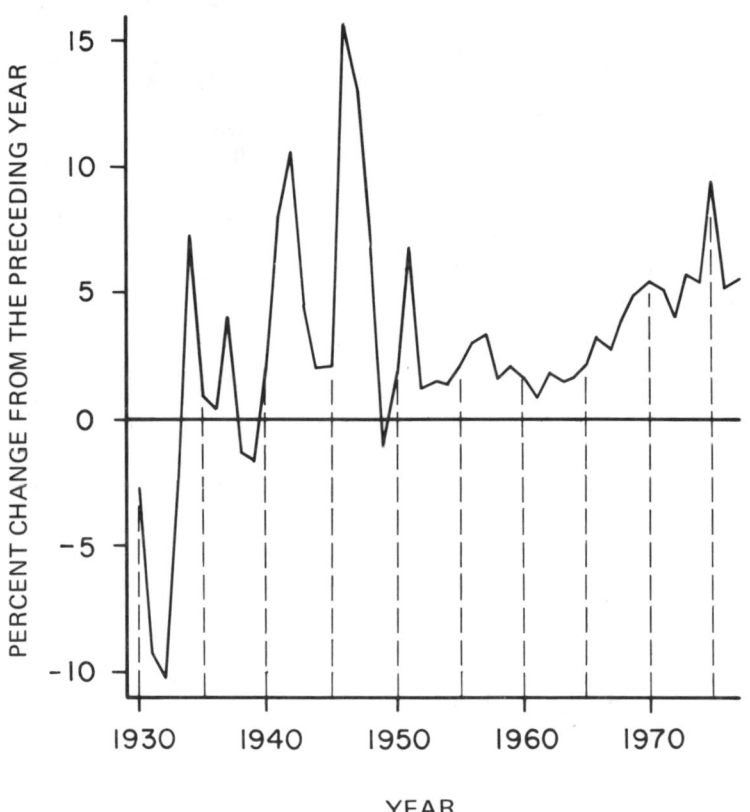

YEAR

The division of the period into the decades of disturbance and the decades of stability is shown even more strikingly in Figure 2-3.   It shows the components of the gross capacity product

expressed as a division of 100 percent gross capacity product
into its various parts. This is what I have called a "layer cake"
diagram, which shows how the relative structure of the economy
changes as time goes on. The vertical distance between the 100
percent line and Line 1 is the unrealized product, measured by
the proportion of the labor force unemployed. The distance
between Line 1 and Line 2 is net exports. Between Lines 2 and 3
is gross private domestic investment; that is, the dollar value of
the additions to capital structure of businesses. The distance
between Line 3 and Line 6 is total government purchases, divided
into national defense (between 3 and 4), federal civilian
purchases (between 4 and 5) and state and local purchases
(between 5 and 6). The extraordinary stability of this total after
1953 is very striking. We find a decline in defense being almost
exactly offset by the increase in state and local purchases, the
federal civilian purchases being rather stable and fairly small.
The distance between Line 6 and the bottom axis is personal
consumption expenditures, which, again, are extraordinarily stable as a proportion of the total (about 60 percent since 1950).

We see the decades of disturbance expressed first of all in
the Great Depression, with unemployment going to 25 percent of
the labor force. Gross private domestic investment almost
disappeared in 1932 and 1933 and then made a halting recovery,
interrupted by the depression of 1938. Then after 1940 we see
the enormous expansion of national defense, which reached 42
percent of the gross capacity product in World War II virtually
eliminating unemployment. It also severely squeezed personal
consumption, state and local government, and gross private
domestic investment. The little bump of the Korean war is seen
in the early 1950s and the hardly noticeable bump of Vietnam in
the late 1960s, which economically was a much smaller operation, being largely offset by the decline in other defense
expenditures. The little business cycle in the 1950s and 1960s in
unemployment was almost wholly the result of fluctuations in
gross private domestic investment, especially in inventories;
personal plus government consumption or purchases are remarkably stable. The crucial role of gross private domestic investment
in unemployment is seen very clearly.

Figure 2-4 shows another layer cake diagram, this time
showing the distribution of national income by type of income.
It would be more satisfactory if we had this distribution by, say,
net national product, but this is not available. National income
is a very odd statistic. It is roughly equal to gross national

Figure 2-3.   Unrealized Product and Major Components of the
Gross National Product Expressed as a Percentage
of the Gross National Product, 1929-1977.

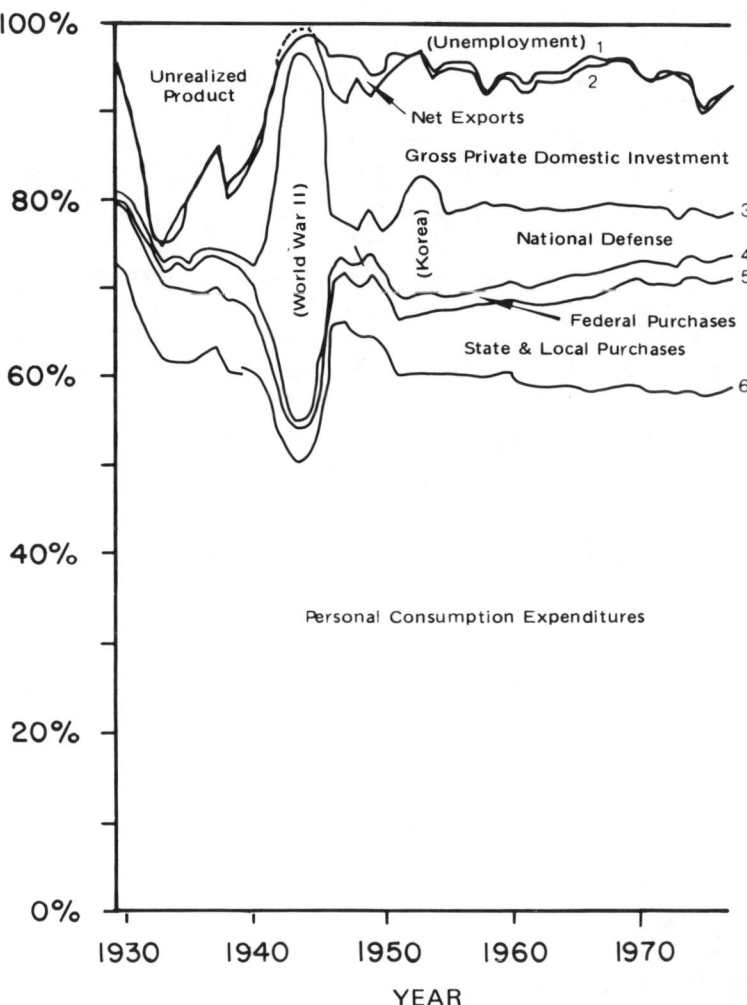

product minus capital consumption allowance for depreciation of fixed capital and minus direct taxes.   Unfortunately, it is a rather meaningless aggregate, but we started with it in 1929 and seem to be stuck with it.   The distribution in Figure 2-4, however, is probably not greatly different from that of net national product.   Here again, the layers of the cake consist of corporate profits between the 100 percent line and Line 1, net interest between Line 1 and Line 2, rent and royalties between Line 2 and Line 3, non-farm proprietors' income between Line 3 and Line 4, farm proprietors' income between Line 4 and Line 5, and compensation to employees between Line 5 and the bottom axis.

The enormous disturbance of the Great Depression is highly visible.   Corporate profits were negative in 1932 and 1933, the proportion of national income going to employees rose sharply in the Great Depression in spite of unemployment because the real wages of the employed rose sharply.   Money wages fell much more slowly than consumer prices in almost the whole industrial sector.   Over the long haul, we see a reasonably steady rise in compensation to employees and a corresponding shrinking in farm income, with the great decline in agriculture, and also in non-farm proprietors' income, with the increase in the corporate structure of the economy.   Farm proprietors' and non-farm proprietors' incomes include a fair amount of labor income, though one suspects that the rise in the compensation to employees is more a reflection of the increase in corporate employment rather than of a change in the proportion of national income going to labor, which would probably lie somewhere between Line 3 and Line 4.   Rent and royalties represent a very miscellaneous item of not very much interest.   It also declined, probably again as a result of an increase in incorporation in real estate.

The difference between profits and net interest is of great importance, as shown dramatically in Figure 2-5.   We see here the near doubling of the burden of net interest in the Great Depression from 1929 to 1932.   With deflation reducing the price level by almost half, with interest payments continuing, and with long-term interest at the level of 1929, this burden became almost intolerable.   Coupled with this we see profits becoming negative in 1932 and 1933.   Then we see net interest very low from the mid-1940s to 1960, for nominal rates of interest had not caught up with even the modest inflation of that period.   Then from about 1965 on we see a roughly steady decline in profits and a rise in interest.

Figure 2-4.   National Income by Type of Income, 1929-1977.

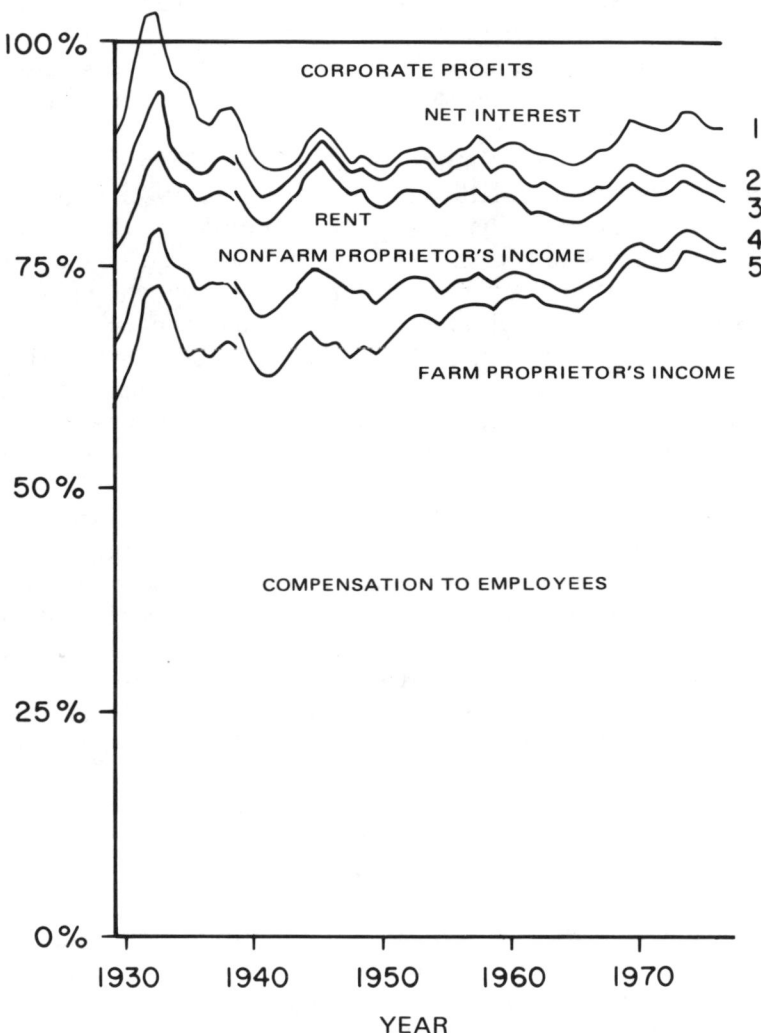

Figure 2-5.   Corporate Profits and Net Interest as a Percentage
of the National Income, 1929-1977.

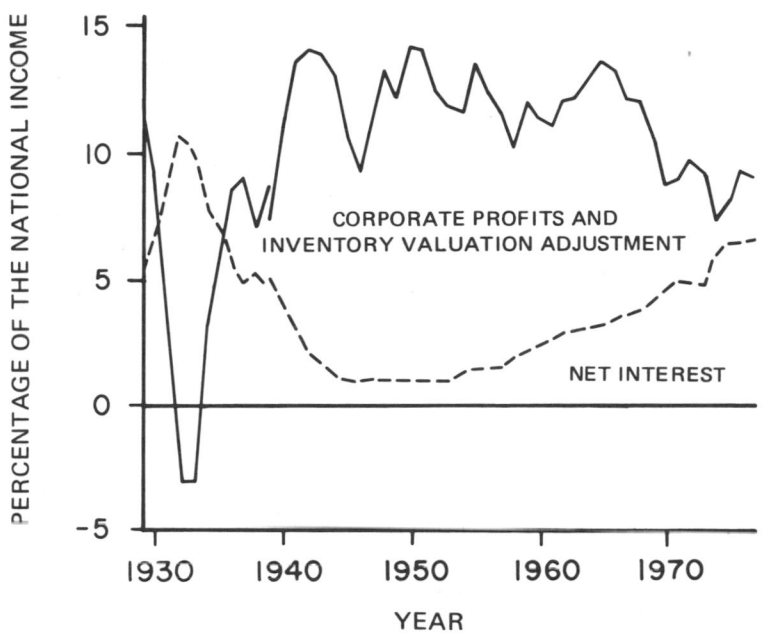

Figure 2-6 again separates out two items of Figure 2-3: unemployment and national defense expenditures. The dramatic and catastrophic nature of the Great Depression is very clearly shown between 1929 and 1940 as are the little business cycles of the 1950s and early 1960s and the alarmingly rising unemployment of the 1970s. This figure at least dispells one illusion—that the only thing that saves us from unemployment is military expenditures. Even in the 1930s unemployment began to fall long before the advent of World War II, although it is certainly true that that war coincided with the lowest level of unemployment on record. The Korean war also produced a decline in unemployment, but we see the period from about 1958 through 1965, before the Vietnam war, when the proportion of the GNP devoted to the military declined fairly sharply and unemployment declined along with it. It is clear that only the substantial military expenditure of a major war has any large effect on unemployment.

Figure 2-6.   Federal Purchases of Goods and Services for
National Defense, Expressed as a Percentage of
the Gross National Product, and Percentage of
the Civilian Labor Force Unemployed, 1929-1977.

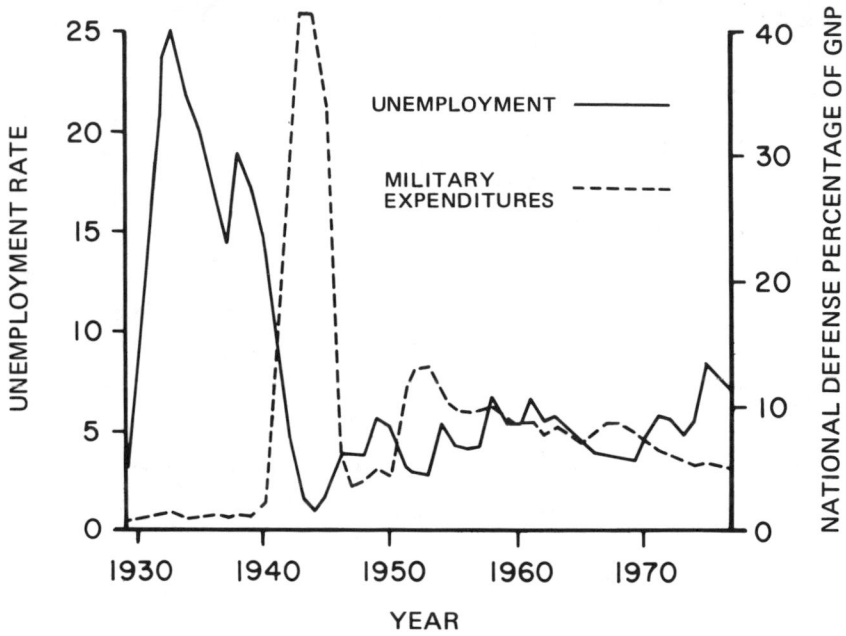

AN OLD-FASHIONED THEORY

At this point it is perhaps time to stop and ask what the time
maps have to tell us and to introduce a little rather old-
fashioned theory.   We see that unemployment is related very
closely to two things: gross private domestic investment on the
one hand and the gap between profits and interest on the other.
Several considerations indicate that this relationship is no accident.   A wage earner is employed when there is an exchange
between the wage earner and an employer, who may be a single
person or a person acting on behalf of an organization, such as a
corporation, a nonprofit organization, or a government.   In this
exchange the employer pays out money in the form of wages in
return for some fairly well-specified activity on the part of the
wage earner.   The activity of the wage earner produces some

oort of change in assets of the employer. In the case of a profit-making organization, this change in the value of assets constitutes the profit resulting from employing the wage earner. With the money that is paid to the wage earner, the employer could have bought an interest-bearing security of some kind, so in the case of a profit-making organization the act of employing a wage earner involves the sacrifice of potential interest for the hope of profit.   In the case of a nonprofit organization or a government, the wage still diminishes the liquid assets of the organization, and presumably the work of the wage earner does something for it.   In this case the liquid assets may be replaced by a grant or a one-way transfer either charitable or through taxes and does not have to be realized through the sale of a product.

In the United States between 60 and 70 percent of the labor force is hired by profit-making organizations, and it is a deficiency in these transactions which is the main source of unemployment. Because of the risks and uncertainties involved in a profit-making operation, it is reasonable to suppose that a wage earner will not be hired unless the profit on the transaction is somewhat greater than the interest that would otherwise be earned by buying interest-bearing securities with the wage. Liquid assets (cash), we can suppose, bear a virtual rate of interest in the form of convenience, measured by the interest foregone. In 1932 and 1933 it is clear that any profit-maker who hired anybody was in retrospect either a philanthropist or a fool, for he was bound to lose on the transaction. It is extraordinary indeed that unemployment did not go far beyond 25 percent under these circumstances. The only reason why it did not was just habit and the hope of holding an organization together in anticipation of better times to come. If the conditions of 1932 and 1933 had continued for another two or three years, employment in the private sector might well have collapsed altogether.

In this respect, the erosion of profit by interest, which has been apparent since the middle 1960s, is very ominous. If we couple this with the fact that the risks of giving employment have almost certainly increased sharply in the 1970s as a result of government regulation, it almost looks as if the level of unemployment that we have is even now partly the result of habit, and it is not surprising that we are running into an unemployment-inflation dilemma, often referred to, a little fallaciously, as the "Phillips curve dilemma."

Inflation may be expected to reduce unemployment simply

because it reduces the real rate of interest. If I lend you $100 today and you pay me back $110 at this time next year because interest is 10 percent per annum and if in the interim we have a 7 percent inflation, then your $110 next year is only worth $103 of this year (roughly). Consequently, the real rate of interest is only 3 percent. If inflation is pushing up the price of products, then rates of profit should actually rise as we earn profit on something at one time and sell it later at a higher price, or a price above its cost. If in the interval all prices have risen, then the probability of profit is higher. Inflation, therefore, makes real profit rates higher and real interest rates lower than they otherwise would have been. It is a little hard to estimate by how much, however, especially in the case of profit.

INFLATION: A POLICY OF GOVERNMENT

We would not be surprised, therefore, to find that inflation is a fairly deliberate policy on the part of a government which fears a further rise in unemployment. There are three closely related mechanisms involved here. The first is the overall surplus, or deficit, of government, strictly at all levels. The second is the extent to which this surplus or deficit is divided directly between an increase or a decrease in the money supply or in the issuance or repayment of government securities. The third is that the total money supply is related not only to monetized government deficits but also to Federal Reserve policy and the behavior of the banking system.

The following time maps show something of what has been happening. Figure 2-7 indicates the relation between the money supply M_1, which is the most liquid part of liquid assets, and the consumer price index. The relation, as might be expected, is very direct. It is a little surprising that from the mid-1960s forward the consumer price index lags behind the money supply, suggesting that there may actually have been a fall in the velocity of circulation. This possibility seems very surprising in light of the rising credit card economy, which certainly econo-mizes money in the wallet, and in light of the inflation itself, which normally would be expected to diminish the demand for cash balances (on which, after all, there then arises a negative rate of interest). We would expect these factors to increase the velocity of circulation.

The relation between the consumer price index and the federal surplus or deficit is shown in Figure 2-8. The delayed effect of the deficit of World War II is shown clearly. So is the fact that the federal surplus or deficit was virtually zero on the average between 1947 and 1970, which is a little astonishing, and thus the relatively mild inflation of that period cannot be attributed to it. It must be attributed, as we see in Figure 2-7, to the rise in the money supply, mainly as a result of Federal Reserve and banking policy. From 1970 on, however, we witness a most alarming escalation in the federal deficit, to a point even beyond the World War II level in current dollars, and this factor is undoubtedly responsible for the acceleration in inflation that we see after 1970. This deficit is not due to military expenditure. Indeed military expenditure as a proportion of the economy was actually declining in this period. Instead, it is almost wholly due to social welfare expenditures not financed by any increase in taxation. One rather surprising aspect of the 1970s is that the federal deficit created a quite substantial state and local surplus. We see this by the dotted line in Figure 2-8. This surplus to some extent offset the federal deficit, but it evidently produced the "tax revolt" symbolized by Proposition 13 in California. This, of course, may not last. The cumulative effect of government deficit is seen in Figure 2-9, which shows the public debt against the consumer price index. Here again, the relation is very striking and certainly suggests that there is a very strong tendency for a public debt either to be monetized or to be regarded as liquid assets.

"COST PUSH" OR "DEMAND PULL"?

What these time maps do not resolve is the old controversy about whether inflation is "cost-push" or "demand-pull." Certainly, without the demand-pull provided by the increase in the money supply and the government deficits, the inflation would not have taken place short of a very improbable rise in the velocity of circulation. However, whether this increase in money supply, and therefore money demand, is a reaction to previous increases in money-wages and money-prices is something which cannot be assessed from mere statistical data. Needed is a much more detailed investigation of the actual decisions which resulted in the public deficits, especially by Congress, which has the fundamental control of the public purse strings. But how far these decisions are a result of factors quite extraneous to the inflation, like tax resistance or demands for more public expenditure, and how far they are a response to a rise either in the wage-price level or in unemployment, only a very detailed analysis could reveal.

Figure 2-7.   Money Stock M_1 and the Consumer Price Index, 1929-1977.

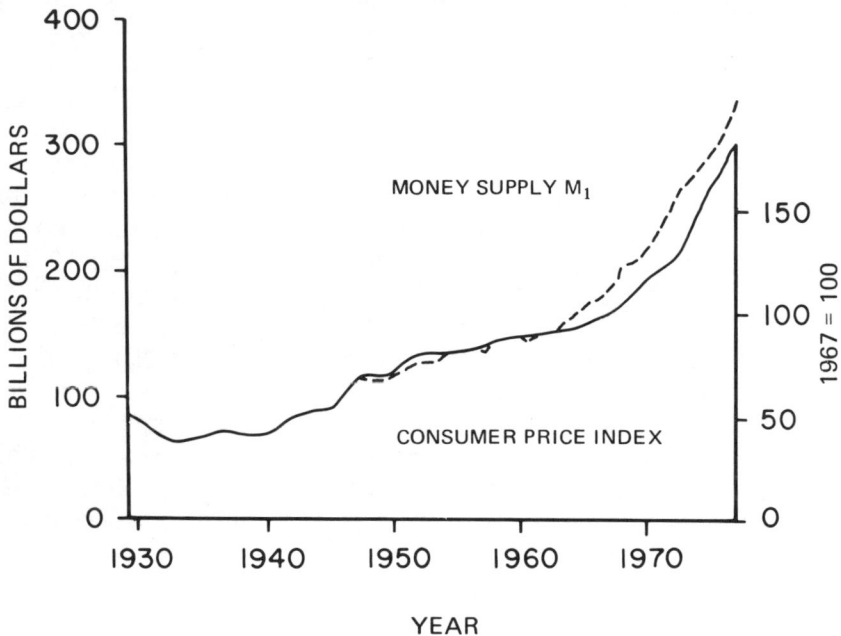

Even here, we would not be out of the woods, because a rise in money-prices or money-wages is always a result of somebody's decision or a collection of decisions, either in collective bargaining or even in competitive markets. These decisions in turn may be influenced by the anticipation of future increases in the government deficit or the money supply in response to the decision to raise money prices or wages. Even if congressional decisions to increase the public deficit and Federal Reserve decisions to increase the money supply were independent of previous inflationary pressures, the anticipation of them might still create a rise in money prices and money wages. This is a chicken-and-egg problem that is extraordinarily hard to solve. We certainly cannot assume that schemes devised merely to restrain the rise of money-prices and money-wages would necessarily hold back inflation if Congress were in a deficit-spending

mood for other reasons. Here the time maps fail us, and we need
a level of analysis that is much more detailed and "micro" than
anything we have achieved up to date.

Figure 2-8.   Federal Government Surplus (+) or Deficit (−) and
the Consumer Price Index, 1929-1977.

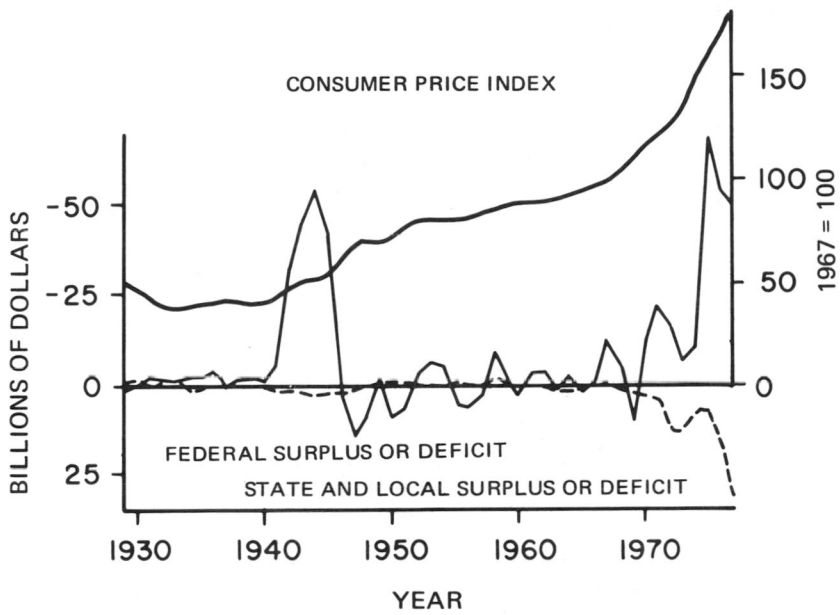

PROSPECTS FOR INFLATION CONTROL

In all this analysis, it is hard to avoid a rather pessimistic
conclusion that the prospects for control of inflation are not
very good. The real heart of the matter is our very understand-
able unwillingness to interfere with financial contracts. Nevertheless, the phenomenon that makes inflation almost inevitable
is the fact that interest rates have now adjusted to it, and thus
nominal interest rates are now running on the order of 12
percent on long-term contracts and mortgages. Even quite
short-term rates are running 8 or 9 percent, which with the rate
of inflation somewhere between 7 and 9 percent makes real rates
of interest vary from close to zero on short-term bonds (negative, of course, on savings deposits) to not much more than 3 or 4
percent on long-term contracts and mortgages, which is about
what the society can bear.

Figure 2-9.   Total Public Debt and the Consumer Price Index, 1929-1977.

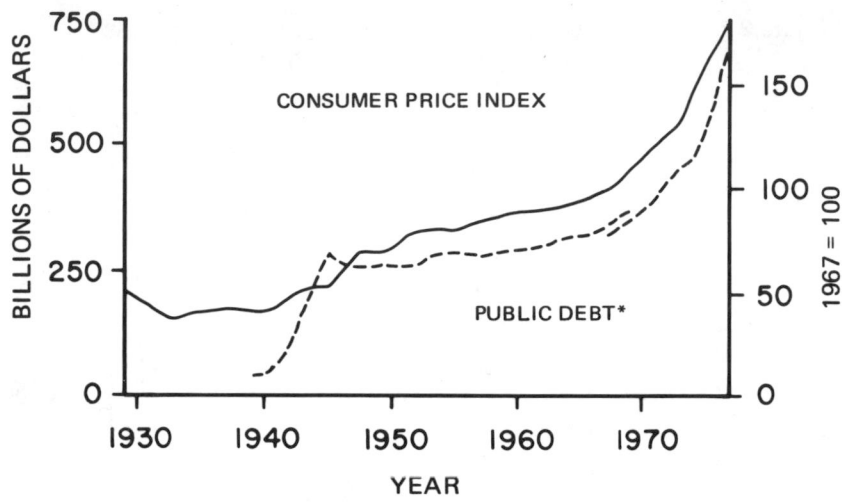

*1939-1969 = TOTAL PUBLIC DEBT SECURITIES
1967-1977 = TOTAL INTEREST BEARING PUBLIC DEBT

We could stop the inflation tomorrow by sufficiently Draconian measures; for instance, raising the income tax by 10 or 20 percent, which would have an immediate effect on take-home pay, and perhaps having a temporary wage-price freeze, or even rollback, that would create a suitable psychological atmosphere. If we did this and nothing else, however, it would almost be impossible to avoid a very sharp rise in unemployment and a serious depression simply because interest rates, especially on long-term contracts, would then be running at real rates of 12 percent, which would be intolerable, as we can hardly conceive of profits rising sufficiently above this level. Interest would rise above profit, with the same potentially catastrophic results which we saw for the early 1930s. If we are going to stop the inflation, therefore, we must intervene in existing financial contracts.   There is, fortunately, a precedent for this in the abrogation of the gold clause in 1934, when many financial contracts at that time had a clause saying that debts would be repaid in the dollar value at the time of so many ounces of gold. When the price of gold was raised from $20.67 per ounce to $35 per ounce, these contracts obviously would have become intolerably burdensome; therefore the federal government, exercising its prerogative as a source of contract law, simply abrogated these clauses. We could do the same sort of thing today. We could, for instance, say that all financial contracts are null and void as of this date unless the rate of interest in them is, shall we say, halved. Then we could stop the inflation without much fear of catastrophic unemployment.

QUESTIONS, QUESTIONS

Still open is the question as to what really determines the proportion of the national income that goes to nonlabor income in general and to profit and interest in particular. Also open is the question as to what determines the volume of gross private domestic investment. A sharp decline in this, for instance, would lead us into serious trouble no matter what we did on the monetary scene even in regard to rates of interest. The relations are subtle and extremely complex. I have argued for many years without much effect that the "widow's cruse" effect, first formulated by Keynes in the *Treatise on Money* [2], is a very important explanation of the total volume of nonlabor income and that distributions in dividends and in interest tend to flow back through the financial system again into profits. Without this relationship, it is very hard to interpret what happened between 1929 and 1932, which on this theory is quite intelligible as positive feedback. Decline in investment, triggered perhaps by the stock market collapse, resulted in diminution in profit, which resulted in a further diminution in investment, and so on until the catastrophic state of 1932–33 emerged, with profits negative, gross private domestic investment virtually zero, and net investment actually negative.

The gap between interest and profit undoubtedly played a part in this process. A rather puzzling question is why a move into interest-bearing securities did not raise their prices to the point where interest rates fell very low. One reason for this perhaps is that in deflationary periods even cash has a positive real rate of interest, and it is therefore difficult for nominal rates to fall much below 2 percent, as Keynes himself observed as a "liquidity trap." The relation between the interest-profit gap and employment, however, is much more direct than Keynes supposed. It is not merely mediated through gross private domestic investment. It has a direct effect even on employment that replaces inventories sold, so that even the willingness to hold *any* inventories declines and firms simply shut down.

A RETURN OF THE PAST?

We are by no means necessarily exempt from the kind of perverse positive feedback that went on between 1929 and 1933. It is even conceivable that we might have a speculative collapse either in real estate or even in the stock market. The return on stocks is so low now compared with interest rates that the stock market only stays up where it is out of sheer institutional habit. If this habit ever begins to break, we could see a very massive shift, or at least attempted shift, out of stocks into bonds, thereby bringing about a collapse of stock prices to the point where rates of return at current rates of profit would be commensurate with interest rates. If this happened, however, the volume of profit itself might shrink, resulting in still further shrinkage in the rate of profit. These are very complex processes which have been quite imperfectly analyzed in the past, and much more work needs to be done on them.

All of this suggests that a full-employment, antiinflation policy is feasible. It requires, however, more knowledge than we now have, a somewhat different data base, and a very different political image and political will. The latter is what it is hard to be optimistic about. Inflation is very much like heroin--it is an easy way out of depression, it gives a false euphoria, but it is addictive and requires increasing doses to produce the same effect. Furthermore, the withdrawal symptoms could be very severe. What we need is a kind of economic methadone in the way of intervention into financial markets. But politically we are simply not prepared to do this at the moment, and so there is every prospect that the inflation will continue.

NOTES

1. Data for all figures come either from selected issues of U.S., President, *Economic Report of the President* (Washington, D.C.: U.S. Government Printing Office) or from U.S., Department of Commerce, *Historical Statistics of the United States* (Washington, D.C.: U.S. Government Printing Office).

2. John M. Keynes, *A Treatise on Money*, 2 vols. (New York: Harcourt, Brace and Company, 1930).

＊   *Chapter 3*

THE DOMESTIC AND INTERNATIONAL
ASPECTS OF STRUCTURAL INFLATION

Leonard A. Rapping*

POLITICAL UNDERLAY OF INFLATION

The American defeat in Indochina, the development of
the Soviet SS-9 which ended the American nuclear monopolies,
and the breakdown of the Bretton Woods system, which, broadly
conceived, defined the monetary, commercial, military and political rules governing the relations among member nations,
signaled the end of *Pax Americana*. The disjuncture between the
domestic economic and political system organized and predicated on American power and global order, and the reality of
declining power and international economic and political incoherence, explain the emergence of stagnation and accompanying
inflation in this decade.   Moreover, as the American global
position wanes, it is increasingly obvious that economic and
political events around the world impact on American society in
ways previously thought unimaginable. The decline of the dollar,
reflecting a loss of confidence in the United States, and the
increase in the price of oil, reflecting an inability of the United
States to control external events, are perhaps the most salient
examples of this unpleasant and destabilizing relationship. The
monetary manifestation of these international events is domestic
inflation.
The period between the Korean war and the Vietnam war was
one of creeping inflation throughout most of the capitalist world.

---

*Professor of Economics, University of Massachusetts.

Then came accelerating inflation. While the experience of each country shown in Table 3-1 varies in detail, there is clearly a general pattern of accelerating inflation starting in the late 1960s. For the United States, this process was temporarily arrested during the period of wage-price controls, 1971-73, and again during the sharp economic decline in the winter of 1974-75. However, accelerating rates of inflation are clearly in evidence in 1978. One might reasonably suppose that the 1970s are distinctly different from the earlier era. Indeed, except for the inflations associated with the American involvement in World Wars I and II, covering the years 1917-19 and 1941-48, the United States has not, in the twentieth century, experienced so intense an inflation as that of the 1970s.

The creeping inflation of the years 1950 to the middle or late 1960s is usually explained by relatively high level of employment maintained by means of expansionary monetary and fiscal policies which were implemented under temporarily fortuitous circumstances. The inflationary bias in the system was viewed as resulting from the wage-price setting process which harbored an inflationary thrust once the threat and reality of mass unemployment faded from memory. Some economists saw creeping inflation replacing mass unemployment as an instrument of "labor discipline" [1]. This interpretation was too sanguine, since unemployment continued to function in its historic role, albeit in a less extreme form than in earlier decades. The Eisenhower recession of 1957-59 was a kind of muted "Austrian" remedy for the excesses of the prior expansion. The use of full-scale liquidation and unemployment was unnecessary in the favorable domestic and international environment that existed, and, in any event, might have been politically constrained by the New Deal coalition which at that time had considerable cohesion.

The acceleration of inflation in the late 1960s marked an important structural break in the post World-War II era. In my judgment, it is inadequate to explain this acceleration as either the result of adaptation to inflation, so that larger doses of it were necessary to maintain employment, or as the result of the changing age-sex composition of the labor force. These explanations assume secular structural cohesion, and are too linear and technical in light of the political and economic events of the 1970s. The institutional conditions which facilitated growth and prosperity in the post war years were ruptured by the breakdown of the Bretton Woods order.

TABLE 3-1. INFLATION RATES FOR
SELECTED COUNTRIES BY PERIOD[a]

Post-World War II Inflation Rates
(Average Annual Percentage Increase in CPI)

Country	1945-48	1960-71	1971-78[b]
W. Germany		3.3	6.1
France	58.0[c]	4.3	13.2
Italy	57.0	5.0	21.9
U.K.		4.6	21.3
U.S.	11.3	3.3	9.0
Canada		3.1	11.1
Major oil exporters	(8.0)[d]	(17.0)	
Non-oil developing nations		(10.1)	(32.3)

Post-World War I Inflation Rates
(Average Annual Percentage Increase in Consumer Prices)

Year	France	Germany
1914-18	138.0	140.0
1919	21.0	223.0
1920	37.7	68.0
1921	-21.6	144.0
1922	-1.0	5,470
1923	17.8	75×10^9
1923-26	16.9	
1927	-6.3	

Sources:
a. *Economic Report of the President*, 1979; C.S. Maier, "The Politics of Inflation in the Twentieth Century," in *The Political Economy of Inflation*, eds. Fred Hirsch and John H. Goldthorpe (1978); and International Monetary Fund and World Bank, *Finance and Development*, 5:2 June 1978.
b. Computed through the third quarter of 1978.
c. Retail food prices only.
d. Figures in parentheses are for the periods 1967-72 and 1974-77.

The collapse of the fragile gold exchange standard in September 1931 and the resulting breakdown of commercial and political relations among the countries integrated by this system of fixed exchange rates, converted a deep depression into the Great Depression [2]. The breakdown of the Bretton Woods system in 1971 has strained and discombobulated nations bound together by this post-World War II dollar standard. The crisis now manifests itself as accelerating inflation, not mass unemployment. The displacement of mass unemployment by inflation is attributable to the principle of the unbalanced budget and willingness to flood the system with credit. While accelerating inflation and high unemployment are undoubtedly serious problems, they are not the catastrophe of mass unemployment. Yet the system is fragile, as evidenced by the collapse in industrial production in the winter of 1974-75 and by the stock market and international money market panic in October of 1978. Moreover, the failure of growth has left its trail of wreckage: stagnate real wages, excessive unemployment and excess capacity, urban decay, regional economic disparities, and the usual signs of social disintegration among the weak and the poor.

During the twentieth century, rapid inflations in both Western Europe and the United States have been associated with war or its aftermath. They have occurred when growth has been problematic and when the preconditions for growth have been politically contested. In each case the dynamic issue of growth is intensely intertwined with the immediate problem of distributing a low or slowly growing social product. Thus, not only are the distributional and other institutional preconditions for growth subject to political contention, but the distribution of the existing product is similarly contested. Inflation proceeds so long as there is no political and economic structural resolution to the problem of distribution and growth.

In the present period, not unlike the years after the two World Wars, the preconditions for stability, the *sine qua non* for growth, are only slowly being formulated. Specific problems giving rise to instability include unsettled international commercial and monetary arrangements, the disposition of international and domestic debt, uncertainty arising from the emergence of expensive energy and food, and the distributional conflict emerging from the relocation of industry which requires massive readjustments. In addition, these problems are compounded by the need for higher levels of both public and private investment requiring further containment in the standard of living. These challenges cannot be met under the ground rules which defined the mix of social and private activity after World War II. Logic would suggest the need for extension in economic planning, yet there remains a powerful political thrust to contend with these problems through the workings of an unfettered market. Ultimately, without consensus or without sufficient authority these problems are unresolvable. Under these circumstances, the inflation proceeds, perhaps awaiting some national or international crisis which will force a resolution.

It is in the above sense that continuous inflation is often a reflection of a weak or disoriented government lacking sufficient power to impose solutions. Inflation is never a technical economic problem. The technical details of stabilization policy depend on specific historical circumstances, but the standard list includes tax increases, expenditure cuts, credit restriction, direct or indirect price and wage controls, and the confiscation of excess currency holdings. Recognizing the important political underlay of inflation, it is useful to consider several different visions of the inflationary process which can be expressed in technical terms but each of which has an ideological undertone which is clearly recognized when stabilization problems are considered within the framework of the respective theories.

ECONOMIC THEORIES OF INFLATION

The accelerating rate of inflation following the escalation of the Indochina war has as its proximate cause both corporate and government deficit spending financed by the expansion of credit. For the government's part, it was the failure to raise taxes, a time-honored political necessity during war, which was the cause of its contribution to the inflation [3]; for the corporations, it was declining profitability coupled with a sustained desire to accumulate physical assets. In summary, for the period 1965 to 1969 the inflation was a result of classic "demand-pull" pressures. It is for the next nine years that the reasons for continuing inflation are less obvious.

A view common enough among economists of the monetarist persuasion is that the accelerating inflation during the 1970s results from adaptive inflationary expectations coupled with the insistence on the part of state authorities to maintain too low an unemployment rate. For monetarists, larger and larger doses of monetary injection are necessary to maintain employment, although eventually this process is viewed as self-defeating in the sense that employment no longer responds to inflation. Explosive inflation is the price of commitment to high employment. If one accepts all of the necessary assumptions, accelerating inflation and rising unemployment in the 1970s are consistent with this theory. However, it would seem that excessive monetary expansion is at best a proximate cause of inflation. Why is it that such monetary expansion occurs? For some monetarists it is simply "error," or "bad economics," which accounts for the behavior of the state. For others it is a defect in the democratic process defined in a narrow electoral sense. Vote maximizing governments accede to the pressures from potential beneficiaries of inflation.

There are several difficulties with the monetarist view [4]. It is assumed that the stock of narrowly defined money is supply determined; that changes in this stock determine changes in effective demand; and that changes in effective demand impact on prices, not quantities. There is nothing obvious about any of these three assumptions. However, even if these assumptions are accepted, one is also required to adopt a Walrasian vision of the underlying economic process, for the theory proceeds to analyze the impact of price changes on production and employment under the assumption of atomistic competition. The view that market participants engage in neat and orderly calculations might have some appeal in periods of international prosperity and peace—perhaps it was appropriate for the years 1870 to 1913 when Britain dominated the world's economic scene or for the years 1950 to the middle or late 1960s, when the United States imbued the capitalist world with order and growth. In such periods, market participants might have some basis upon which to contemplate, formulate and extrapolate in response to current market events. When the underlying process is stable and knowable, they may have some basis upon which to "see" the future. But this is hardly the situation in the 1970s. Modern economies are deeply embedded in a global financial and commercial system. Wars, revolutions, mass starvation, racial and nationalistic conflict, global political realignments, or the breakdown of imperial systems, have no special importance in this Walrasian vision, except perhaps to alter the exchange rate. More likely, in the conflict-ridden world of the 1970s, uncertainty abounds. Determinate, well-specified models of future price developments simply do not exist. No one, not even the CIA, could have predicted recent Iranian events which are currently impacting on prices.

There are other problems with the monetarist view. The
Central Bank does not control credit; it simply controls the
elements in its balance sheet. Rapid financial innovations during
the late 1960s and throughout the 1970s have created financial
markets in which the Central Bank has only loose and imperfect
influence. The development and expansion of Euro-currency
markets, commercial paper markets, commercial bank liability
management, and trade credit in its numerous forms have
created a loose and uncertain relationship between changes in
the composition of the Central Bank's balance sheet and the
volume of credit. In the present financial environment, the
Central Bank can "pull on a string," but only at the risk of
breaking it.

Finally, Central Bank decision-making does not come directly
under the influence of the electoral process. The decision-
making apparatus of this institution is dominated by bankers and
large industrialists. Unless one is to argue that, like
Mr. Dooley's Supreme Court, the central bankers follow election
returns, the voters have no way of coercing these men. Moreover, the democratic process is more complex than that implied
by a narrow electoral vision. Admittedly, the electoral process
plays a role in influencing policy but so does group "pressure
politics." Graft, corruption, ideology, strikes and street demonstrations are all in evidence in western democracies. Witness
the striking gains of the civil rights movement in the 1960s
which were based on marches, demonstrations, and general
political pressure. Or consider the current struggle over nuclear
power. It is not limited to the electoral process. Finally, the
narrow electoral view cannot explain the failure of the Eisenhower Administration to stimulate the economy in 1960. While
the electoral trade cycle model contains an important insight
concerning the role of elections, it remains far too incomplete.

Opposed to the Walrasian view is a bewildering variety of
theories all of which parade under the banner of "price-wage"
equations. These theories have in common the assumption that
effective demand determines quantities, not prices. These
quantities discipline the wage and price setting process. If
unemployment and excess capacity are increased sufficiently,
wage and price increases are attenuated. Once quantities are
set, money wages are determined by power relations in the labor
market. Prices are set by a mark-up pricing equation with
product market power establishing the mark-up. In this
approach, money and credit are seen as endogenous and elastic,

partly because of the institutional characteristics of the credit markets and partly because of political considerations which guide the monetary authorities [5]. Borrowing from natural rate theorists, adaptive inflationary expectations are recognized, and as individuals, unions and corporations adjust to the experience of inflation the inflationary process becomes self-generating.

The approach which sees inflation as the monetary manifestation of a wage-price process requires an explanation of why inflation is intense in some periods, as in the 1970s, and modest in others, as in the years from 1950 to 1965. What causes shifts in either the wage or price equation? A variety of explanations has been offered, most of which stress the notion of union "wage-push" rather than monopoly "price-push," probably because of a belief that despite widespread mergers and conglomeration, the degree of product market power has not significantly increased in the past fifteen years [6]. These explanations differ widely in their emphases but all seem to stress the unacceptability of existing income differences and the resulting distributional dissent. There are theories of "new consciousness" and "frustration," and more complex theories of ongoing sociopolitical structural processes that undermine the necessary status or hierarchical ordering of capitalist society [7]. While these arguments and theories provide important insights into the workings of capitalist economies, they do not address the transition from creeping inflation to rapid inflation. After all, the sociopolitical forces at work have been operative for well over a hundred years. Why do they now manifest themselves as rapid inflation? Moreover, any theory of the underlying structural causes of inflation must account for the occurrence of rapid inflation and slowly growing product.

Far more promising is the idea that accelerating inflation is rooted in the concept of an "aspirations gap." When the rise in the living standard is halted by the failure of growth or a deterioration in the terms of trade (defined here as the total quantity of exports necessary to acquire a given quantity of imports), it is assumed that if real demands are maintained, an "inflationary gap" arises. As individuals, unions, and corporations attempt to maintain their standard of living and their real profits (or their growth rates), they lay claim, through the price-wage setting process, to a larger share of the declining (or less rapidly rising) social product. The result is inflation.

In broad terms, something akin to this may have occurred in the industrialized capitalist world during the decade starting in the late 1960s. The terms of trade deteriorated and growth in output slowed. Table 3-2 shows the growth rates in real Gross National Product for the years 1960-78. Clearly there has been a slowdown in recent years. According to the aspirations view, whatever explains this slowdown explains the accelerating inflation.

TABLE 3-2. ANNUAL PERCENTAGE GROWTH IN
REAL GNP FOR SEVERAL COUNTRIES,
1960-1978

Country	1960-73 (Average)	1974-78 (Average)
U.S.	3.9	2.3
Japan	10.5	3.7
West Germany	4.8	1.7
France	5.7	2.8
U.K.	3.2	1.0
Canada	5.4	3.4
Italy	5.2	1.9

Source : *Economic Report of the President*, 1979, p. 139.

The poor performance of real wages and profits are consistent with the idea that distributional strife has intensified in the 1970s. Despite the rather impressive performance of profits in the past year, a variety of statistics measuring the profitability of the capital stock indicate that profits, like real wages, have performed poorly in the 1970s as compared to earlier years [8]. This is indicated, for example, by the rate of return on depreciable assets for nonfinancial corporations which averaged 10.7 percent between 1970 and 1978 as compared to 13.0 percent over the period 1955 to 1970 [9]. This reflects the slow growth rates in real output in the 1970s as compared to the earlier decade.

In the United States this slowdown in growth is seen in the failure of real wages to grow at their traditional rate. Between 1950 and 1965 real wages, as measured by average hourly earnings, grew at the rate of 2.6 percent per annum, while in the period 1966 through 1978 they grew at only 0.8 percent per annum.   If we measure real wages in terms of real take-home pay, they have not grown in over a decade [10].

We may view the issue in terms of a different statistic.   A short-term decline in either the level or rate of increase in real per capita consumption will not in general intensify conflict. Rather, what is required is a long term or permanent decline in this measure.   When this occurs, antagonisms are heightened and workers at all levels of the wage hierarchy struggle to maintain their living standards.   For the United States, the statistics on real per capita consumption indicate that the rate of growth in the 1970s has fallen short of its 1960s performance.   In the earlier decade this statistic grew at the rate of about 5 percent per annum.   In the latter decade it grew at a rate of only about 3 percent per annum.   However, this comparison belies the true decline in the standard of living during the 1970s for the average American.

The population figures on which this statistic is based do not include illegal aliens who have been entering this country at what may well have been an accelerating rate since the early 1970s when economic conditions deteriorated in many parts of Latin America, from whence the great majority have come. To this factor should be added the point that since the advent of high inflation rates there has been a marked deterioration in the quality of many commodities.   Henry Ford's Pintos and good old Harvey Firestone's radials are the more deadly examples of this phenomenon.   But in less flagrant ways, plastics, polyesters, and other chemicals invade and degrade almost every aspect of American consumption.   These phenomena result from cost-cutting efforts throughout American industry and although they are not easily accounted for in the price index, it is plausible to conclude that measured price statistics understate the rate of inflation.   Consequently, the rate of growth in real per capita consumption is overstated for the 1970s, perhaps by a very wide margin.

There are two other reasons why the data on real consumption growth in this decade overstate the improvement in the standard of living.   Between 1974 and 1975 there occurred a rather sharp and unexpected increase in the female labor force participation rates.   As a result, part of the subsequent improvement in consumption has been achieved through an increase in the number of multiple worker families.   Finally, a not insignificant part of the growth in real consumption after the spring of

1975 has been financed by installment credit rather than from current income or past savings.

Increased distributional conflict, which manifests itself as rising wages and prices, will necessitate the expansion of credit in order to finance a higher level of nominal income. In recent years endogenous credit has served to finance even higher levels of income. Moreover, in inflationary times speculative fever rises. Changing relative prices in existing assets like land, real estate, jewelry, and many other items which are the traditional objects of speculation excite and tempt those in quest of a fast buck. Speculation is often credit financed as the banks see an opportunity to make large profits in their role as speculative brokers. The credits granted by banks, once used in a speculative venture, may find their way into the more normal channels of trade. In this way, speculation in existing assets will alter the demand for newly produced commodities. But this is not the only channel whereby speculation in existing assets can influence the price and wage structure. Increased land prices, as well as that part of the increase in interest rates associated with the speculative demand for credit, will be incorporated into the general price of housing and foodstuffs. Whether this incorporation is quantitatively significant remains a matter of conjecture.

Within the price-wage vision of the inflationary process, then, we have a situation in which money wages, prices, and credit are all expanding apace. The price-wage process, however initiated, has self-generating properties, for once the process is in motion, inflationary expectations undoubtedly take hold and propel prices upward. During the 1970s this process has been continuously refueled by the deteriorating terms of trade and slow growth. In turn, both the terms of trade and the growth rate have been impaired by international instability and the decline in American hegemony.

THE DECLINE IN THE DOLLAR

The dollar has declined about 25 percent on a trade weighted basis between 1970 and 1978. This decline has increased the domestic price of internationally traded commodities, including agricultural products. From 1970 through 1978, U.S. agricultural exports rose from $7.2 billion to $28.0 billion, an event that undoubtedly raised domestic food prices. During the same period, the increased dollar price of oil has raised the price of all oil-based products and has significantly contributed to the increased cost of oil imports. In 1970, the dollar value of oil imports was $3.1 billion; in 1978, over $40 billion. Both the decline in the dollar and the OPEC price increases are rooted in the decline of American hegemony. This is obvious in the case of oil, but I would also ascribe dollar devaluation to the weakening of confidence in the United States as a military, political, and economic power. This loss of confidence has impacted on the dollar primarily through short-term capital flows reflecting an unwillingness to hold dollar denominated assets as a store of value [11].

While the relative price increases in food and energy have been large (see Table 3-3) these externally caused shocks by themselves cannot account for the inflation of the 1970s [12]. But a rise in the price of internationally traded commodities can affect domestic prices by altering wage and price decisions which impact on domestically traded commodities.

TABLE 3-3. PERCENTAGE GROWTH RATES OF FOOD, ENERGY AND OTHER PRICES, 1971-1978

Period	Food Prices	Energy Prices	Prices of All Items Less Food and Energy
II/71-IV/72	3.9%	3.7%	3.1%
IV/72-I/74	19.6	22.3	4.6
I/74-III/75	8.8	13.9	9.7
III/75-II/78	6.2	6.9	6.6
IV/77-IV/78	11.3	7.0	8.6

Sources: *Economic Report of the President*, 1979, and *St. Louis Federal Reserve Review* (December 1978).

It is best to study the effects of deteriorating terms of trade in real rather than price terms. A decline in the terms of trade will, like a slowdown in the growth rate, generate price inflation to the extent that the deterioration is quantitatively significant and that it impacts on workers and corporations who attempt to defend their standard of living and maintain their profits. Between 1970 and 1978, United States import prices (in dollars) have risen by 30 percent relative to U.S. export prices, which means that the U.S. must now export 30 percent more commodities or attain foreign credits in order to finance a given quantity of imports. In 1978, the United States imported $170 billion in merchandise which required $51 billion more per year in exports or in trade credits than in 1967 ($234 per person or $936 per family of four per year) [13]. Deteriorating terms of trade have impacted significantly on the American standard of living.

DOMESTIC INVESTMENT AND INTERNATIONAL INSTABILITY

There are other less obvious but important inflationary effects of international instability and declining U.S. power. Domestic investment, along with global investment, may have been contained by increasing international instability and uncertainty. Investment both creates effective demand and increases effective supply. For any given growth rate of the labor force, the higher the level of net investment, the higher the growth rate in labor productivity. Weakness in investment relative to labor force growth may partially account for the poor performance in labor productivity in this decade. It can also partially account for the slow growth rates in output since 1973.

The breakdown of the Bretton Woods system and the emergence by default of floating exchange rates, increased trade restrictions, and currency controls have fundamentally altered the basic institutional environment in which world-wide investment occurs [14]. Perhaps more than anything else, the 1970s is a period of uncertainty with respect to the international flow of financial capital and commodities. In the absence of reasonable predictability concerning the world-wide distribution of production, flow of commodities, and movement of financial resources, it is difficult for multinational or indeed even national corporations to embark on long range investment projects anywhere in the world. In short, the recent efforts at competitive devaluations, exchange controls, and import restrictions, as well as the heightened conflict of developed and developing nations and oil producing and consuming nations, not only affect the level of international trade but provide a partial but significant explanation of the failure of investment in the capitalist world economy to recover vigorously from its low point in 1975.

The problem of evaluating the impact of uncertainty on investment is certainly not a new one. It was widely discussed in the 1930s. One of Keynes' major theoretical contributions was

to stress the potential importance of uncertainty on the investment decision. In the *General Theory* [15] he said:

> The state of long-term expectation, upon which our
> decisions are based, does not solely depend. . .on the most
> probable forecast we can make. It also depends on the
> *confidence* with which we can make this forecast--on how
> highly we rate the likelihood of our best forecast turning
> out quite wrong. *If we expect large changes but are very
> uncertain as to what precise form these changes will take,
> then our confidence will be weak.*
>   The *state of confidence,* as they term it, is a matter
> to which practical men always pay the closest and most
> anxious attention. But economists have not analyzed it
> carefully and have been content, as a rule, to discuss it in
> general terms. In particular it has not been made clear
> that its relevance to economic problems comes in through
> its important influence on the schedule of the marginal
> efficiency of capital. . . .*The state confidence. . .is one of
> the major factors determining the. . .investment demand-
> schedule.* (Emphases inserted.)

Keynes is arguing that a perceived potential for large
changes in the environment for which no firmly held probabilities
can be attached is the essence of a weak "state of confidence."
And the "state of confidence" is one of the main determinants of
investment demand. To Keynes the impact of risk and uncertainty was *the* problem of the 1930s. Both his theory of liquidity
preference and of the marginal efficiency of investment dealt
with the problem of risk and uncertainty and their relation to
investment and, ultimately, employment and growth. Although
there are striking differences between the 1930s and the 1970s,
the impact of uncertainty on investment is one of the major
problems of both eras. It may be an important explanation for
slowly growing productivity both in the United States and abroad
elsewhere.

INTERNAL AND EXTERNAL STABILIZATION

The term stabilization has both a narrow and a broad interpretation. When the underlying structure of both the domestic and
the international economy is stable and ordered, in the sense
that the potential for profitable growth exists, stabilization

means simply demand management, sometimes combined with minor institutional adjustments required to facilitate growth following stabilization. Perhaps this is best exemplified by the Eisenhower stabilization effort in the late 1950s; or, going further back in time, one can cite the stabilization policies in France in the mid 1920s, when a sound bourgeois government under Poincare replaced a left coalition. In the latter instance, a 15 percent per year inflation (see Table 3-1) was suddenly halted by the technical device of a mild tax increase and more importantly by the restoration of confidence. In both instances, stabilization was achieved in the framework of relatively stable international conditions and, in a broader sense, domestic and international conditions conducive to growth. There was no need to significantly alter the proportion of income devoted to investment, no need to reestablish workplace productivity, no need to alter real wages, no need to reconstruct international financial and commercial order, and no need to adjust to a significant alteration in the relative prices of the two major sources of energy, food, and oil.

Both the Walrasian and the "price-wage" visions of the inflationary process are in a strict sense concerned with stabilization in the narrow usage of this term. Within the pure logic of these theories, any reduction in nominal spending, however caused, will moderate the inflationary thrust of the system [16]. The price of this reduction is unemployment and excess capacity. However, the theories are too general and the world is too complex to permit anything other than the qualitative judgment that declining demand will necessitate additional unemployment. There is, however, a strong presumption present in the Walrasian view that when the stabilization effort by the state is definitive and credible, the resulting unemployment will not be too severe [17]. On the other hand, within the "price-wage" vision there is the presumption that those forces generating an inflationary thrust in the system will be resistant to the disciplinary impact of unemployment and excess capacity [18]. The necessary level and duration of disciplinary unemployment could be so high and so long as to create a political and economic crisis far deeper and less predictable in its impact than the inflationary crisis itself.

In retrospect it is now clear that throughout the 1970s, demand restraint never represented a real antiinflationary option, although I would not express this position in terms of the deterioration in the trade-off between inflation and unemployment (i.e., a shifting Phillips curve). This vehicle of expression implies a stability and predictability in the underlying process that simply does not exist. It seems preferable simply to assert that the financial process and the production-employment process are too unstable to contemplate demand restraint as a means to reverse the inflationary thrust of the system.

Since the middle of the 1960s, financial and production processes have become increasingly resistant to antiinflationary demand management. In the "fragile" financial sector, "Near Panics" occurred in the "Crunch" of 1966, in the "Second Crunch" of 1971, and in 1974-75, when OPEC price increases and foreign exchange speculation caused the collapse of the Herstatt and Franklin National Banks [19]. The intense drive in October 1978 to unload both ownership claims in American industry and the dollar revealed the continued underlying instability of the financial system.

The fragility of the financial process is paralleled by the unsoundness of the production-employment process. Four years ago when a Republican administration attempted an orderly retrenchment of the economy by means of monetary and fiscal restraint, industrial production collapsed and unemployment rose to its highest level since the 1930s. They quickly retraced their steps. Taxes were cut and money was thrown at the economy. With the help of monetary ease and a $60 billion deficit, depression was avoided both here and abroad [20]. The economy is no less vulnerable to rapid descent now than it was in 1974-75. So long as there remains uncertainty concerning such matters as the relative price of energy, the parameters of the international system, the limits of state activity, and the distribution of income, the economy will exhibit instabiity and unpredictability.

The inflation is an alternative to a worse outcome, mass unemployment. The inflation unfolds under the impetus of the distributional struggle over wages, prices, and taxes and the process of national and international restructuring proceed under the inflationary umbrella [21]. When or if the preconditions for growth are established and when there is sufficient power to impose an explicit parliamentary or authoritarian distributional solution through tax, credit and state expenditure policy, stabilization will follow. But stabilization will fail unless there is a resolution to issues relating to real wages, authority at the work place, parliamentary incoherence and international disorder. Stabilization in the broad sense of the term involves the internal settlement of relations among the numerous levels of workers and between capital and labor generally. It involves also the external settlement of relations among national interests. In a general sense, stabilization in the large means institutional change, not demand management. Keynes himself was aware of this distinction. Discouraged by the experience of ending mass unemployment in the 1930s, except in the case of Nazi Germany, he wrote in 1940 [22]: "It appears to be politically impossible for a capitalistic democracy to organize expenditure on a scale necessary to make the grand experiment which would prove my case, except in war conditions."

STABILIZATION AFTER THE TWO GREAT WARS

Inflation associated with slow growth or abnormally low output is containable when the preconditions for rapid growth are reestablished. This structural interpretation of inflation is consistent with the experience after World Wars I and II, when rapid inflations were ended by a combination of domestic and international reconstruction. Internationally, the reestablishment of order entailed agreements to contain the use of certain competitive tactics, especially devaluation, quotas, and tariffs. The objects were to create order and predictability within the framework of an integrated world economy. These agreements were embodied in rules which restrained nationalistic policies. These rules were defined by the gold exchange system, which was partially erected by 1926, and later by the Bretton Woods system, which was well established by the early 1950s.

The achievement of the fragile international order after World War I, and the more durable order after World War II, facilitated and were facilitated by domestic stabilization. In the most general terms, domestic stabilization required a resolution concerning the mix of collective and private activites and the role of labor organizations in the workplace and in the parliamentary system. The resolution of these issues defined the ideological and distributional preconditions for growth. After both wars, domestic inflation proceeded at extremely high rates, both in Western Europe and the United States, until these issues were resolved in either conflict or compromise. In the post-World War II years, resolution came under the auspices of the social democratic compromise which entailed a significant role for both the state and the unions. This is to be distinguished from the post-World War I solution in which labor organizations were either severely contained—as in the cases of Germany and Great Britain—or excluded from the mass production industries as in the cases of the United States and France [23].

CONCLUSIONS

The stabilization of prices requires the restructuring of both the domestic and international economy. Restructuring is required to create the conditions necessary for economic growth, an absolute prerequisite for calming distributional strife. At the international level, government restructuring is presently predicated on large military expenditures and a continuation of the American internationalist thrust, defined within a system of freely moving commodities and financial capital. The alternative, American retrenchment within the context of a smaller dollar block, a lower level of military expenditures, restrictions on the movement of commodities as well as direct and financial investment, has not been widely articulated. However, there is no logical reason to base stabilization on the concept of internationalization. Free trade and economic growth are by no means necessary partners.

Domestically, restructuring seems to be moving in the direction of an earlier, bygone era. This is seen in the efforts to extend market relations and to reduce collective activity. These efforts include the call for deregulation, a reduction in the social wage, the elimination or attenuation of health and safety standards, the push for right-to-work laws and the support for other antiunion legislation, tax reductions, and a variety of other proposals to extend market relations. The alternative, of course, is to extend the role of the government in democratic planning for energy, health, food, credit allocation and a host of other areas. Planning entails the logical extension of the macro-planning system of the post World War II years and it is only within the framework of a broader system of planning that wage and price controls are workable. The challenge is how to blend the unique American experience into a democratic planning system. The danger, of course, is the emergence of planning in the service of a selected few.

The issue, it seems, is whether the United States will move to the political right or left. The inflation has increased ideological and political tensions that have long been suppressed by economic growth. Economists who are unwilling to take the broad view will be unqualified to deal with these problems.

NOTES

1. Martin Bronfenbrenner provides this interpretation in his essay, "Some Neglected Implications of Secular Inflation," in *Post Keynesian Economics*, ed. K.K. Kurihara (New Brunswick, N.J.: Rutgers University Press, 1954).

2. Charles Kindleberger develops this interpretation in his book *The World in Depression, 1929-1939* (University of California Press, 1973). The argument traces back to William A. Brown, Jr., *The International Gold Standard Reinterpreted, 1914-1934*, Vol. I (National Bureau of Economic Research, Inc., 1940).

3. The choice of wartime inflation as in World War I, or of price controls followed by postwar inflation as in World War II, as opposed to tax increases during the war, represents the substitution of a distributionally uncertain inflation tax burden for a distributionally certain income and corporate tax burden.

4. In a previous incarnation, I found monetarist theories compelling. Age and experience have altered my perceptions of the world.

5. The issues raised by the Walrasian versus the wage-price visions of the inflationary process hark back to an old controversy in Anglo-Saxon economics between the Currency School represented by Ricardo, and the Banking School, represented by Tooke. One wonders how much the science of economics has progressed since the Napoleonic Wars.

6. Within the framework of the wage-price view of the inflationary process, many economists ascribe causal primacy to the excessive money wage demands of organized workers. Price increases are primarily a reflection of these union excesses. The inflationary process unfolds on the basis of the numbers trade union leaders pluck from the air. This stress on union wage policy rather than the corporate determined mark-up is a curiosity most charitably explained by theoretical inconsistency. By accepting a determinate theory of corporate pricing behavior— the theory of continuous profit maximization--economists eschew a monopoly theory of inflation unless the extent of monopoly significantly increases prior to or during an inflationary episode. But, by similar reasoning, one would eschew a union theory of inflation if it were assumed that unions, like monopoly corporations, attempted to maximize an objective function containing the single argument, total economic rents. This would freeze union power, but admittedly at considerable cost in terms of realism. I would judge that unions sometimes sacrifice rents

for employment gains while at other times rents per worker rather than total rents might be of primary concern.   But by similar reasoning, profit maximization might not be appropriate under all circumstances either.   As argued by Herbert Simon, corporations are complex political and social units seeking numerous goals which can only tautologically be expressed as profit maximization.   Were corporations to shift from, say, share maximization to profit maximization, the level or rate of increase in product market prices would increase.   In this event, increased mark-ups would precede wage increases.   Of course, as a practical matter wages and prices rise together during inflationary episodes.   Nonetheless, it is only the willingness of many economists to accept corporate profit maximization while at the same time holding no firm theoretical position on union wage policy that biases them toward a "wage-push" rather than a "price-pull" theory of inflation.

7.   An excellent exposition of these ideas can be found in Fred Hirsch, *Social Limits to Growth* (Cambridge, Mass.: Harvard University Press, 1976). See also John H. Goldthorpe, "The Current Inflation: Towards a Sociological Account," in *The Political Economy of Inflation*, eds. Fred Hirsch and John H. Goldthorpe (Martin Robertson, 1978).

8.   The cyclical upswing beginning in the spring of 1975 has, as usual, contributed to an improvement in profitability.   Moreover, in 1978 the rapid increase in prices might well have benefited capital as opposed to labor in the distributional struggle.   It should also be added that data on average profitability belie   the performance of profits in many industries.   In particular, the profits of energy companies have performed comfortably since the OPEC price increase in the fall of 1973.

9.   See *Economic Report of the President*, 1979, p. 128. While the measurement of profitability is notoriously inaccurate, especially in inflationary periods, other measures of profitability such as cash flow as a percent of GNP indicate profit problems in the 1970s.

10.   Of course, *measured* real family consumption has grown during this period, but that is because of an increase in multiple workers and consumer installment credit, especially after 1975.

11.   I recognize that domestic inflation has some impact on the exchange value of the dollar, but I wish to stress that it is incorrect to assume that the willingness to hold a particular currency as a store of value depends only on its expected purchasing power in terms of commodities of the country of

issue.   Among other things, in periods of uncertainty, asset
holders have no basis upon which to formulate price expectations. Moreover, in unsettled times it is unclear what the future
rules of convertibility will be.   After all, there are historical
examples of nations which have blocked foreign holdings of
domestic currency. Great Britain after World War II prevented
exports by blocking the sterling holdings of Commonwealth
nations. In general, it is difficult to predict the resolution to the
problem of the dollar overhang, an issue which has been elevated
to primary concern in the 1970s.

12.   Presumably using a model with fixed coefficients in
consumption and production, the Council of Economic Advisers
estimates that a 10 percent devaluation of the dollar "will
generally result in a roughly 1.5 percent increase in prices by the
end of a 2- to 3-year period. . . " (*Economic Report of the
President*, 1979, p. 43).

13.   In 1978 the United States was in deficit on commodity
account, and the excess of imports over exports was financed by
foreign central banks which were accumulating short-term treasury paper.   In effect, the United States continues to act as
though the dollar is still *the* reserve currency. For an interesting
discussion of this behavior, see E. Ray Canterbery, "The International Monetary Crisis and the Delayed Peg," *Challenge*
(Nov/Dec. 1978).

14.   This section is based on a study jointly conducted with
Professor James Crotty.

15.   John M. Keynes, *The General Theory of Employment,
Interest, and Money* (New York: Harcourt, Brace and World, Inc.,
1936), pp. 148-49.

16.   The level of government expenditures has by itself no
sacrosanct impact on the rate of inflation. If the government is
pursuing an antiinflationary policy, it can just as effectively
impact on the inflation by raising taxes as opposed to cutting
relief spending.   Indeed, there is no technical reason why a
reduction in spending must be achieved through the government
sector. Consumer installment credit, which permits some workers to deficit finance, or business credits which permit some
corporations to deficit finance, are no less candidates for budget
balancing than the federal government, if the sole objective is to
moderate inflationary pressure. Indeed, the government sector,
including both the federal and state sectors, has at the present
time a balanced budget with the federal deficit roughly offset by

state government surpluses. Were it not for matching grants and other federal transfers to the state governments, it would be the states rather than the federal budget which would be in deficit. The political conflict revolving around state and federal budgets--as seen in Proposition 13 pathology is best understood as reflecting distributional strife and it is only peripherally related to the problem of terminating the current inflation.

17. There is, of course, a difficult problem in specifying what constitutes a credible program and this raises issues of stabilization in the large.

18. At no point in the post-World War II era has recession failed to moderate advancing prices. The issue is not whether recession is deflationary, but rather its cost in terms of employment and overall political and social stability, both here and abroad.

19. The best treatment of the financial fragility hypothesis is found in Hyman Minsky's *John Maynard Keynes* (New York: Columbia University Press, 1975).

20. I use the term depression rather than recession in the sense in which the term was used in the pre-World War II period. The term recession is of post-World War II coinage and has meaning only in the context of effective Keynesian-style stabilization policies. I take it as obvious that under current circumstances no one seriously proposes fine-tuning the economy. I also presume that the reader is sensitive to the economic and political distinctions between the term depression and the events of the 1930s, the Great Depression. The latter term should be reserved to identify a global event in which the commercial, financial and political institutions of capitalism are wrenched from their moorings.

21. The distributional outcome of inflation is uncertain because the process is blind and arbitrary. It is the simultaneous underlying restructuring that is the significant distributional process during an inflationary episode. Thus, the distributional effect of inflation is best studied after its conclusion. This does not deny the fact that some groups benefit (at the expense of others) from inflation *per se*, but these distributional effects will vary from one inflationary experience to another. Although the distributional effects of the current inflation are difficult to identify because tax evasion has significantly increased in the past decade, I have little doubt that a redistribution from low to high income groups has occurred. For an insightful discussion of

this and related issues, see Bernard Malamud, "Keynes and the German Inflation" (unpublished, University of Nevada, Las Vegas).

22. John M. Keynes, "The United States and the Keynes Plan," *New Republic* 103 (July 29 1940): 158.

23. In Germany, the return to the ten-hour workday in late 1923 signified the loss of parliamentary power by the Social Democratic party and its union allies. It signified also the demise in the authority of the factory councils. In both France and the United States, organized labor was excluded from any significant role in the mass production industries by their resounding losses in the strikes of 1919 and 1920, and by the depression of 1920-22. In the case of France, their strike defeats and the depression of 1920 "...effectively subdued proletarian militancy for a decade and a half." (C. Maier, *Recasting Bourgeois Europe* (Princeton, N.J.: Princeton University Press, 1978: 158). For the United States, the events of 1919-22 ushered in the heyday of the open shop movement, labor injunctions, antitrust laws applied to labor, the American Plan, and Taylorization.

Chapter 4

ON SOME MICROECONOMIC ISSUES IN INFLATION THEORY

William J. Baumol*

INTRODUCTION

A curious ambiguity pervades popular discussions of inflation policy and to some extent is reflected even in the professional literature. On the one hand, we think of inflation as an intertemporal process driven by some continuing force whose consequences are properly evaluated in terms of rate of change in the overall price level. On the other hand, price changes which are essentially once-and-for-all adjustments are spoken of as "inflationary." Analogously, writings on the comparative statics of macro theory refer to a self-limiting transition from one equilibrium to another as an inflationary process.

There is certainly little point in quibbling about terms and accordingly there can be no overwhelming objection to the use of the word "inflation" to refer both to a continuing process and to independent price jumps or self-terminating price movements which may fortuitously be closely bunched so as to produce disquietingly large and protracted changes in price levels. However, it is important, if we use the term to include the latter, to recognize that the corresponding analyses still leave inflation *processes* unexplained. And inflation processes, even if they are not the only source of concern over price behavior, are surely a significant part of the policymaker's concerns. When economists

---

*Joseph Douglas Green Professor of Economics, Princeton University, and Professor of Economics, New York University.

assert that it is probably going to be very difficult for the rate of inflation to fall below 6 percent during the next few years they presumably do not have in mind a set of coincidental price raising events. They must believe that there is some mechanism at work which is acting as a continuing force driving prices upward. This, in turn, implies that the nature of this mechanism must be determined before a counteracting program can be designed.

This chapter will first examine some comparative static views of inflation showing that while their limitations are fairly obvious in microeconomic discussions, they have less obvious counterparts in macroeconomic analysis. Next, I will describe several process analysis models of inflation, indicating their mechanism and their implications for policy. This will lead the discussion to the interpretation of inflation as an externalities or prisoners'-dilemma problem and to the policy measures that this view suggests. Specifically, the analogy with environmental policy suggests two measures: a tax on wage or price increases and a market in permits to increase wages and prices. In environmental theory these measures are considered close substitutes for one another, and there are good reasons to expect either of them to be effective in suitable circumstances. I will end by suggesting that in the theory of inflation policy, the analogy does not hold. The theoretical foundation for a market in price-raising permits seems considerably stronger than that for an inflation tax and, indeed, there seems to be a serious question about the analytic foundation for the latter.

STATIC ATTRIBUTIONS OF INFLATION

In popular discussions, almost all micropolicy measures are evaluated at least partly in terms of their effects upon inflation. Environmental protection programs are often said to be "inflationary," while an increase in competition resulting from deregulation of entry and pricing in air transportation is described as "deflationary."

Each of these changes can, indeed, be expected to have an effect upon prices. But in the absence of other contributing forces they are likely to bring the affected prices to a new plateau rather than imparting to them any protracted upward motion. Each such change involves a shift in one or more of the economy's cost functions and consequently leads to a change in the equilibrium values of prices. The process of transition to the new equilibrium may be subject to lags, and this can give the appearance of a protracted process of price movement to something that amounts to a once-and-for-all change in prices. It involves nothing more than the time path taken by the process of adjustment to the new equilibrium. It is properly the subject of a comparative statics analysis rather than of true dynamic theory.

Once said, this is all obvious. One can hardly attribute any role in the *persistence* of a 7 percent rate of inflation to the adoption of a measure such as a piece of consumer-protection legislation. Continuing price movements must be a result of continuing forces.

It is only worth saying this about the microeconomic side of the matter because it has its macroeconomic counterpart whose inadequacy as an explanation of the inflation process is perhaps less obvious. If we consider the discussions which deal with the subject in terms of an inflationary gap, it soon becomes obvious that they involve no more than a lagged adjustment to a new equilibrium which, once reached, should be characterized by steady prices.

The argument runs something as follows. Suppose, starting with an equilibrium, there is some exogenous change, such as a fall in the marginal propensity to save or an influx of money from abroad. This leads to an equilibrium level of national income higher than that corresponding to full employment. The resulting excess demand for labor can be interpreted as an inflationary gap. It induces rises in wages and prices which cut down the purchasing power of the stock of money. In the absence of continuing injections of money supplies or destabilizing expectations, this must ultimately eliminate the gap, thus bringing the economy to a new equilibrium in which no further change in price level is to be expected in the absence of a new disturbance from exogenous sources.

This story is very similar in structure to that describing the effects of a change in micropolicy upon equilibrium price. There is, once more, an autonomous shift in one of the pertinent relationships. That, in turn, leads to a lagged transition to higher equilibrium prices. Those prices, once attained, exhibit no tendency to return to their old levels, but they also do not tend to rise any further. The lags in the macroeconomic process may, perhaps characteristically, be longer than the microeconomic ones, although that is by no means self evident. But aside from that, there is no fundamental difference in structure between the two analyses. In that sense they seem equally unconvincing as explanations of an inflationary *process*. The inflationary gap analysis, by itself, just does not seem up to the task.

SOME MODELS OF INFLATIONARY PROCESSES

The preceding discussion is not meant to imply that dynamic models of an inflationary process are unavailable. Rather, it is meant only to suggest that some of the more standard discussions of inflation have adopted approaches unsuited to the analysis of inflation as process. Let me, therefore, turn next to several models which do seek to account for the persistence of inflationary pressures.

I will describe two models which are very different in character. Each provides a set of conditions sufficient but not necessary for an inflation process. These, therefore, are not rival models because at different times reality may sometimes best be represented by one, sometimes by another, of the models, or it may involve forces which are an amalgam of the two.

Two themes recur: First, the role of public policy decisions, particularly those involving employment goals. Second, the role of expectations, miscalculations, and illusions. There are some ways in which these elements can affect an inflationary process that are very obvious. But in the models that follow, the parts they play are rather more subtle and less widely recognized.

A MINIMUM-WAGE INFLATION PROCESS (MACHLUP)

We begin with a model which is very easy to describe, one which Fritz Machlup proposed in conversation with me. Its starting point is the view common among economists (and to which I also subscribe) that the high rates of unemployment of teenagers (particularly those who are black or Hispanic) is ascribable to a considerable degree to the minimum wage laws, which raise wages above the value of the marginal product of more than a relatively small number of unskilled workers. This high unemployment is politically unacceptable to policymakers. Even if the overall rate of unemployment is quite low, this persistent and large body of joblessness is so serious a problem that politicians feel themselves forced to do something about it. But the typical program undertaken in response to this problem relies heavily on stimulation of effective demand.

With overall unemployment low, measures to increase demand inevitably stimulate inflation. The rise in prices serves to erode the real value of the minimum wage. But this, too, is politically unacceptable. In effect, the minimum wage is indexed; that is, with minor lags, it is revised periodically to keep it more or less constant in real terms. Once this is done, we are back at the initial situation. High minimum wages will have restored the initial level of unemployment of the unskilled if injections of fiscal or monetary stimuli have not continued. Political pressures then force resumption of such injections, and the upward pressure upon prices will be resumed. This process can go on indefinitely.

The crucial role of public policy in this process is clear. Decisionmakers have a bear by the tail and are unable to let go. They can neither abandon the minimum wage law nor can they live with the huge pocket of persistent unemployment that results. Given this dilemma, they are driven to a continuous but hopeless program of deficit spending and expansion of the money supply. The rest then follows inevitably.

Observers will undoubtedly differ in the degree to which they accept this model as an explanation of the inflation which now plagues the United States and other countries. But whatever our views on this subject, it must be agreed that the model does at least formally meet our requirements. It is sufficient to account for a persistent inflation.

While it would be easy to provide a formal version of the model that has just been described, its structure is so simple that the exercise seems pointless. That is, however, not true of the model to which we turn next.

INFLATION UNDER A LONG-RUN PHILLIPS CURVE

Despite the doubts that have been expressed about the possibility of a stable long-run Phillips curve, I have recently proved [1] that such a curve is not only possible but also is easily derivable from a widely proposed line of argument. I will next indicate the general character of the model and outline the formal proof of its stability.

But first the relevance of this result for our discussion should be made clear. The point is that if the menu of employment-inflation rate choices available to the policymaker is really governed by a Phillips curve and if policymakers choose or are forced to choose some maximum level of unemployment which they are unwilling to exceed for any substantial period, then the rest follows.   This combination of assumptions condemns the economy to an inflation rate which it may sometimes or even often exceed, but of which it will rarely fall short.   This set of conditions is, then, sufficient to keep the economy in an inflationary process which will continue until there is change in one of the underlying relationships.   That is, under the conditions postulated, the inflationary process will cease only when policy-makers give up their employment goals or if there is a substantial shift in the position of the long-run Phillips curve.

This brings up a crucial distinction.   A stable Phillips curve need, of course, not be unshiftable.   Just as a stable supply-demand equilibrium can shift in response to changes in taste, productive techniques, or other exogenous influences, a stable Phillips curve can be moved by changes in institutional arrangements—the power or behavior of unions, the degree of concentration of industry, and the like.   In other words, there is no inconsistency between stability of the long-run Phillips curve and the view that in recent decades the Phillips curve has been shifting in a direction which increases the rate of inflation corresponding to any given level of unemployment.   We will return later to these microeconomic influences upon the position of the curve.

The validity of our argument then hinges upon the validity of the hypothesis that a long-run Phillips curve exists.

This last hypothesis is an empirical issue which I will make no attempt to investigate [2].   Rather, I will pursue a more modest goal: to show that long-run stability of the model is not impossible, and to provide a plausible construct with this property.

HEURISTIC OUTLINE OF THE MODEL

The model follows a line of argument apparently first offered by Lipsey [3] and then expanded upon by Archibald [4] and by Tobin [5].   The basic assumption is that any given unemployment rate is normally not distributed evenly through the economy.   With, say, a 5 percent level of unemployment some industries will, perhaps, have a 7 percent excess supply of labor, some a 3 percent excess supply, and some even an excess demand for labor.   The lower the overall rate of unemployment in the economy the greater will be the ratio of the number of industries with excess demand for labor to the number of industries with an excess supply.

Such a situation will automatically generate forces that tend to eliminate these interindustry disparities. However, random and exogenous changes will constantly produce changes in tastes, in productive techniques, and so forth, which constantly change the labor supply-demand status of the various industries so that new disparities in the labor supply-demand status of various industries will constantly replace those that are eliminated by the mobility of labor. In this way at any time there will be an expected probability distribution of rates of excess demands and supplies of labor in the economy.

The argument requires only one additional element. In line with the widely held hypothesis that prices and wages are more rigid in the downward than in the upward direction (see, for example, Schultze [6]), we postulate an asymmetry in the response of prices and wages to excess demand for labor vis-a-vis an equal excess supply. That is, we assume, given two industries A and B, the former with an excess demand for labor of R percent and the latter with an R percent excess supply, that the average wages and prices in the two industries will rise because A's wages and prices will rise more rapidly than those of B will fall.

The logic of the model should now be clear. If fiscal or monetary measures succeed in reducing the level of unemployment, then the expected number of industries with excess demand for labor will rise relative to the number in excess supply. Random shifts in supply and demand functions will make this expected ratio permanent, offsetting the effects of mobility of labor from excess supply to excess demand industries. Finally, the asymmetry in rates of change of wages and prices assures that the increase in the relative frequency of cases of excess demand will increase the rate of inflation in the economy. Thus, corresponding to each level of overall unemployment in the economy as a whole there will be a fixed and stable rate of inflation. Moreover, the smaller the level of unemployment the greater will be the corresponding inflation rate. This, of course, is precisely what is asserted by the Phillips curve hypothesis [7].

In the Appendix it is shown rigorously that these loosely-described relationships do yield the results I have just claimed for them and, in particular, that the resulting Phillips curve is demonstrably stable in the long run.

ON THE ROLE OF EXPECTATIONS

Expectations play a crucial part in the microeconomic process underlying inflation. When contracts are drawn up or other arrangements are made for the future, all participants can be relied upon to take inflation prospects into account, and the resulting prices will inevitably reflect these anticipations. As far as I know, no one denies the importance of expectations or disagrees sharply about this general description of the way they affect the inflationary process.

The outstanding issues relating to expectations, rather, concern the role of other influences. Are expectations, in the end, all-powerful? Are there no other variables whose values affect the rate of inflation? And, if any such variables exist, how much emphasis do they deserve?

The issue is crucial for policy formulation and for the degree to which it can be aided by economic analysis. The critical role of expectations is an observation which is not terribly helpful for the design of a program to deal with inflation because we do not know any measures which can change expectations quickly and painlessly. They just do not respond readily to government actions. It is for precisely this reason, I believe, that Keynes, having granted the power of expectations to affect investment and hence employment, proceeds nevertheless to assign a central part in his discussion to interest rates, whose influence is, in some sense, probably much weaker. Governments can affect interest rates quickly and reliably. Massive propaganda machines have not been able to move expectations. Policy analysis is, therefore, quixotic if it focuses upon expectations despite the admitted strength of their influence.

In looking for alternative influences upon the rate of inflation, we quickly find a number of candidates. For example, restriction of the money supply, it is generally agreed, will slow inflation down. But the issue here is whether money supply adjustment can do the job, as it were, independently or whether it must work *through its effect on expectations*. If, as some believe, it can only work via expectations a restrictive monetary policy may not only be painful but also extremely slow. A program of monetary restriction may at first be greeted with skepticism by the general public as yet another brief stop in a long-run stop-go policy in which inflationary "goes" are likely to overwhelm the occasional "stops." Only after some years of determined reining of the money supply and its devastating effects upon output and employment will the government's determination achieve credibility, and only then will expectations and the rate of increase in prices be affected significantly [8].

This dismal scenario may perhaps be all we can accept with confidence. It is certainly not something to which we will aspire. Hence, the search for other direct influences upon the rate of inflation.

There are some standard candidates which offer as little promise as expectations for public policy. The rate of growth of productivity and the degree of militancy of the trade unions are frequently mentioned in discussions of inflation. But no one pretends to be sure about means that will stimulate growth in productivity, particularly means that will increase it sharply and quickly. Union behavior has given rise to measures such as wage guidelines in the United States or "social contracts" in Great Britain, all examples of so-called incomes policies, whose performance has been far from inspiring.

Our Phillips curve model suggests one possibility which may merit exploration. Obviously, one may hope ideally not to be forced to move along the Phillips curve, trading reduced inflation for increased unemployment. Rather, on the widely credited conjecture that the Phillips curve can shift (and, indeed, *has* shifted), one may hope to find means to move the entire curve so that it permits lower inflation rates at any given level of employment.

If my Phillips curve model deserves credence, then there is at least one key element to which it should attract our attention. It is the asymmetry in the upward and downward flexibility in wages and prices. For this purpose we turn next to the mechanism that may underlie it. While no one seems to dispute the occurrence of this phenomenon, there seems to be no generally accepted explanation. Yet, without understanding its workings, we can hardly hope to do much about it.

INFLATION AS AN EXTERNALITY PROBLEM OR PRISONERS' DILEMMA

Nearly thirty years ago, I first discussed the asymmetry in upward and downward flexibility of wages and prices and its role in the inflationary process. I sought to explain this phenomenon in terms of externalities or the free rider problem. The analogy with pollution is direct. Assume that everyone would be better off under a social contract while requiring everyone to reduce emissions. But in the absence of an enforcement mechanism, any one individual will gain the most for himself if everyone else adheres to the contract while he pollutes to whatever degree is most convenient for himself. If everyone reasons in this way, no one will adhere to the social contract or have any reason to expect anyone else to adhere to it. That is precisely why government intervention is required to coerce the group into acting in its own interests.

In the case of inflation, society is entrapped in exactly the same way, and the analysis helps to explain the asymmetry in upward and downward price and wage movements. As I wrote in my earlier publication [9]:

> [R]igid wages and prices in (say) an industry will, in times of falling prices, tend to result in relative unemployment there. [But] in some industries where the various inputs are employed in quite rigidly fixed proportion and where the prices of the factors are more or less independently controlled, there may be some reluctance on the part of the owner of any particular factor of production to permit a reduction in its remuneration, for while the reduction in remuneration will adversely affect him directly, any benefits resulting from a subsequent reduction in prices and the consequent increase in the scale of operations of the industry will only partially accrue to him. In other words, his lowered money income will have benefits falling indiscriminately on all those connected with the particular industry, which are entirely analogous to external economies of scale. This serves partially to explain the tendency towards (downward) rigidity in the (money) remuneration received by some of the factors of production. . . .
>
> Similar reasoning indicates that a situation such as this may result in finished product prices which are exceedingly flexible in an upward direction, for if there is a loss of demand resulting from the rise in price of any one component, this may be quite small and more than offset by the consequent rise in per unit profit. . . . This suggests that our analysis may have some bearing on the problem of inflation . . .

[It] may well be rational for individual trade unions and others to press their claims for higher remuneration in times of inflationary pressure even though inflation affects them adversely. A voluntary abstention from wage-raise demands by one particular union will do little to relieve the overall inflationary pressure, and will indeed put its members completely at the mercy of rising prices.

This externalities analysis (which Shlomo Maital and Yael Benjamini have recently reinterpreted as a prisoners'-dilemma game), then, may account for the crucial asymmetry in the Phillips curve model. But it may do more than this. For it seems to indicate an appropriate avenue for antiinflation policy.

PIGOUVIAN TAXES AND A MARKET IN RIGHTS AS ANTIINFLATION MEASURES

The analogy between the inflationary process and the pollution problem at once suggests something that can be done about the former. Pigou, as we know, long ago proposed taxes and subsidies as the appropriate means to control externalities. More recently, strong arguments have been offered suggesting that there is a second measure which can achieve the same results and more. It is proposed that the environmental protection agency issue a presumably fixed number of pollution rights serving as a substitute fiscal inducement for reduced emissions, with all the efficiency properties of Pigouvian taxes and, in addition, with some certainty about the equilibrium level of pollution and with some resistance to erosion of the fiscal penalties upon emissions by the process of inflation [10].

As we all know, analogous measures for inflation policy have in fact been proposed. Sidney Weintraub and Arthur Okun have presented plans analogous to Pigouvian taxes while Abba Lerner's alternative proposal closely resembles the market in pollution rights. (Weintraub and Lerner discuss their programs later in this volume.)

The externalities model of the inflationary process would seem to provide a rigorous theoretical underpinning to this approach. I must conclude, with some regret, by arguing that this is not quite true. In saying this, I do not want to be taken as an opponent of these approaches. On the contrary, as a matter of instinct, for whatever it may be worth, I consider them to be the most promising proposals now before us. *Faute de mieux,* surely inflation policy should not reject such measures simply because of their novelty.

But this endorsement does not rest on the belief that the theoretical underpinnings of these programs are firm. There is a crucial imperfection in the analogy between fiscal penalities upon pollution and fiscal penalities upon price and wage increases. The effectiveness of the former relies upon the consequence of, say, pollution taxes for *relative* prices and the subsequent effect on resource allocation. A Pigouvian tax on a commodity whose production causes pollution has several consequences upon which its effectiveness depends: (a) it makes it relatively cheaper for consumers to devote more of their budget to nonpolluting commodities, (b) it makes it profitable to producers to invest more in nonpolluting outputs and less in polluting outputs, (c) it makes it relatively cheaper for producers to adopt productive processes which are less polluting or to adopt emissions-reducing measures.

The equivalents on the inflation front are rather less obvious, and the reason is not hard to seek. Here, as elsewhere in inflation policy, expectations can play a debilitating role. To bring out this point, suppose for concreteness that the government were to adopt a tax strictly proportionate to the wage or price increases that occur in each period (of some fixed length) [11]. Then, if in period t a seller's price rises from p_t to p_{t+1}, his tax bill will be

$$B = (p_t - p_{t-1})b, \quad b > 0 \tag{1}$$

where b represents the tax rate.

But then suppose that buyers and sellers build this into their expectations as a cost, so that if r is the expected rate of inflation, price in period $t+1$ for commodity i settles at a level that satisfies

$$p_{it+1} = (1 + r)p_{it} + b(p_{it+1} - p_{it}). \tag{2}$$

Then, solving for p_{it+1}, we obtain directly

$$p_{it+1} = \frac{1 + i - b}{1 - b}p_{it} = (1 + \frac{i}{1-b})p_{it} > (1 + i)p_{it} \quad if \ 0 < b < 1. \tag{3}$$

Thus, if there is an attempt by sellers to compensate themselves for the tax rise, they can all do so, at least in theory.

Naturally, the result will be a *greater* rise in prices than would have occurred without the tax.

If the price of another commodity, *j*, behaves similarly, we will end up—dividing the equation (3) for good *i* by that for good *j*—with

$$\frac{p_{it+1}}{p_{jt+1}} = \frac{p_{it}}{p_{jt}}.$$

In other words, despite such a Pigouvian tax on price increases, it is perfectly possible for rising prices to absorb the tax completely and for relative prices to be left unchanged. The implication is that there need be no motivation for anyone to behave in a manner different from what he would have in the absence of a tax. Because relative prices are unaffected and because the purchasing power of prices need not be affected, the theoretical basis for the inflation tax proposal remains cloudy.

But that is not the worst possible scenario. For it is possible that the greater rapidity of the rise in price will, in turn, affect inflationary expectations and so increase planned prices for the following period. This will automatically raise the total inflation tax payment, reraise the following period's expectations and so on, *ad infinitum*. Specifically, let i_t be the rate of inflation expected in period *t*. Then, under this scenario, from the equation (3), we have

$$i_{t+1} = i_t/(1-b)$$

or

$$i_t = i_0(1/1 - b)^t,$$

which is an explosive time series. That is, under this last scenario, the tax, far from dampening inflation, can transform an inflation proceeding at the steady rate, *i*, into one whose rate increases steadily and exponentially.

So far, the discussion has assumed, implicitly, that it is possible for sellers (including sellers of labor and other inputs) to shift the entire tax to buyers. In principle, this will be possible since each member of the economy will benefit in the same way from the process in his role as an earner of income, whether through higher prices for his labor or for the other resources he sells or through higher prices for the products he provides [12].

In practice we would perhaps expect only some proportion of the tax to prove shiftable. But even then it is easy to see that all of the preceding argument holds unchanged. However, the inflation stimulus provided by the tax will be decreased proportionately to the share of the tax that can be shifted.

Even in the extreme case where none of the tax can be shifted, while it will not cause the inflation to accelerate, at least in theory it will do nothing to slow it down. For then there will clearly be no more reason than without the tax for buyers to resist the price increases. Moreover, sellers will still be motivated to press for the price increases unless the tax is 100 percent or higher. After all, even if the tax is, say, 50 percent, every dollar increase in pretax earnings resulting from a price rise still brings in 20 cents, and so it must be more lucrative than not raising price.

Matters do, of course, work out quite another way if the inflation tax is so large as to wipe out all gains from a wage or price increase. This means that the legislation will set $b > 1$ in the tax relationship (1). If $b = 1$, it will simply be impossible for people to make up the tax by price increases. Indeed, they will be unable to obtain any net gains from price or wage increases, and the inflationary process must come to an end. Thus, equation (2) must degenerate into

$$p_{it+1} = (1 + r)p_{it} + p_{it+1} - p_{it}$$

or

$$rp_{it} = 0,$$

so that r, the expected rate of inflation, may be reduced to zero. This drastic solution, however, has two pitfalls: its extreme political unpalatability and its impartial preclusion of all price adjustments, inflationary or noninflationary. For example, it would effectively preclude a rise in the price of a mineral whose supply was running out or any other price adjustment called for by changes in demand or production conditions [13].

The theory pertinent to the inflation permit proposal is, however, considerably different. If the government holds the line and resists pressures to increase the number of permits issued, then, unless the law is widely flouted, the rate of growth of the price level must be kept down to the level selected by policymakers. For if no more than x dollars in price increases [14] are authorized, no more of a rise than x dollars can occur. The obvious issue is whether this process will merely succeed in *suppressing* inflation, with the attendant social costs.

One distinction immediately must be noted. The garden-variety process for inflation suppression, say via price and wage controls, is notorious for its distortion of relative prices and for the resulting misallocation of resources. But a system of inflation permits should have no such effects. The free market proposed for such permits should assign them to those products where they are needed most urgently, as measured by their marginal profit contribution. This, of course, is one of the great merits of the proposal [15].

One particular manifestation of this phenomenon is the plague of shortages which inevitably accompanies a standard process of inflation suppression. Goods whose prices are most strongly repressed below their equilibrium levels will naturally manifest excess demands and this is merely another way of saying that they are in short supply. Under a system of inflation permits, this is at least less likely to occur because of the flexibility of relative prices which it allows. But one may well ask whether this merely redistributes the problem, leading to universality of small amounts of excess demand, rather than a relatively small number of cases of spectacular shortages.

In principle, there is no reason why even the small shortages should occur. If inflation is in fact eliminated or sharply reduced, the rate of increase in costs must closely parallel the decline in the rate of increase in prices, since rising production costs are merely another side of rising input prices.

But we are still not at the end of our story which, once again, must return to the role of expectations and credibility. These will manifest themselves in the market price of the inflation permits. If the program establishes credibility and is widely expected to succeed, the urgency of the demand for permits will be reduced sharply. On the other hand, if inflation is expected to continue or to recur in the near future, the price of a permit is likely to be very high. It may be argued that even then the program is likely to succeed, but it may do so in a somewhat surprising manner. The absorption of purchasing power by the permits will have effects very similar to a reduction in the stock of money. Both may restrict effective demand, reduce employment and thus attack inflation by moving along the Phillips curve rather than shifting it, as might have been preferred.

This all suggests that, unlike their analogues in pollution control policy, the workings of an inflation tax and a system of inflation permits are fundamentally different from one another. At least theoretically, the advantages in terms of potential effectiveness all lie with the latter, although we do not yet fully understand the workings of a system of pollution permits and so one must not conclude that the case for them is open and shut.

CONCLUDING COMMENT

This essay leaves undiscussed many issues in the microeconomics of inflation which still badly need to be studied. It has merely undertaken to deal selectively with a few illustrative problems to suggest how they can be approached analytically and to indicate how their policy implications can be examined. The discussion has revealed some major gaps in the theoretical underpinnings of inflation policy, though perhaps it has contributed slightly to their elimination.

APPENDIX: THE FORMAL MODEL

Let us describe more rigorously the Phillips curve model discussed heuristically in the text. For ease of exposition, I will deal with a particularly simple two sector case. However, the generalization of the argument will be obvious throughout. In any event, I have elsewhere [1] described the corresponding general model.

For this purpose, let

x_{it} = excess demand for labor by industry i in period t as a percentage of the labor force in i,

w_{it} = hourly wage in industry i in period t expressed in nominal terms,

x^* = target percentage excess total demand for labor aimed at by government policy (explained below),

w_t = average money wage in the economy,

p_t = overall price level,

r_{it} = a random variable with expected value zero,

$g =$ the operator of discrete *expected* growth rates which yields,

$$gw_{it} = E \frac{w_{it+1} - w_{it}}{w_{it}}$$

the expected percentage rate of growth of money wages in industry i in period t, and, similarly

$gp_t =$ the percentage expected rate of growth in the price level.

In our comparative dynamic analysis we take the government to select the value of the parameter x^*; that is, to select its overall excess demand target for labor and then stick to that target value "forever." Only in this way can we compare the long-run equilibria (if they exist) corresponding to the alternative values of x^*.

Our asymmetrical wage response function is for illustration, assumed to be linear in past prices and excess demands, so the function for industry i is

$$gw_{it} = agp_{t-1} + k_j x_{it-1}, \tag{A.1}$$

$$\text{where } k_j = \begin{cases} k_1 \text{ if } x_{it-1} > 0 \\ k_2 \text{ if } x_{it-1} \le 0, \end{cases}$$

$0 < a < 1$, and $k_1 > k_2 > 0$,

so that an excess demand for labor raises wages more than an equal excess supply reduces them. The excess demand for labor in industry i is the average level for the economy plus a random variable:

$$x_{it} = x^* + r_{it}. \tag{A.2}$$

Let us assume for simplicity that the economy is composed of two industries, identical in size and in average wage rates, however those may be measured, and that the random variable r_{it} always takes one of two values: $r_{it} = +r$ or $r_{it} = -r$, with

$$r_{1t} + r_{2t} = 0 \text{ in each period } t. \tag{A.3}$$

Let us consider the range of values of x^* for which $x^* + r > 0$, $x^* - r < 0$. Then, substituting equation (A.2) into (A.1) we have, for the economy as a whole (since the two industries are identical in size and begin with equal money wages),

$$gw_t = 0.5gw_{1t} + 0.5gw_{2t}$$
$$= agp_{t-1} + 0.5k_1 (x^* + r) + 0.5k_2(x^* - r). \tag{A.4}$$

Using as an illustrative price adjustment equation

$$gp_t = gw_{t-1}, \tag{A.5}$$

we have

$$gp_{t+1} = agp_{t-1} + 0.5k_1(x^* + r) + 0.5k_2(x^* - r). \tag{A.6}$$

This is a first-order linear difference equation whose solution is

$$gp_t = [a^{t/2}gp_0 + 0.5(k_1 - k_2)r] (1-a)^{-1} + 0.5(k_1 + k_2)x^*(1-a)^{-1} \tag{A.7}$$

or

$$= a^{t/2}gp_0 + gp_e(x^*, r),$$

where the first term on the right-hand side represents the transitory component of the rate of growth of price and the remaining term, $gp_e(x^*, r)$, represents the equilibrium rate of growth of prices. By our premise $a < 1$, equation (A.6) is stable and does possess an equilibrium value which can be written simply as

$$gp_e = mr + nx^*, \tag{A.8}$$

where m and n are constants and $n > 0$. That is, these equilibrium growth rates of prices are a rising function of expected excess demand for labor.

A numerical illustration will bring out the workings of the model a bit more clearly, while highlighting the relationship of x^* to the actual equilibrium rate of unemployment in the economy.

Let us assume the illustrative values $r = 11$; that is, r_{it} equals either $+11$ or -11. $k_1 = 0.4$, $k_2 = 0.2$, and $a = 0.8$. Let x^*, the

governmental target for excess demand for labor, range over
integer values from -3 to +3; that is, from the labor demand
generated by a budget surplus to one corresponding to a substantial deficit.

We will use i' to indicate the industry that happens to have an
excess demand for labor in a particular period and i'' to designate
the industry in which there is an excess supply in that period
(where each of our industries will move in a random pattern
between these categories in accord with the values of r_{lt} and
r_{2t}).

Consider first the lower end of our policy range, the case x^*
= -3. Then we have in each period, by equation (A.2)

$$x_{i't-1} = -3 + 11 = 8 \text{ percent excess demand for labor}$$

$$x_{i''t-1} = -3 - 11 = -14 \text{ percent excess supply of labor,}$$

so that (since there can be no negative unemployment in industry
i') the overall unemployment rate equals 14/2 or 7 percent. With
both industries of the same size, we can then take the overall
rate of growth of wages in the economy to be the (unweighted)
average of the growth rates in the two sectors; that is, equation
(A.5) becomes

$$gw_t = 0.5gw_{i't} + 0.5gw_{i''t} = 0.8gp_{t-1} + 0.2(8) - 0.1(14)$$

or, by (A.5),

$$gp_t = gw_t = 0.8gp_{t-1} + 0.2. \tag{A.9}$$

It follows from the solution to the difference equation (A.9) that
the equilibrium rate of inflation corresponding to $x^* = -3$ must
be $gp_e = 0.2/(1 - 0.8) = 1$.

Exactly the same procedure can be used to determine the
equilibrium values of our variables for the other values of x^* in
the relevant range. Table 4-1 summarizes the results for the
cases corresponding to all integer values of the government
policy variable x^* in the interval from $x^* = -3$ through $x^* = +3$.
In particular, it shows the different values of gp_e associated with
the different values of x^*, which vary up to a $gp_e = 10$ percent
rate of growth of price level when $x^* = +3$.

We see from the last two rows of the table that the premises
of our illustrative example yield a long-run Phillips curve relat-

ing different inflation rates to different levels of unemployment. This curve happens to be linear in our example, but that is just a consequence of the piecewise linearity of the relationships (A.1) and (A.2) on which we based our illustrative calculation.

Table 4-1. Inflation Rates, Unemployment Levels, and Other Variable Values Corresponding to Different Values of Government Contributions to Excess Demand for Labour *(x*)*

x^* (%)	$x_{i't}$ (%)	$x_{i''t}$ (%)	gw_t	gp_e (%)	Unemployment Rate (%)
-3	8	-14	$0.8p_{t-1} + 0.2$	1.0	7.0
-2	9	-13	$0.8p_{t-1} + 0.5$	2.5	6.5
-1	10	-12	$0.8p_{t-1} + 0.8$	4.0	6.0
0	11	-11	$0.8p_{t-1} + 1.1$	5.5	5.5
1	12	-10	$0.8p_{t-1} + 1.4$	7.0	5.0
2	13	-9	$0.8p_{t-1} + 1.7$	8.5	4.5
3	14	-8	$0.8p_{t-1} + 2.0$	10.0	4.0

It has been suggested that a model such as the one just described cannot work without reliance, explicit or implicit, on the assumption that individuals base their decisions at least partly on nominal rather than on real values of the pertinent economic variables. To give concreteness to the discussion it is convenient to deal with it in terms of the preceding illustrative model.

Equations (A.1) and (A.2) suggest that our model deals with a Phillips curve relationship of the form

$$gw_t = agp_{t-1} + F(x^*, r), \tag{A.10}$$

where $0<a<1$ and F is a function whose form will presently be specified.

Since we are trying to deal with a *long-run* Phillips curve, equation (A.10), like all of our other relationships, must be taken to refer exclusively to a situation of stochastic equilibrium. That is to say, apart from random deviations resulting from the stochastic elements built into the model, all of the growth rates in question are equilibrium growth rates. Thus, the time subscripts such as t and $t-1$ in equation (A.10) and in our other relationships must be taken to relate only to random departures from the corresponding equilibrium relationships.

The premise $a<1$ in (A.1) is, of course, required for the stability of the solution. But it is this assumption that appears to entail some sort of money illusion, for it seems to imply that growth in wages only *partially* reflects the rate of increase in the price level.

But further consideration of our postulate $a<1$ shows clearly that it does *not* imply the presence of money illusion, for if we mean by this that in equilibrium and in the absence of productivity increases workers make certain that their incomes follow the rate of increase in the general price level, despite the assumption $a<1$, our model will guarantee precisely that—random year-to-year fluctuations apart. To see this, note that from (A.5) and (A.10) we have an interpretation of $F(x^*, r)$ in terms of the equilibrium rate of growth of prices as

$$F(x^*, r) = (1 - a)gp_e(x^*, r). \tag{A.11}$$

Substituting this back into equation (A.10), that basic relationship becomes

$$gw_t = agp_{t-1} + (1 - a)gp_e(x^*, r). \tag{A.12}$$

Equation (A.12) and hence (A.10) embody a "permanent inflation rate" hypothesis which implies that wage bargains do not follow slavishly every *transitory* change in the rate of inflation, but that they also take into account longer-term price behavior. In particular, it means that in the long-term equilibrium with which our discussion is exclusively concerned, the apparent role of the premise $a<1$ as a bearer of money illusion disappears completely.

NOTES

1. W.J. Baumol, "On the Stochastic Unemployment Distribution Model and the Long Run Phillips Curve," in *Stability and Inflation*, Essays in Honour of Professor A.W.H. Phillips, eds. A.R. Bergstrom et al. (New York: John Wiley and Sons, 1978), pp. 3-20.

2. For a recent study and a review of some of the literature, see William Craig Riddell, "The Empirical Foundations of the Phillips Curve: Evidence from Canadian Wage Contract Data," *Econometrica* 47 (January 1979): 1-24.

3. R.G. Lipsey, "The Relation Between Unemployment and the Rate of Change of Money Wages in the United Kingdom, 1862-1957: A Further Analysis," *Economica* (N.S.) 27 (February 1960):1-31.

4. G.C. Archibald, "The Structure of Excess Demand for Labour," in *Microeconomic Foundations of Employment and Inflation Theory*, ed. E.S. Phelps, (New York: W.W. Norton and Company, Inc., 1970), pp. 212-23.

5. James Tobin, "Inflation and Unemployment," *American Economic Review* 62 (March 1972):1-18.

6. C.L. Schultze, "Recent Inflation in the United States," in *Employment, Growth, and Price Levels*, Study Paper No. 1 (Washington, D.C.: U.S. Congress Joint Economic Committee, 1959).

7. The model is expressed in terms of mobility of labor and the asymmetry in upward and downward flexibility of wages. However, it can just as easily be formulated in terms of mobility of capital and differences in upward and downward rates of adjustment of prices.

8. See Robert Barro, "Unanticipated Money, Output, and the Price Level in the United States," *Journal of Political Economy* 86 (August 1978): 549-580 as discussed by Robert E. Hall, "Controlling Inflation," Stanford University, November 1978 (mimeographed.)

9. W. J. Baumol, *Welfare Economics and the Theory of the State*, 1st ed. (London: Longmans Green, 1952); 2nd ed. (Cambridge, Mass.: Harvard University Press, 1965), pp. 139-41.

10. This is not the place to go into the comparative advantages and disadvantages of the two types of fiscal controls over pollution. It is sufficient to note that the arguments do not all go one way, and that there are also some attributes of the Pigouvian tax approach which seem to be superior to the

corresponding characteristics of the market in pollution rights
However, it is interesting to note that, despite the earlier
contrary judgment of some observers (including myself), there
are preliminary indications that a market in rights, appropriately
disguised, may prove more palatable politically than a system of
Pigouvian taxes. For example, the EPA recently ruled that in
areas of the country where the air is dirtier than national
pollution standards allow, industries may construct new polluting
facilities only if they buy off a number of other polluters in the
vicinity and persuade the latter to agree to a reduction in
emissions which at least offsets those of the new installation. A
moment's thought shows that this is nothing more than a market
in pollution rights, however imperfect and restricted. Sue Anne
Batey Blackman and I are working on a study of these and other
fiscal devices now used by environmental agencies, looking for
early indications of their effectiveness in practice.

11. This assumption is adopted only for simplicity of representation and does not affect the substance of the argument.

12. In all this I assume that the tax does not increase the government's fiscal surplus or reduce its deficit. That is, I assume that the government (immediately) spends the proceeds of the tax. Otherwise, the tax may, indeed, help to reduce inflation by the conventional process of functional finance—by cutting down effective demand. But then, *any* increase in taxes might work as well.

13. If b is set at a level greater than unity the results become absolutely perverse. Equation (3) suggests that the equilibrium value of p_{t+1} would be negative! This means only that if the tax were permitted to work both ways, offering a reward for actual price reductions, a negative price in the next period would be required to offset the effects of the tax.

14. Presumably, a price-raising permit will take into account the volume of sales affected by a given price rise so that it will, perhaps, be expressed in terms of price increase multiplied by (initial) volume of sales, and it may be expressed in terms of percentage rather than absolute increases. The choice of words in the text should not be taken as a serious attempt to suggest the structure of an inflation permit.

15. The microeconomic process underlying the rebounding of the price level that seems inevitably to follow the end of a period of price controls is not entirely clear. Three explanatory hypotheses come to mind. First, some price rises, notably those of imported commodities, will inevitably escape the controls,

and the remainder of the economy may be awaiting the opportunity to make up for these. Second, people may be subject to
the illusion that the price and wage rises of which the controls
deprived them were in fact merited for reasons other than
compensation for inflation, and so the end of inflation may
induce them to strike for their just desserts. Finally, a process
of inflation suppression inevitably prevents changes in relative
prices which are called for by real changes in real economic
conditions. When controls are abolished, because of the asymmetry in price flexibility, there will be a rapid rise in the prices
of items the demand for which exceeds supply, but no offsetting
fall in the prices of items in excess supply. At least this last
source of renewed price rises should be absent when a market for
inflation rights is used to restrain the price level.

Chapter 5

INFLATION, NECESSITIES AND DISTRIBUTIVE EFFICIENCY

*E. Ray Canterbery**

INTRODUCTION

Thirty-five years ago Abba P. Lerner advanced the remarkable idea of distributive efficiency [1]. As the concept hypothesized a diminishing marginal utility of income, it contained an ingenious defense of egalitarianism because utility could only be maximized by transferring income from the higher to the lower intervals. As economists thought the redistribution of income would threaten productive efficiency, they generally dismissed the idea of distributive efficiency even though Lerner argued recently that since the labor supply curve is upward-sloping some unnecessary rewards are paid to labor [2]. That is, the first few hours of labor need not be paid any marginal revenue at all. This would leave a "surplus" in the labor market, a surplus which could be allocated in such a way as to meet the distributive efficiency conditions as well.

In this chapter, I go one step beyond Lerner and argue that distributive efficiency has priority over productive efficiency in the manufacturing sector of the advanced capitalistic economy. As a result, the productive efficiency condition is no longer relevant. Moreover, the struggle (or mock battle) between workers and management over distributive shares is a force that sustains inflation even when its root causes are elsewhere in the economy. I view this process, not so much as a class struggle,

---

*Professor of Economics, Florida State University.

but as a struggle for class. In showing how the marginal utility of income concept relates to recent developments in demand theory, I find the basis for dividing goods and services between necessities and non-necessities, a division which sheds some additional light on today's inflation. Such a division, achieved by the combined forces of labor and management, complicates the welfare effects of inflation because rising prices redistribute *real* income.

LERNER'S FORMULATION OF THE DIMINISHING MARGINAL UTILITY OF INCOME

Lerner's distributive efficiency principle governs the division of national income among individuals. He sees distributive efficiency as exactly parallel to productive efficiency, a principle governing the efficient allocation of resources among their different possible uses. In this analogy the efficient allocation of income requires the equalization of the marginal utilities of different expenditures on the various consumption goods in a situation in which the marginal utility of income is diminishing. Throughout his argument, Lerner presumes that the marginal utility of income is derived from the marginal utility of *expenditures* on consumer goods and services.

Lerner is quick to admit that there is no way of discovering whether any particular individual's marginal utility of income is greater than that of any other individual. Every individual could declare that he has an exceptionally high capacity for satisfaction and so the marginal utilities of income could be equalized only by giving him more income than anybody else; and there is no way of testing the validity of such claims. Nevertheless, Lerner contends that it is possible to redistribute income so as to maximize the *probable* gain. In his even more controversial conclusion, Lerner contends that the probable gain from any redistribution is maximized by dividing the income equally. This conclusion is derived from the principle of marginal utilitarianism; namely, all increments of output should be allocated wherever they will enjoy the highest utility [2].

The Lerner proposition rests on—at the least—the following assumptions: (1) all consumers are capable of feeling satisfactions; (2) every individual receives more satisfaction from a larger income than from a smaller income; (3) whenever a consumer can choose among two or more alternatives, he or she chooses the one that yields the greatest satisfaction; (4) the satisfactions experienced by different people are similar, so that it is not meaningless to say that the satisfaction which one individual derives from an additional unit of income is greater, or that it is less than, a satisfaction that would be derived from it by another individual.

From these asssumptions, Lerner concludes that the marginal utility of income is diminishing. The extra satisfaction that the individual obtains from a given increase in his income (the marginal utility of income) is less if his original income is greater. Lerner closes the gate with a telling argument. If, indeed, consumers spend their income in such a way that it maximizes their satisfaction, the things bought give a greater satisfaction than the other things that could have been bought instead with the same income, but were not bought for this very reason. If income were greater, the additional things that would be bought would be "next best"--the things that are rejected when incomes are smaller because they give less satisfaction. And, if income were greater still, even less satisfactory things would be bought. This, essentially, is what Lerner means by the principle of diminishing marginal utility of income.

Lerner reduces the principle of diminishing marginal utility to a *probability* because of three possible complications. (1) Goods and services may have complementary relationships. If so, it is possible for the marginal utility of income to rise with increased income. Lerner attempts to deal with this complication, but not to everyone's satisfaction. (2) The experience of having a larger or smaller income may develop or dull a person's taste or capacity for enjoying the income. The net gain (which is a certainty in the case of equal capacity) then becomes only a *probable* gain because of the possible increase or diminution of the gain which arises with unequal capacities. (3) An individual may receive more satisfaction from an extra $1.00 of income for someone else than from an extra $1.00 of income for herself. The third condition is only a problem if the poor derive more satisfaction from seeing the splendors of the rich increase by $1.00 than from the alleviation of their own poverty by $1.00, a kind of rationality that would throw virtually all of economic analysis out of the window. Irrespective of these three qualifications, only the original three assumptions need to hold to sustain Lerner's conclusion. The first extra condition is really a measurement problem, the second an issue about the timing and magnitude of transfers, and the third a pathological case. Even though the soundness of Lerner's logic has not eroded with time, many economists (including Lerner himself) are convinced that marginal utilities of incomes cannot be measured.

THE HIERARCHY OF NEEDS AND WANTS

I would agree that the marginal utility of income for *every individual* cannot be determined. However, that is not the issue. We are concerned only with probabilities, and for that it is sufficient to measure marginal utility between one income interval and another.

The Lexicographical Utility Function

Suppose that individuals have a hierarchy of needs and wants. Preferences are expressed in terms of the ranking of needs and wants. The ranking of goods and services only enters insofar as they become bundles which, in turn, roughly satisfy the needs and wants. Within any one of these bundles, traditional demand theory would apply in which substitutes and complements would bounce back and forth in response to price changes as the consumer attempts to maximize utility by minimizing expenditures for the bundle.

It is easier to imagine a hierarchy of bundles than it is to measure it. The following societal rank order of bundles is provisional, and the *exact* ordering does not affect my basic arguments. The first bundle, ranked highest in the hierarchy, would be food goods supplying minimal nutrition. The second would be clothing to supply minimal warmth. The third would be sufficient shelter to sustain life. Ranked number four would be the minimal transportation required to move wage and salary earners to and from their workplace. (If these four were judged "equally necessary," the quartet would consist of one subsistence parcel.) After bundle four we move into nonnecessities, goods and services not absolutely essential for sustaining life minimally. This, however, does not prevent the first tier of such nonnecessities from being *culturally* necessary because of what members of society have been conditioned to believe essential for the "good life." Nonetheless, the bundles beyond bundle four satisfy *wants*, rather than absolute necessities [3].

In bundle five would be extra increments (purely quantitative) of food, clothing and shelter above subsistence requirements. In bundle six would be additional increments of food, clothing, and housing which are of improved quality or else *perceived* of a quality above those in the lower-ranked bundles. In bundle seven would be extra transportation units of higher actual or imaginod quality. In bundle eight would be goods and services that would amuse and entertain or in other ways enhance one's health (including medical services). After bundle eight the individual has to be increasingly imaginative in his or her search for additional wants that are not fulfilled. Increasingly, as we go into the lower reaches of the hierarchy (or depths of marginal utility), the individual must be bombarded by external stimuli in order to desire to buy more goods and services. Otherwise, after earnings are sufficient to satisfy absolute necessities plus several steps down the hierarchy of wants, income would tend to go into savings. In fact, income does precisely that.

Properly defined, the hierarchy of bundles of goods and services can be lexicographically ordered. That is, individuals would rather have some goods and services (hereafter referred to as simply goods) from bundle-type one than to have any at all from the bundle-type ranked two, and this holds for all subsequent rankings [4]. Imagine these bundles of goods stacked like the sandbags on a levee with the water level representing the level of income. All the goods and services in each bag will not be consumed until the income level rises to the top of the bag. The other bags remain dry. As income (water) rises, the contents of the higher bags stacked on the initial necessities base are consumed.

The essential theory can be stated in terms of two needs or wants $W(1)$, $W(2)$ and quantities $x(1)$, $x(2)$ of two bundles $X(1)$, $X(2)$ of goods specific, respectively, to the satisfaction of these two wants [5]. A person in a particular income interval will attempt to minimize his or her expenditures for goods in a bundle (in the order of priority). Assume that the technology available to the consumer in combining goods to satisfy a given want is constant and that the qualities of goods are fixed. The consumer has complete knowledge regarding his or her income, the prices of available commodities, and his or her wants, and has no knowledge or expectations regarding future prices. Only the current planning period is considered and all values are per unit of time.

The regions of wants (I, II) are in two nonoverlapping spaces, as in Figure 5-1. The higher the income interval, the greater the level of satisfaction of the want because the individual can purchase a greater number of bundles of the goods which are used to produce satisfaction. Therefore, the level of satisfaction of the want can be represented as $W(1, y(m))$ or $W(2, y(m))$, $m=0$,

Figure 5-1. Lexicographical Wants in Two Space

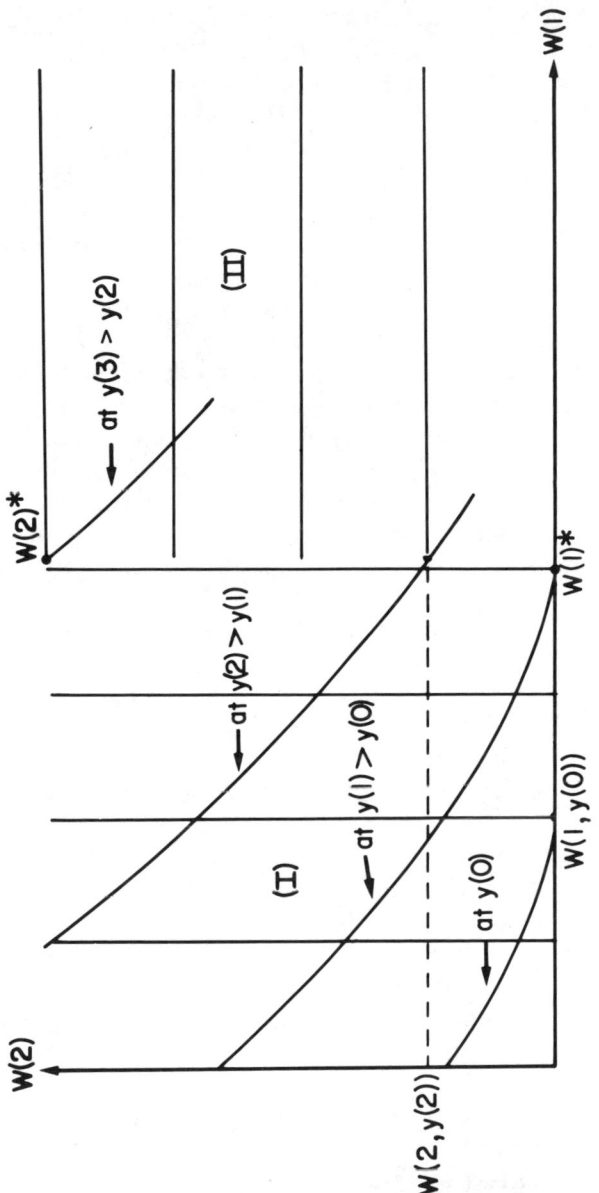

$1, \ldots, t-1$. Vertical and horizontal satistaction mapplngs reflect the lack of substitutability of wants and thus the lexicographical nature of the utility function. The convex-to-origin budget curves represent the most efficient combinations of goods from the bundles allowable at the indicated income level. In each want region, I or II, only one marginal utility is positive at a time and therefore all "optimal" outcomes are corner solutions.

The priority want $W(1)$ has a satiation level $W^*(1)$ which can be achieved in the income interval $y(1)$, so that at $y(0) > 0 < y(1)$, $0 < W(1, y(0)) < W(1)^*$, $W(2, y(0)) = 0$, where $\partial W(1, y(0))/\partial x(1) > 0$ and $\partial W(2, y(0))/\partial x(2) = 0$. Satiation of the priority want occurs where $x(1) = y(1)/p(1)$ at $W(1)^*$, $p(1)$ being the price of bundle $X(1)$. Then, where $y(2) > y(1)$, $W(1, y(2)) = W(1)^*$, $W(2, y(2)) > 0$, $\partial W(1), y(2))/\partial x(1) = 0$ and $\partial W(2, y(2))/\partial x(2) > 0$. At a sufficiently high income—$y(3) > y(2) > y(1) > y(0)$ at which expenditures are sufficient to buy enough bundles to completely satisfy $W(1)$ and $W(2)$—the second-ranked want is satiated. This analysis can be repeated for any number of wants.

The Engel curves implied by these utility relations are illustrated in Figure 5-2. The threshold level of income for bundle-type two equals the satiation level of income for bundle-type one so that the satiation level of income in each case specifies the kink in the Engel curve. Again, these relations can be extended over n bundle types [6].

Once the kink in the Engel curve is reached for any bundle type whatsoever specifically satisfying a particular want, this bundle becomes a necessities candidate. When a large share of persons or families of the society achieves an income interval sufficient to reach the kink in the Engel curve for the bundle type in question, such a bundle type is usually considered a cultural necessity.

Let us now consider the meaning of a lexicographical utility function of bundles for consumer demand. Total consumption is a function of per capita money income and average budget shares. Price indices enter indirectly insofar as bundle price index changes cause money budget shares to change. The bundles cannot exhibit complementarity. For example, automobiles and their fuel would have to be in the same bundle. (This incidentally satisfies one of the complexities raised by Lerner.) If the price of one or more bundles changes substantially as a share of per capita income, substitution is possible. However, the nature of such substitution is unconventional, being based

Figure 5-2.   Lexicographical Engel Curves in Three Space

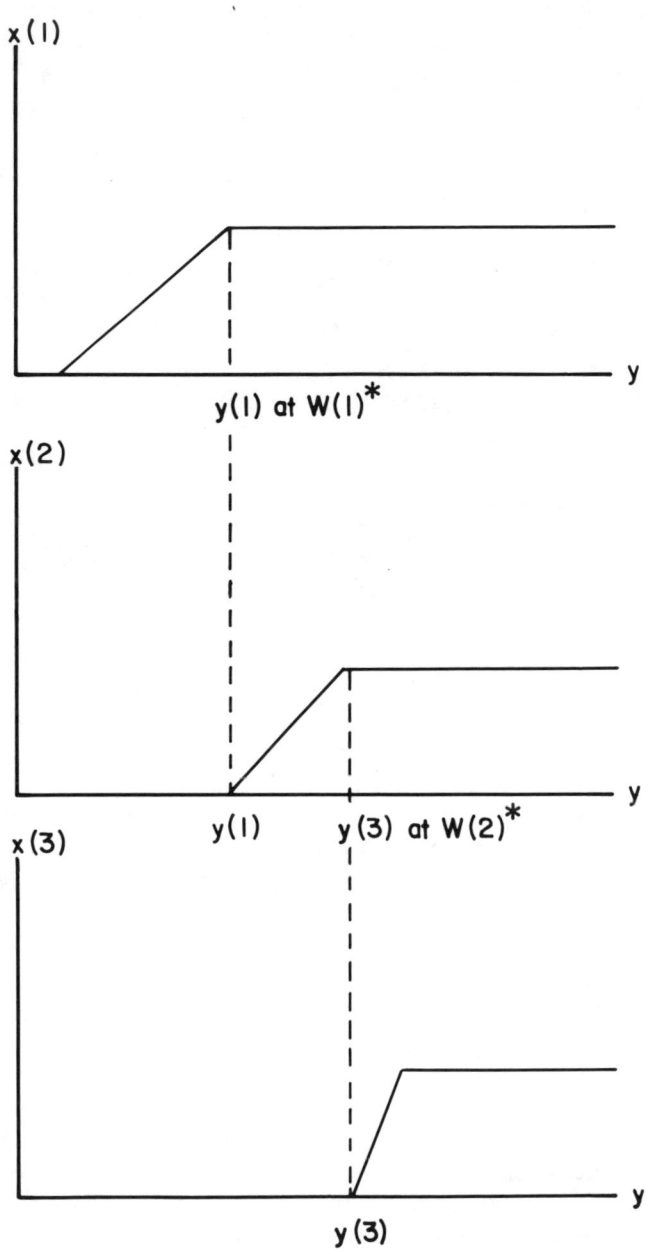

upon the income rather than the substitution effect. That is, demand adjustments are made through the budget constraint. Moreover, the compensated cross-price elasticities are non-symmetric. This condition holds at a given money income level because—when prices change—the consumers' goal is at least to maintain their budget shares in *physical* terms of higher-ranked bundles. If the price of bundle one rises sharply, the quantities of bundle two would be diminished so that individuals could "afford" bundle one. However, if the price of bundle two declines, the numbers of bundle one purchased *do not decrease*. Consumers never substitute lower-ranked for higher-regarded bundles. Rather, the quantities demanded of bundle two will increase only because real per capita income has advanced. In general, if the prices of lower-ranked bundle types rise, consumers retreat into higher-priority bundles.

Thus, two conditions preclude the specification of a continuous utility function even though the utilities are additive. First, the cross-partial derivatives are non-symmetrical. Second, utility can only be represented as a components-ordered vector rather than as a real number. However, this mathematical difficulty does not alter our main conclusion; namely, a properly ordered lexicographical utility function of bundles of commodities and services exhibit diminished marginal utility as income increments are sufficient to purchase the next lower-ordered bundle!

THE MEASURABILITY OF MARGINAL UTILITY

The Extended Linear Expenditure System (ELES)
As far as I can surmise, we cannot move directly from the set theory of lexicographic functions to an econometric estimate of the implied parameters. Fortunately, this appears to be both unnecessary as well as unwise. Our initial problem is deciding what the bundles are. Recent advances in modern demand theory have given us a tool for estimating the value of subsistence expenditures in the presence of positive savings, which is all that is required for gaining an estimate of a marginal utility of income.

The main breakthrough in terms of measuring the marginal utility of income is the formulation of the extended linear expenditure system (ELES). The method can be traced back to A.C. Pigou [7] who thought that consumer responsiveness to price changes would likely be related in a fairly straightforward way to consumer reponsiveness to changes in income. Pigou's idea was followed up by Milton Friedman [8] and incorporated rigorously into demand theory by Ragnar Frisch [9] and by H. Houthakker [10].

The utility function is directly additive. Namely,

$$U = \Sigma f(i)(x(i)), \qquad i = 1, \ldots, n \tag{1}$$

where (in the above argument) the $x's$ represent quantities of the bundles consumed. The maximization of this utility function subject to a budget constraint involves homogeneity of degree zero of the demand functions. The "representative consumer's" utility function is written as the sum of a set of individual partial utility functions, each having as its only argument the quantities of a particular bundle type. There are no net complementary bundles. However, the income-compensated cross-price effects are symmetrical in violation of a strict lexicographical ordering.

Assume that household decisions are made on a per capita basis. Then, given a spendable amount of per capita disposable income per unit of time (y) and a set of n bundles whose quantities are denoted $x(1), \ldots, x(n)$ with prices $p(1), \ldots, p(n)$, the amount spent on each bundle is $v(i) = p(i)q(i)$, total expenditure is $u = \Sigma v(i)$, so that savings are $s = y - u$. The ELES equation is

$$v(i) = p(i)a(i) + b(i)(y - \Sigma p(j)a(j)), \tag{2}$$

where the $a(i)'s$ and $b(i)'s$ are parameters to be estimated [11].

The $a(i)$ parameters may be interpreted as representing subsistence quantities in a less developed country and culturally determined basic needs in an advanced economy. The value of $\Sigma p(j)a(j)$ $(j = 1, \ldots, s)$ is total subsistence or culturally basic expenditure. The value $(y - \Sigma p(j)a(j))$ represents supernumerary or purely discretionary income. The $b's$ are marginal propensities to consume each commodity out of income, so that $\Sigma b(i) = c$, the aggregate marginal propensity to consume. Therefore, equation two says that the total actually spent on the ith bundle type is related to its own price, the prices of all other bundle types, per capita disposable income, and (indirectly) the marginal propensity to save.

There are several explanations for the introduction of savings in this particular way. I prefer the possibility advanced by

Constantino Lluch [11]. In his view, equation two represents optimal behavior at the beginning of the consumption plan. The plan is defined as the maximization of the present value of utility, discounted at the fixed rate $d>0$, subject to the constraint that the present value of expenditure cannot exceed initial wealth. The initial wealth consists of nonhuman wealth that yields an income flow at the rate of interest *(r)*, and human wealth or the flow of expected labor income over the plan, discounted to the present at the rate of interest. The expectations about prices and the interest rate are stationary and the present value of expected changes in labor income is zero.

The supernumerary function, $-f$, is

$$-f = (u - \Sigma p(j)a(j))/u, \tag{3}$$

or the ratio of expenditures on nonnecessities to total expenditures. One would expect the absolute value of this ratio to be higher in higher income countries. By the same token, the ratio presumably would be higher for high income individuals and lower for low income persons in the *same* country.

The expenditure elasticity of the marginal utility of expenditure, e, is the function

$$e = 1/f, \tag{4}$$

or the negative of the inverse supernumerary ratio, the original Frisch parameter. As savings are accounted for, the income elasticity of the marginal utility of income, e^*, is the linear transformation of e,

$$e^* = ce - (1 - c). \tag{5}$$

The directly additive utility function has several advantages in dealing with the issues raised in this chapter. (1) The approach is usable for interpreting demands for broad groups of goods. (2) It focuses upon the importance of relative prices in which the main influence consists of the income effects of price changes; that is, where the defined "good" represents a large budget share. (3) As the marginal utility of income is the integral of the income elasticity (e^*), ELES provides a direct estimate of the marginal utility of income.

Empirical Indicators of Diminishing Marginal Utility

The ELES specification and the above derivations provide several measures which are potential indicators of the diminishing marginal utility of income. The following discussion of these measures will describe their behavior when the marginal utility of income is diminishing.

The Relation of Subsistence to Total Expenditures. The expenditures for basic commodity bundles of food, clothing, and shelter should increase with rising per capita incomes but should decline as a share of total actual expenditures. The proper measure from ELES is $\Sigma p(j)a(j)/u$.

Marginal Budget Shares. The marginal budget share for the "most necessary" bundle type should decline as per capita income rises. The marginal budget shares are the $b(i)'s$ in the ELES equation, equation two above. The marginal budget shares of "less necessary" bundles should rise with per capita income until such bundles are considered cultural necessities and then fall as incomes continue to rise.

The Engel Elasticities. The Engel elasticity or income elasticity for the "most necessary" bundle should decline as per capita income goes up. The Engel elasticity for nonessentials should exceed one and rise until the non-necessities become "cultural necessities" (at very high per capita incomes). In the ELES formulation the Engel elasticity (e') is equal to $b(i)/B(i)$, where $B(i) = v(i)/u$. That is, the Engel elasticity is equal to the marginal budget share divided by the average budget share.

The Frisch Parameter. The Frisch parameter (e), the elasticity of the marginal utility of total expenditure with respect to total expenditure and correspondingly the income elasticity of the marginal utility of income (e^*), should decline (in absolute terms) as per capita income rises, reflecting the greater price responsiveness for bundles where incomes are highest.

Savings and the Marginal Propensity to Save. Savings should be sensitive to the price of the "most necessary" bundle, but this sensitivity should decline as per capita income rises. Stated alternatively, as absolute necessities become a smaller share of incomes, saving becomes less responsive to price changes in the highest ranked bundle. As a corollary of this, one would expect the marginal propensity to save to rise at higher levels of per capita income, as Keynes surmised.

Recent ELES Estimates

Lluch, Powell, and Williams [12] have estimated the ELES parameters from time series data within countries as well as from cross-sectional data between countries. Their results tend to confirm a diminishing marginal utility of income according to the above measures.

The authors use eight commodity bundles: food (food, beverages, and tobacco), clothing (clothing and other personal effects), housing (household operation, rent, water, fuel, and light), durables (furniture, furnishings, and household equipment), personal care (personal care and health expenses), transport (transportation and communication), recreation (recreation and entertainment), and other services (financial services, education and research, and other). Among these bundles, the food bundle would come closest to fitting the description of our highest ranked bundle, with other necessities expenditures distributed *among* subsistence spending on clothing, housing, transport, personal care, and (regretably) durables. The least necessary bundle would consist most probably of "other services." As the ELES model suggests, some share (measured by the $a(i)'s$) of each commodity bundle include either subsistence or culturally determined necessities.

It must be emphasized that the ELES measures subsistence only at lower income levels, a calibration of the expenditures required to survive. At higher income levels or in nations with higher per capita incomes, the same term becomes a measure for "culturally determined subsistence." The latter is a *perceived* subsistence measure. In both the time series and cross-section results, the level of "subsistence" consumption increased with income levels, but those for food and *total subsistence* declined relative to actual spending. From the time series results, total subsistence is estimated to be around 62 percent of GNP at per capita GNP levels of $100 to $500, but this declines to around 25 percent at levels of GNP per capita of about $2,500. Subsistence expenditure on food, as a percentage of total subsistence expenditure, falls from around 63 percent at the per capita GNP interval of $100 to $500, to 50 percent at higher levels.

The empirical result that occurs with most frequency and strength from all data bases is a fall in the marginal budget share for food as income levels rise. In the time series results, the marginal budget share for food in high income countries is only 50 percent of that for lower income countries. Estimates of the marginal budget share for housing increase with income. The marginal budget share for transport, which includes expenditure on motor vehicles, increases significantly with income levels over the whole range of per capita incomes.

The Engel elasticity for food was found to be less than one and "in general" declined with increases in per capita GNP. The expenditure elasticity for clothing trended toward greater than unity and sometimes declined. Estimates of the expenditure elasticity for housing tended to be centered on unity.

In the time series data, implied values of the Frisch parameter (e) at different levels of GNP per capita were -7.5 at $100, -4 at $500, -3 at $1,000, and -2 at $3,000. (Each of these values can be transformed by the appropriate marginal propensity to consume into the income elasticity of the marginal utility of income *(e*).)* Therefore, at low per capita income levels the estimates of the Frisch parameter are much higher in absolute terms than the value of -2 which is frequently reported by various researchers for high income countries. The cross-sectional results for individual countries tended to conform with the time series findings.

NECESSITIES AND INFLATION

The division of expenditures between subsistence and nonessentials is important for assessing the welfare effects of inflation. Given the individual's income level, expenditures are budgeted according to needs and wants in great part conditioned by the person's position in the income distribution. This explains the regularity in the way households allocate expenditure on food, clothing, transportation, and other items. If goods and services that are need-and-want-specific are grouped and aggregated at a sufficiently high level, no physical substitution between groups is possible. Substitution occurs by expenditure transfers from lower ranked to higher-ranked priority items which maintain the necessities' quantities. In turn, the budget shares in money terms are altered.

It follows that a knowledge of which prices are rising is as important--perhaps more important--as the fact that prices in general are rising. The relative price changes between necessities and non-essentials--between bread and pleasure boats--reveals the quality of the inflation. The inflation in recent years has been most severe in the food, public utilities, housing, fuel, and medical care sectors. A general rise in the price of necessities (at a given money income) requires a diversion of income away from discretionary items. In marginal utility terms the household shifts expenditures away from those items yielding lower marginal utility and toward those providing higher marginal utility. The consequence of such inflation is to reduce the total utility of all those who do not anticipate the inflation or expect it but cannot offset its adverse effects. The subsistence share of total expenditures rises.

The impact of necessities' inflation is uneven. The market basket of goods is more necessities-intensive, the lower the family in the income distribution. According to a 1972-73 study by the U.S. Bureau of Labor Statistics, 136 percent of family income from the lowest decile was spent on (one measure of) basic necessities (food, energy, shelter, and medical care). In contrast, only 44 percent of the eighth decile's income was spent on necessities. As the inflation of necessities can push the middle class into subsistence, it is hardly surprising that the working class resists the efforts of prices in making them poor.

Inflation in the prices of necessities also has adverse production and employment implications in the affluent society. The required diversion of money income away from discretionary goods and services results in sales declining in such industries, in production slowdowns and in unemployment. Such shortfalls are not offset in the necessities sector because the diversion of money expenditures does not result in higher output levels.

The production relation leads directly to the issue of productive efficiency in the manufacturing sector of the advanced economy. Are the aforementioned money income increments based upon marginal products? If not, productive efficiency fades into the background and distributive efficiency or the income-utility equity issue dominates the landscape.

BUDGET SHARES AND LABOR MARKET RETURNS

If labor is paid its marginal revenue product, we would expect to find conditions conducive to such returns in the labor markets. In this regard, the marginal product theory supposes that employment and wages are determined at the same time in the same place by the same forces. The purpose of labor markets is to match producers' labor requirements with quantities of human capital that have various qualitative characteristics. However, there are numerous institutions involved over long periods of time in many different places. The probability that all these institutions would facilitate the convergence of labor demands and supplies to equilibria simultaneously everywhere appears low. Moreover, for labor to be paid its marginal revenue product everywhere requires that short- and long-run equilibria coincide. The foregoing discussion of subsistence expenditures suggests still another requirement; namely, labor market returns must be independent of consumers' or workers' needs, a more transparent way of saying that wage rates must be based on worker productivity rather than on needs, physically *or* culturally determined.

The Classical Versus Neoclassical Views

The classical economists had workers being paid subsistence wages in which subsistence was often defined in cultural terms. Wage goods provided subsistence. For these economists, necessity was the mother of convention. The producer was saved only by the excessive sexual appetites of the working class who—reproducing without limit—were always in abundant supply. Of perhaps equal importance, the workers were not organized.

The classical view of necessities versus luxuries was lost with the neoclassical economists, most of whom came from the upper middle class. Income was presumed to be above subsistence. All commodities looked alike to the neoclassicals and all income was discretionary. Without the burden of having to worry about purchasing necessities, the imaginary consumers were free to choose any set of goods and services they desired. Income was a "given" and—with the neoclassicals snubbing necessities—income for *everyone* was always adequate. The poor were not simply invisible, they were not there to be seen. For the neoclassicals, discretion was the better part of value.

Discretionary Spending in Advanced Capitalism

In the advanced capitalistic system, however, the existence of discretionary spending and the production of nonessentials is not independent of the wage rate. Just as with the agricultural economy in which the classicals saw labor being paid in food supplies, the wage earner in manufacturing is paid in terms of the goods he or she produces. Unlike the classical system, however, there is, in part, a revised sequence in which the producer stimulates wants and defines what the worker will demand in wage goods. Also, unlike the classical system, the wage earner in manufacturing is organized.

General Labor Market Conditions

As the concentrated manufacturing sector and industrial unions are the pace-setters in the modern industrialized economy, I will focus exclusively on what John Kenneth Galbraith has called the "planning system." This sector also is most frequently cited as a source of chronic inflation [13].

Noncompeting Labor Markets and the Labor Supply. It is useful to think of labor markets as non-competing with respect to human capital types. The labor force, the supply side of the labor market, consists of those persons who are of working age, wish to work and have sufficient job-related skills to enter a labor market. The persons' human capital types are decided simultaneously at any time, $t(0)$, by individual's characteristics and training and by the labor markets and occupations currently available in the economy.

Initially assume a one-to-one correspondence between general human capital classifications (HC's) and labor market types. There are many homogeneous and, thus, noncompeting national labor types. A homogeneous noncompeting labor market is defined as one bounded geographically and one in which the elasticity of substitution in production between the labor of its type and the other types within the area approaches zero. The geographic limits are set by "reasonable" commuting distances (at current state of transportation technology) from the selected labor population center. The short run is a period of complete labor immobility among homogeneous labor markets.

The long run is a period sufficient for persons to accept employment in a lower yielding homogeneous market within or outside of the geographical area, to move spatially to a labor market with "like" but higher paid HC types or to increase their human capital and in this way "qualify" for a higher return labor market.

In general, the number of persons geared to a labor market decreases with increases in the skills, special aptitudes, and credentials requirements of the market. For example, the number of persons who can qualify as unskilled labor greatly exceeds the number who can qualify as medical doctors.

We can think of the members of the labor supply of a human capital type as being in rank order (for example, 1, 2, . . . , g) from most to least preferred employee characteristics, a labor force queue at either a local or national level.

There is no assurance that all participants will be employed at any particular time. The employment levels depend upon product demand and the technology of production. It is presumed that wherever involuntary unemployment exists it will involve the persons lowest ranked within the HC classification. This would include young persons who lack job training or are being newly considered for on-the-job training.

Population growth is the main source of the total labor supply. Changes in labor force participation rates also will affect many if not all labor markets. In the interest of simplicity, I will abstract from those factors which alter the overall labor force size and its participation rate. Suffice it to say that most new entrants will appear at the end of this labor queue.

The Industrial Union

The industrial union organizes an entire industry. Therefore, the industrial union population comprises many different human capital types and occupations, including both unskilled and semi-skilled workers. The main economic effect of the industrial union is negotiation of a wage-rate floor for its members.

The Demand for Labor. In the short run the wage rate and the employment level are decided by different forces. Essentially, this separation of forces stems from the static nature of production processes combined with union regulations in the short run. Union rules usually specify the number of workers assigned to a machine and floor area as well as their work speed. The production process--otherwise designed by technology--cannot be altered in the short run.

Thus, in the short run the state of technology, industrial competition and product prices ($p(i)$'s) are given. Let $h(k)$ be the labor hours required of the kth human capital type per unit of physical output in a selected geographical area. As employment is a fixed proportion of production, the quantity of labor demanded is

$$z(k) = h(k)q(i), \tag{6}$$

where $q(i)$ is the total output of product i, which is assumed to be homogeneous across the labor market.

If labor is paid its value in production, the wage rate is

$$w(k) = p(i)/h(k), \tag{7}$$

where $p(l)$ is the price of the product or service by this labor type. (In Knightian terms, p would be the expected price.) No union worker can influence this price.

Technology and Demand. Technological progress, a change in the production process, can alter directly the demand for a particular labor type by changing labor-quantity requirements. That is, while capital and labor tend to be complements (fixed factor coefficients) in the short run, they potentially are substitutes in the long run. The magnitude of the direct effect of technological progress upon the demand for labor depends upon whether the new technology is labor-using.

In modern capitalism the main purpose of new tools and equipment is to reduce unit labor requirements. Machines are more responsive to managerial commands. Moreover, the long-term trend of wages is known to be upward, especially in the already capital-intensive industrial sector that is unionized.

Technological change can also exert an *indirect* effect. A new, more complex technology can result in a producer's *shifting* to labor that embodies a much greater quantity of human capital, a different human capital type. These shifts are institutionalized via job description changes (often required by union agreements). Those workers with the "older" skills are, in the short run, unemployed, as they cannot move (along with demand) to the alternative labor market. Either direct or indirect shifts in labor demands from technological change can be represented as changes in the values of the $h(k)'s$.

The Wage Rate. The industrial union's instrumental variable is the wage rate rather than the labor supply. The union is aware of the pricing power of the concentrated industry in which higher wage costs can be passed on through a constant or rising mark-up over variable or average costs [14]. The likelihood of full-cost pricing increases with greater product market imperfection. If the labor union had no wage bargaining power, workers would be paid the classical minimum standard, a physically subsistence wage. Even with this minimum standard a general increase in the price of necessities would result in higher wage rates in a given technological state. Whether biological necessities themselves be produced under conditions of competition or by the concentrated sector, the effect upon workers' budgets and the wage bill is the same. The budget allocation of money income for necessities rises and so does the employer's wage bill.

In the affluent society, however, the impact of the consumers' budgets upon the industrial wage bill does not end with physical subsistence needs. Surpluses are production increments in excess of what is required merely to sustain life. While there are American households which exist at the biological subsistence level, ours is indisputably an economy of surpluses. The Bureau of Labor Statistics' estimate for the "higher" consumption budget of a four-person family in the urban United States in 1976 was $17,048, more than twice the lower budget.

Veblen's snob appeal takes on concrete meaning in the face of such a very high ratio. The large gap between the lowest and highest incomes inspires business management to transcend its role as simply a producer of goods and services. While the difference between the necessities' budget and the higher income budget could in theory be devoted entirely to savings, the producer tries to divert these household dollars toward consumer goods. Not surprisingly, in such an economy a large share of the GNP goes to salespersons, marketing efforts, and advertising. Indeed, the very lifeblood of capitalism as we know it is the exchange of surpluses for desired "extras," whether those luxuries are perceived as "needs" or not. Even the relatively low standards of living of the High Middle Ages did not prevent merchants and manufacturers from emulating the nobility in clothes, customs, and tax exemptions. Economic class emulation is simply more sophisticated in the affluent society.

The producers in the manufacturing sector have succeeded all too well in convincing the consumer that he should expand the number of goods which he considers "necessary." The wherewithal to fulfill both the manufacturers' and the workers' dreams is decided at the labor-management bargaining table. In response to these culturally determined desires, the giant labor union demands higher wages so that the workers can pay for the newly defined standard of living. The corporation capitulates, knowing that the higher cost of production from a larger wage can be passed on to the consumer. The illusion that a higher wage is always a good thing—a money illusion—is enjoyed by the worker who does not quite sense the impact of his dual role as both laborer and consumer. In the worker's budget, these increases are merely ones covering the "cost of living." It is not mere historical accident that the highest-paid workers reside in the protected part of the economy, the concentrated sector.

The industrial union does not negotiate a wage rage, rather it settles for a standard of living. Thus, the wage rate is related not only to the prices of the products produced by labor, but also to the prices of goods *consumed* by labor. The cost of the given standard of living has been rising, especially as the prices of basic necessities go up. This widening circle of rising prices, cost of living, wage bill demands and still higher prices for labor-produced goods leads to an acceleration in the rate of inflation.

Employment and the Long Run. The level of employment is decided by the production technique and the level of product demand (output) in the short run. The wage rate selection is a political decision and has been decided independently from these economic forces.

In the long run the connection between productivity and the wage rate is closer but of a different character than often described. The demand for labor is responsive to changes in average product prices and improvements in technology of the employing industry and firms. As the labor supply of a particular HC type usually requires a gestation period of several years, the long-run labor supply is a function of the *expected* wage rate (w^*) rather than the actual. In the manufacturing sector the producer expects the wage rate to move only one direction—upward.

The motives for capital accumulation are not always clearly defined. However, even if producers do not desire growth to maintain market shares or for other reasons, a remaining salutary effect of adopting a new mode of production is the potential it gives for replacing labor. Beyond the reduction of the wage bill, replacement of workers with machines has further advantages: machines do not demand fringe benefits and do not talk back. It is not surprising, therefore, that the price markup is used to generate investment funds for the purpose of acquiring a production process which utilizes less labor.

It is important to distinguish between the usual graph depicting a cause-effect relation between the wage rate and the quantity of labor demanded and a graph of the loci of wage rates and labor quantities. It is the latter that is represented in Figure 5-3, which represents the labor market for one unionized human capital type in a particular geographic area [15]. (Linearity is assumed for simplicity.)

If the growth of technology reduces the labor-output ratio, the loci of $w = p/h$ and $z = hq$, where z is employment and q and p are at given levels, trace out what appears to be a downward-sloping labor demand curve. As fixed production coefficients pertain at each new level of technology, the labor-output ratio equals the marginal labor-output ratio. As more capital-intensive production reduces labor per extra unit of output, *by definition* the marginal physical product of labor rises as z declines. At higher levels of output, the wage-employment loci shift rightward: at higher product price levels, the loci shift upward. However, just as a higher product price and wage rate do not necessarily imply a higher employment level, neither does a lower amount of output necessarily result in a lower wage rate.

Figure 5-3.   Wage-Employment LOCI, An Industrial Union Labor Market

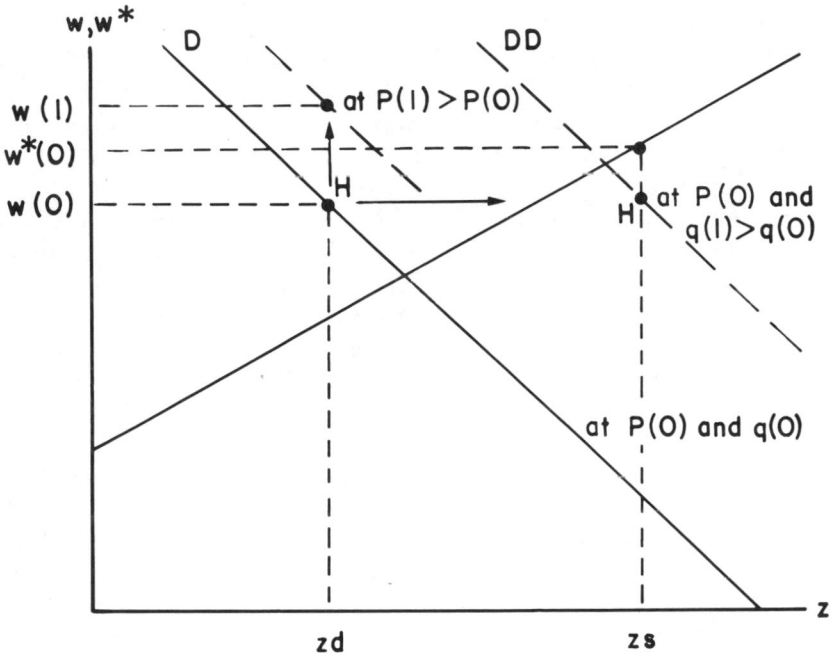

The employers of industrial labor have an incentive and ability to substitute capital for labor in the long run. Thus, the w-z loci trace an "elastic" curve. At any time labor demand, however, is represented by only one point, such as H, which is given by the current state of technology.   The labor supply curve, being based upon wage expectations, tends to be relatively price-elastic. Although the actual *and* expected wage rates may be nearly equal (as illustrated), capital substitution may have advanced to the point where labor demand is *zd* (*h* has declined to *H* so that only an output increase sufficient to shift the demand to *DD* (at *H*) would bring full employment to this labor market). At a constant or rising price markup, a wage increase (motivated by attempts to maintain or increase discretionary income) to *w(1)* will bring along a price rise to *p(1)*. Alternatively, a price rise to *p(1)* may result in an increase in the wage rate to *w(1)*. The direction of cause-to-effect depends upon timing in the bargaining process and may be unrelated to output changes (as illustrated). The wage rate at *t(0)*, the short-run wage rate, may or may not be near the long-term rate.

CONCLUSIONS

Abba Lerner's original instincts, expressed prior to recent developments in demand theory, were correct regarding the requirement that income be redistributed from higher to lower income recipients in order to achieve distributive efficiency. Considerable econometric evidence supports his hypothesis that the marginal utility of income diminishes. However, his retention of the notion of productive efficiency no longer appears either necessary or applicable in the advanced industrial economy. Workers' wage rates can only be geared to marginal products or worker productivity if the wage and employment decision is simultaneous and based upon the same elements. Simultaneity is not the case in the manufacturing sector, the drivewheel of modern capitalism, nor is it evidenced with frequency elsewhere.

The size of the wage demand by the industrial union is determined by the culture-specific needs and wants of the consumer as a union member. The ability of the producer to meet such wage demands—even when spurred by general price inflation—often is assured by his ability to maintain or increase price mark-ups above production costs. The producer has been a participant in the process which leads the worker to strive for a wage rate sufficient to cover newly created or newly attainable (within reach) wants. Therefore, productive-labor efficiency escapes the net of worker and producer alike.

In the long run, the manufacturer reduces his dependence on labor by adopting new capital-intensive processes. These processes are purchased with the investment funds generated by the price mark-up. The long-run physical marginal product of labor is merely an artifact derived from new technologies. The actual relation between labor and capital is that decided by the new human capital required to match the skill requirements for operating the new machines and equipment. As the labor force does not know what these future skill requirements entail, the mismatch of human capital and machines often results in unemployment even when wage rates are rising.

In this view the wage–price spiral runs more deeply through the fabric of society than we once thought. The production and marketing process itself raises the cost of entry into our economy. Once inside, the cost of staying in also accelerates and only wage rates set by monopoly-type powers can keep the income earner from experiencing a decline in his or her formerly attained standard of living. The impacts upon individuals are uneven, and solving the issues related to distributional justice becomes even more difficult.

NOTES

1.   Abba P. Lerner, *The Economics of Control* (New York: The Macmillan Company, 1944, Chapter 3).

2.   Abba P. Lerner, "Utilitarian Marginalism (Nozick, Rawls, Justice, and Welfare)," in E. Ray Canterbery and Harry G. Johnson, eds., Justice, Nozick, and Rawls: A Symposium, *Eastern Economic Journal*, Vol. IV, No. 1 (January, 1978), pp. 54-57.

3.   For a deeper exploration of how needs might be distinguished from wants, see David Braybrooke, "Let Needs Diminish That Preferences May Prosper," in Nicholas Rescher, ed., *Studies in Moral Philosophy* (Monograph No. 1, American Philosophical Quarterly Series, Oxford: Basil Blackwell, 1968), pp. 86-107.

4.   For a mathematically exact definition of lexicographical ordering, see J. S. Chipman, "The Foundation of Utility," *Econometrica*, 28, 1960. pp. 193-224.

5.   In order to confine all equations to one printed line, all subscripts have been written inside parentheses, ( )'s.

6.   Using a different approach and applying it to the introduction of new products, Ironmonger has generated similarly related Engel curves.   See D.S. Ironmonger, *New Commodities and Consumer Behavior* (Cambridge, England: Cambridge University Press, 1972).

7.   A.C. Pigou, "A Method of Determining the Numerical Value of Elasticities of Demand," *Economic Journal*, 20, 1910, pp. 636-40.

8. M. Friedman, "Professor Pigou's Method for Measuring Elasticities of Demand from Budgetary Data," *Quarterly Journal of Economics,* 50, 1935, pp. 151-63.

9. R. Frisch, "A Complete Scheme for Computing All Direct and Cross Price Elasticities in a Model With Many Sectors," *Econometrica,* 27, 1959, pp. 177-96.

10. H.S. Houthakker, "Additive Preference," *Econometrica,* 28, 1960, 244-57.

11. This equation was derived by C. Lluch in the "The Extended Linear Expenditure System," *European Economic Review,* 4, 1973, pp. 21-32 and the steps to solution can be found there.

12. Contantino Lluch, Alan A. Powell and Ross A. Williams, *Patterns in Household Demand and Saving* (Oxford, England: Oxford University Press, 1977). The stochastic specification of equation two is explained on pages 25-35.

13. I do not intend to imply that the marginal product case is any better supported outside of manufacturing. Quite the contrary, a glance at the salaries of professional service workers will be no more reassuring. For a more general theory that explains all personal incomes in non-marginal-product terms, see E. Ray Canterbery, "A Vita Theory of the Personal Income Distribution," *Southern Economic Journal* (July 1979), pp. 12-48.

14. For an early defense of the constant markup view, see Sidney Weintraub, *A General Theory of the Price Level, Output, Income Distribution and Economic Growth* (Philadelphia: Chilton, 1959).

15. See the source in [13] for behavioral descriptions of other labor market types.

 *Part II*

INFLATION: AN INTERNATIONAL PROBLEM

✳ *Chapter 6*

INFLATION'S INTERNATIONAL DIMENSIONS

Martin Bronfenbrenner*

INTRODUCTION

This topic is so broad that all that I can do in the space available is to touch in a less than rigorous way on four specimen problems. These are:

1. How does domestic inflation affect a country's balances of trade and payments?
2. How does inflation in supplier countries affect a country's domestic inflation rate?
3. How does inflation in customer countries affect a country's domestic inflation rate?
4. If we assume the existence of a "world" inflation rate, what are the costs of seeking to inflate more quickly or more slowly than this world rate?

These questions will be considered under both fixed and flexible exchange rate regimes, while trying to dodge the multiplicity of alternative cases that makes Sir James Meade's *Balance of Payments* [1] so notoriously difficult to follow.

———
 *Kenan Professor of Economics, Duke University, and Visiting Scholar, Federal Reserve Bank of San Francisco.

TECHNIQUE

To discuss these questions, let me begin by reviewing: (1) a four-quadrant diagram of balance of payments equilibrium and (2) the determination of domestic income, employment, and price levels by aggregate demand and supply functions within such a system.

Our four-quadrant picture of the balance of payments (Figure 6-1) includes: real trade balance B as an inverse function of the real domestic national income (SE quadrant) with positive values representing net exports; the real capital-movement balance K as an inverse function of the domestic real interest rate (NW quadrant), with positive values representing capital outflows (exports); and the definition of balance-of-payments equilibrium, an identity in which a positive trade balance equals a capital outflow of the same size, and vice versa (SW quadrant). Figure 6-1 shows these relations both singly on the left panel and jointly on the right panel. Also, on the right an equilibrium balance of payments function BP is derived as the locus of real incomes and interest rates at which the preceding three relations are satisfied simultaneously.

Within this model the influence of such factors as relative prices on the balance of trade and the profitability of domestic investment on the balance of capital flows is exogenous. These changes and other important factors are treated as shifts in the b and k functions of the diagram. For example, if higher domestic productivity lowers domestic prices and affects our trade balance as we expect it to do, the b function will shift upward to b' and the BP function downward to BP'. This would mean that payments equilibrium could now be reached at a higher income level and/or at a lower domestic interest rate than previously.

If we are in fact at a point like $P1$ above the BP line, the balance of payments is positive and we are acquiring international resources (gold, convertible currencies, balances with international organizations). If we are in fact at a point like $P2$, we have a passive balance and are losing international resources; when these resources threaten to run out, we have a balance of payments problem. The United States has been losing reserves almost every year since the Korean war, but it has become conscious of a payments problem only a decade later.

I find it easiest to see which case is which by concentrating on the interest rate dimension. Thus an interest rate lower than $r1$ would induce more capital outflow or less capital inflow. If it

Figure 6-1. Balance of Payments Equilibrium.

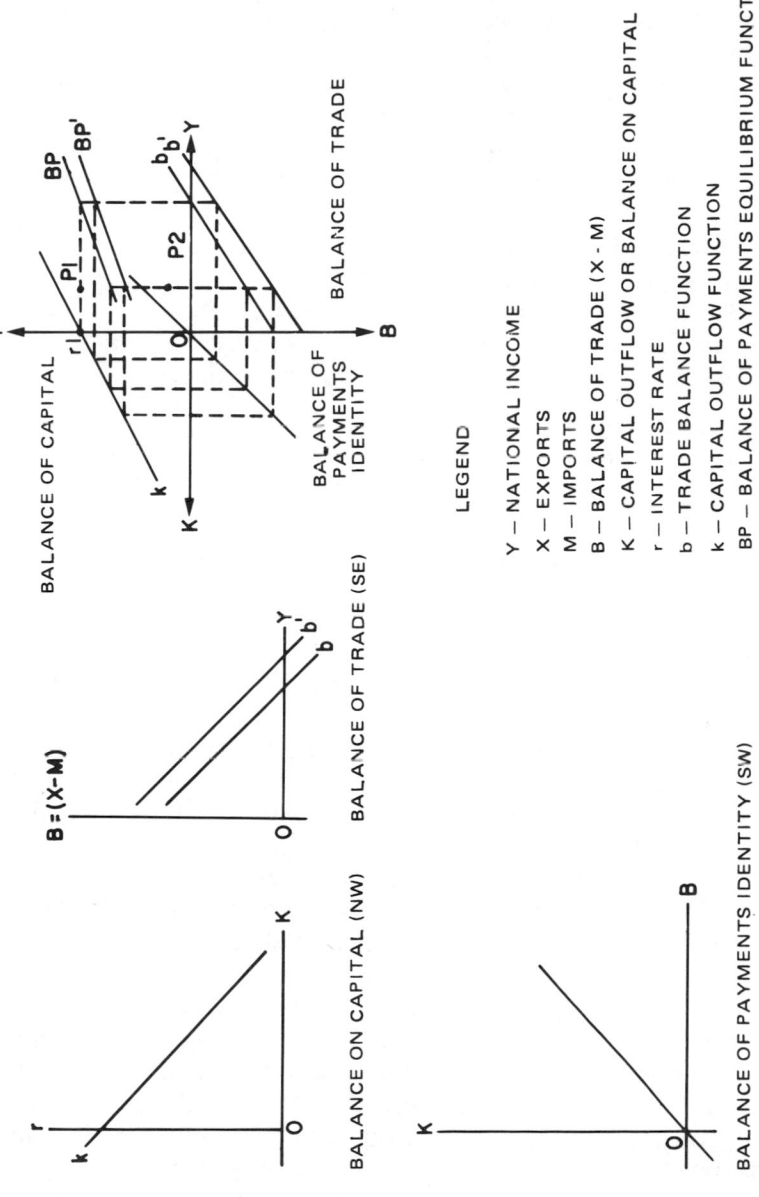

LEGEND

Y — NATIONAL INCOME

X — EXPORTS

M — IMPORTS

B — BALANCE OF TRADE (X - M)

K — CAPITAL OUTFLOW OR BALANCE ON CAPITAL

r — INTEREST RATE

b — TRADE BALANCE FUNCTION

k — CAPITAL OUTFLOW FUNCTION

BP — BALANCE OF PAYMENTS EQUILIBRIUM FUNCTION

would also move us vertically toward the *BP* function, we must have initially been accumulating reserves, so that our balance of payments was positive. (A positive balance is usually called *favorable*, which is obviously silly when a country has no use for the international reserves that it is piling up for the contemplation of God.)

We pass on now to our other bit of technical economics; namely, Figure 6-2. You will be pleased to observe only one quadrant, with its vertical axis representing the domestic price level p and the horizontal axis representing the percentage y of full employment income which the economy is generating. The downward-sloping aggregate demand function *D* is conventional and can be shifted to the right (or left) by expansionary (or contractionary) monetary and fiscal policy. The aggregate supply function *S* is also conventional below the full employment level, but it is drawn vertical above that point. This means that no more than full-employment output can be produced at any price; this might not be quite true in an economy of slavery, brain-washing, or money illusion, or if foreign aid can be secured.

FIRST PROBLEM: DOMESTIC INFLATION AND THE BALANCE

Now we are ready for the first of our four problems without much more geometric apparatus. Suppose, to make the problem a little more concrete, that a country with its payments in balance is suffering from unemployment and desires to raise its income and employment levels by increasing public expenditures and financing these by monetary expansion sufficient to hold the domestic real interest rate steady. As a side effect of these policies, there is a perceptible increase in the inflation rate. What happens to the balances of trade and payments?

We begin by supposing that exchange rates are fixed, as in Figure 6-3. This diagram is Figure 6-1 augmented by Hicksian *IS* and *LM* functions, whose intersection determines equilibrium income and interest rate levels. (*IS* is a locus of points at which the market for goods is in equilibrium, with planned saving *S* equal to planned investment *I*; *LM* is a locus of points at which the market for money is in equilibrium, with the supply of money balances *M* equal to the demand for liquidity *L*.)

The initial intersection of *IS* and *LM* at point *P* on *BP* is one of trade surplus, capital outflow, and payments equilibrium. The final intersection of *IS'* and *LM'* at point *P'*, however, involves a

Figure 6-2. Aggregate Demand and Supply.

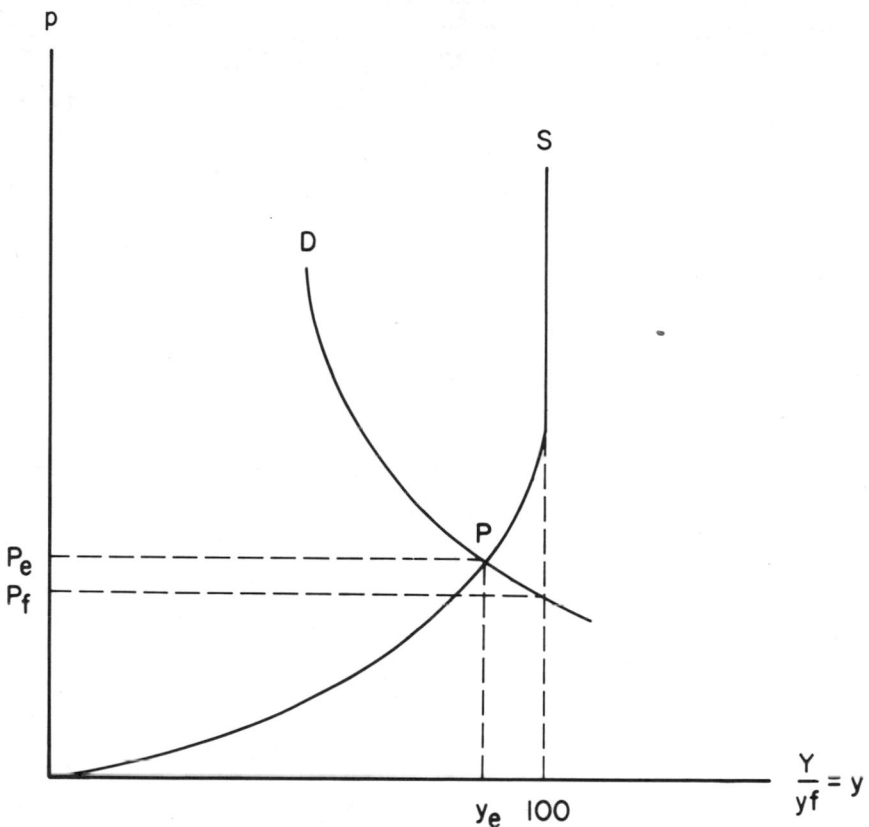

LEGEND

Y — NATIONAL INCOME

yf — FULL EMPLOYMENT VALUE OF Y

y — PROPORTION OF FULL-EMPLOYMENT INCOME $\left(\frac{y}{yf}\right)$

P — PRICE LEVEL

Pe — EQUILIBRIUM VALUE OF

Pf — FULL EMPLOYMENT VALUE OF

D — AGGREGATE DEMAND FUNCTION

S — AGGREGATE SUPPLY FUNCTION

deficit even without other changes, because the interest rate has
been held constant. But there are other changes which operate
to increase the deficit. The "acceleflation" side effect shifts the
capital outflow function k upward and outward, because inflation
discourages capital flowing to or remaining in our country. The
balance of payments function BP therefore shifts upward to BP',
increasing the deficit further.

Figure 6-3.   Inflationary Expansion and the Balance of Payments
(Locomotion Theory)

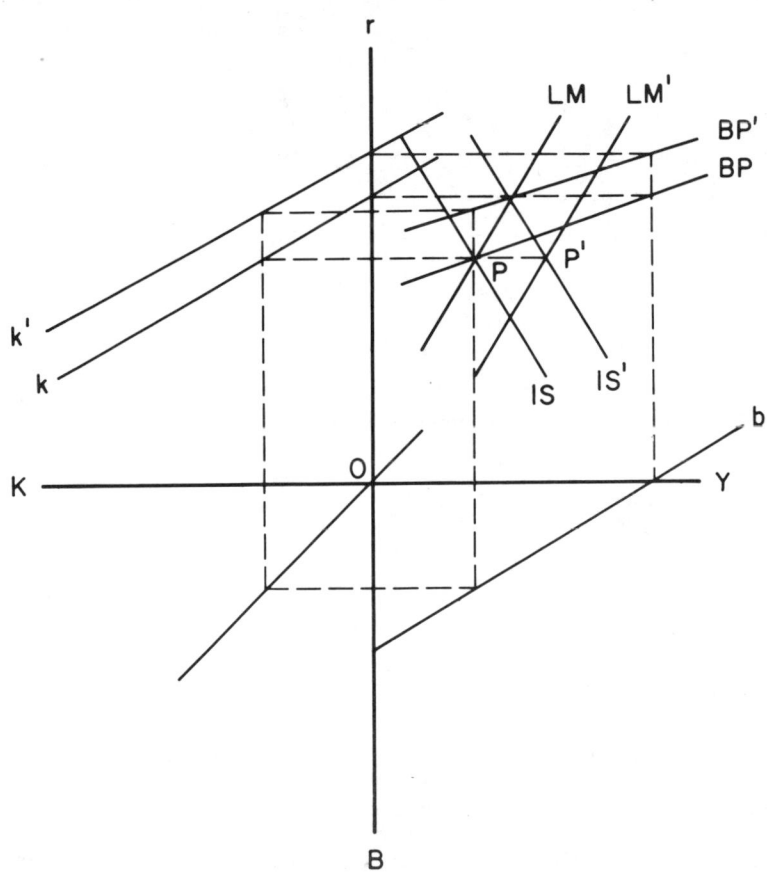

This result is reasonably general unless one or more of four offsets occur: the domestic interest rate is allowed to rise (contrary to our assumptions); the income increase is so highly concentrated on demand for purely domestic and import-competing goods that the marginal propensity to import is zero; the income increase is so highly concentrated in export- and import-substitutes on the supply side that the trade-balance function b shifts upward; and/or the income increase improves profit rates sufficiently to attract or retain capital despite the accelerated inflation or acceleflation.

Let us now introduce exchange-rate flexibility, or "clean float" in the terminology of the financial pages. In this case, any passive payments balance at the initial rate will weaken the domestic currency, causing a depreciation. If this weakening or depreciation increases the foreign demand for this country's exports sufficiently, and reduces the domestic demand for imports sufficiently [2], the resulting shift in the b function will restore trade balance equilibrium after a lapse of time estimated for the United States (by the Brookings Institution's "J-curve" in the mid-1970s) at fifteen to eighteen months (See Figure 6-4). But even here capital flows must not be forgotten. The weakening of the domestic currency will increase capital outflows as investors try to avoid exchange-rate losses. This movement in the "wrong" direction delays further the restoration of payments equilibrium.

These statements put me among the skeptics about the universal efficacy of floating rates as the answer to all our problems. I agree that at *some* positive value of the dollar (before its value falls to zero) the United States balance of payments will surely turn positive, but my refusal to have faith in slight and near-painless depreciations makes me a skeptic, although I think my position on this issue is a minority one among international economists.

A policy application of the foregoing analysis is the "locomotive theory" controversy of the late 1970s. The Carter administration claimed in 1976-78 that the weakening United States dollar was the result of American economic expansion, which some important United States trading partners, particularly West Germany and Japan, failed to support. If they, too, had stimulated their economies and accepted acceleflationary risks, say the Americans, the dollar would not have weakened as it did. Our exposition illustrates this point, so far as it goes. The Germans and Japanese, however, have held out for something they consider even better; namely, disinflation all around, even at some cost in measured growth and employment. In its disinflationary turn of late 1978 and early 1979, the Carter administration appears to have come around at least half way to the German-Japanese position of earlier years.

Figure 6-4.   Brookings J-Curve Analysis

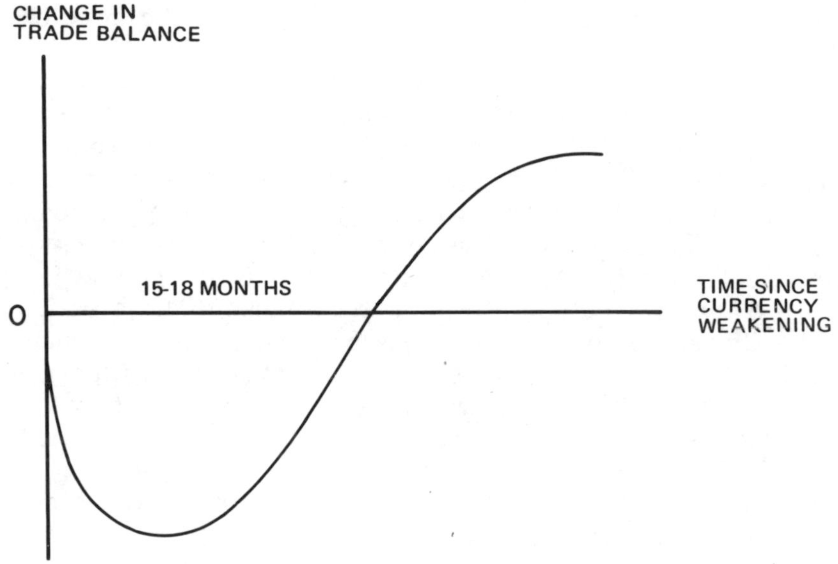

CHANGE IN
TRADE BALANCE

15-18 MONTHS

0

TIME SINCE
CURRENCY
WEAKENING

SECOND PROBLEM: INFLATION IN SUPPLIER COUNTRIES

We pass on now to our second problem, which we can connect immediately to oil and to OPEC. What happens domestically when the import price of an important import like petroleum rises, if that import is complementary rather than competitive with domestic inputs—that is, if it cannot be replaced satisfactorily? (Also, in such cases, the ordinary price elasticity of demand for it is low.) The analysis is identical, by the way, when the import whose price rises is staple food for an industrial country's workers, as in the case of the United Kingdom when they joined the Common Market and became subject to the Common Agricultural Policy.

The relevant analytical apparatus is now Figure 6-5, which is an expansion of Figure 6-2, much as Figure 6-3 was an expansion of Figure 6-1. An increase in the prices of imported raw materials shifts the aggregate supply function S to S'; the shift lowers the employment level while raising prices in the conventional "cost-push" or "stagflation" combination, and the equilibrium point moves from P to P'. (Contrary to what one hears from financial journalists, macroeconomic theory at an intermediate level has no particular difficulty with the analysis of stagflation.)

But now comes the $64 question ($32 in real terms). What should the government do next to counteract the stagflationary move from P to P'? Possibly Andrew Mellon, or his ghost, would propose cutting aggregate demand to D^* and restoring the original price level, but such advice is now discounted (correctly, in my opinion) as economic sadism. President Nixon and later President Ford, after OPEC's assault, apparently hoped to hold aggregate demand at D rather than validating or accommodating macroeconomic policy to the oil price rise and to wait for aggregate supply to return to S by increases in productivity and by voluntary restraint on wages [3] and profit margins; the Mellon policy of 1929-31 formed no part of their strategy. But the result of holding D constant was a more serious recession than the Nixon and Ford Administrations had anticipated, aggregate demand may have fallen for psychological reasons unplanned by the authorities, and the Ford WIN button became the economic joke of 1974. The rival Democratic policy—associated with Senators McGovern, Humphrey, and Kennedy rather than President Carter—was one of accommodation by raising monetary growth and fiscal deficits. This would raise the price level yet further while raising aggregate demand to D' and hopefully regaining at P'' the original employment level which we call y_e.

Let us again change our assumption as to exchange rate regime. Previously we had supposed the rate rigid; now let us let it float freely and flexibly. The expected reaction of our country's exchange rate to a rise in the prices of key imports with inelastic demands is a weakening. This weakening may continue for a considerable time, before the Marshall-Lerner condition and the J-curve bring the balance of payments into equilibrium despite the expected destabilizing reaction of capital movements to the unattractive combination of domestic inflation plus a weakened domestic currency (see appendix). If the required fall in our country's exchange is a large one, the prices of all imports will rise sufficiently to drive the domestic inflation rate considerably higher than it would go under fixed rates.

Figure 6-5.   Inflation in Supplier Countries
(OPEC Case)

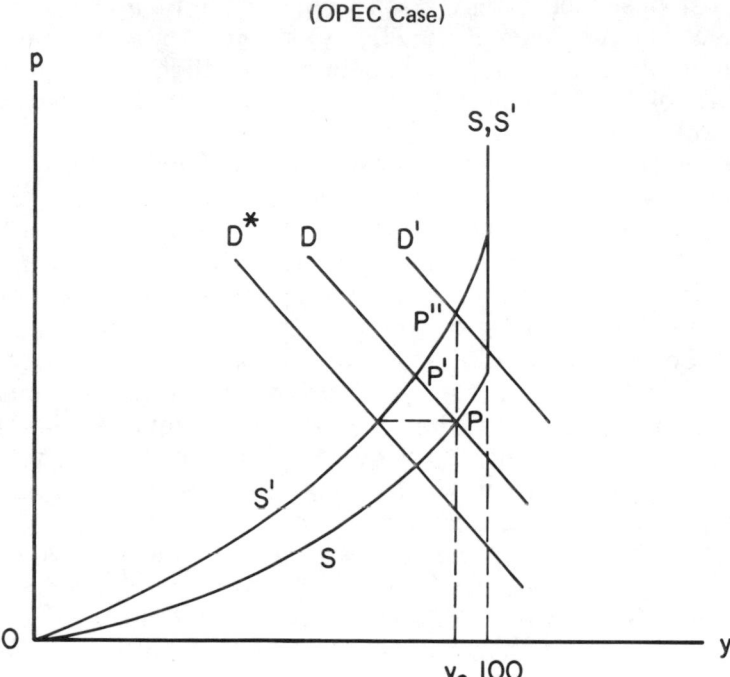

THIRD PROBLEM: INFLATION IN CUSTOMER COUNTRIES

The preceding sections were written with contemporary American situations in mind. The next two are now more relevant to our trading partners, but they were faced frequently by the United States in the past, particularly during periods of American neutrality during European wars from the days of Napoleon to the days of Hitler.

When one's customers engage in war and finance their war by inflationary means, inflation spills over into neutral countries primarily by way of increased demand from belligerent countries for the neutrals' export products. During the Korean war, the Scandinavian countries were neutral, and the Norwegian economist Odd Aukrust revised a special dualistic "Scandinavian" theory of inflation to explain the resulting pattern of events in small countries generally. To take another example, middle-aged Canadians will recall the Canadian hue and cry about "imported inflation" as a consequence of helping to supply the American war effort in Vietnam.

For the appropriate analysis, please look at Figure 6-6. Since aggregate demand for our country's products includes demand by foreigners, the effect of a foreign inflation (whether brought on by war or otherwise) is an increase in aggregate demand from D to D' as our products become relatively cheap abroad in a regime of fixed exchange rates. Increased demand raises the income and employment level, as indicated by the movement from P to P' on the diagram. If this, in turn, sets off rises in our domestic wage rates, profit margins, and raw material costs, there will also be a secondary movement of aggregate supply from S to S', starting from the export industries and speeding throughout the economy by political considerations of fairness and equity. The eventual result may be at a point like P'', with the prior level of employment restored but at a still higher price level than prevailed at P'.

When Canadians complained a dozen or so years ago about such a spillover to their neutral economy of our unpopular Vietnam adventure—which became unpopular in Canada sooner than here!—they could have elected to float the Canadian dollar against the American. By our analysis, the strengthened Canadian dollar would force a reduction in American demand for scarce Canadian goods and services. (Notice that imported *demand* inflation strengthens currencies in floating-rate regimes, whereas imported *cost* inflation weakens them!)

I was once more optimistic than I am today about the *degree* of Canadian dollar appreciation that might have been required to insulate Canada from the Lyndon Johnson phase of American inflation. But supposing that only a small rate change would have been required, let me indicate why Canadians might rationally have hesitated to let the Canadian dollar float upward.

American demand for Canadian exports was both civil and military. It is safe to assume that the civilian demand was more price-elastic in a war situation than was the military demand. Up-valuation of the Canadian dollar would have hurt some Canadian export industries (fish and tourism, for example) which had benefited least from military purchases, and would not have reduced significantly the indirect Canadian economic participation in the VietNam war. Also, those other Canadian industries (wheat and textiles, for example) which compete with imports from America either in Canada itself or in world markets would find themselves less able to take advantage of the American inflation.

Figure 6-6.   Inflation in Customer Countries
(Scandinavian Case)

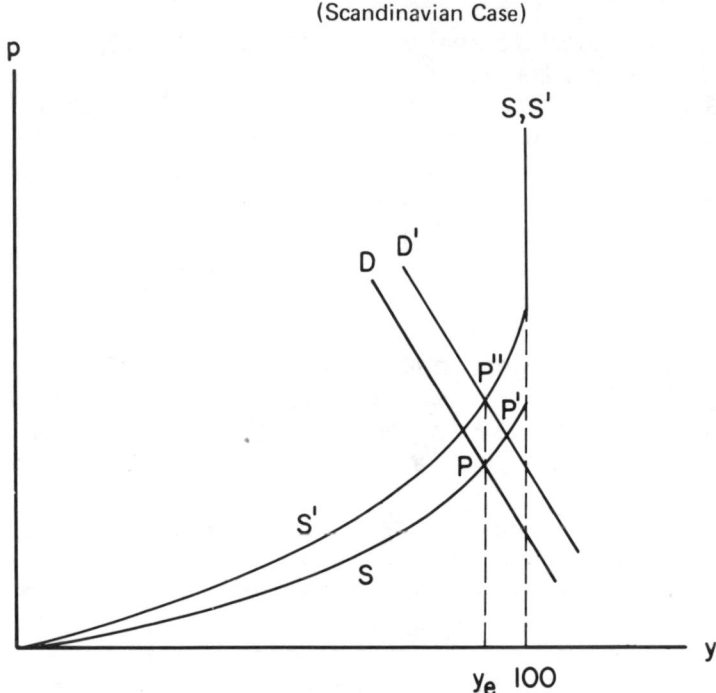

FOURTH PROBLEM: MARCHING TO DIFFERENT DRUMMERS

It is time to take up our final problem, an assessment of the costs of adopting, deliberately or otherwise, an inflation rate different in either direction from the world rate. We can think of our first scenario, the trade and payments consequences of a planned increase in the employment rate with inflationary side effects, as having treated this problem from the viewpoint of a country inflating faster than the rest of the world. We will therefore take up instead the opposite case here, and consider a country like Switzerland or West Germany, which has chosen to disinflate relative to most other countries.

Before going further, let me assure you that the notion of a world rate of inflation is only a convenient statistical artifact. For each country, the world rate of inflation is only a weighted average of the inflation rates of its trade partners, so that it will often be observed differently in every country.

At the present time countries like Argentina or Italy may be inflating at rates above those of nearly all their trade partners--

possibly marching to the beat of a Tobinian drummer and accommodating their macroeconomic policy to workers' and farmers' wage and price demands to avoid both industrial unrest and increasing unemployment. Other countries—we have mentioned Switzerland and West Germany—may be marching to a Friedmanian beat to treat creditors fairly, minimize inflation, and accept a modicum of underemployment and slow measured growth. So we may speak of Argentina as inflating more rapidly than the world rate as seen from Buenos Aires, and of Switzerland as inflating less rapidly than the different world rate seen from Zurich. For purposes of this section of our discussion, we are playing Switzerland rather than Argentina.

If the Swiss, inflating more slowly than the Americans or British, were to hold the Swiss franc at fixed exchange rates in dollars and sterling, the pressures upon them would be as indicated by Figure 6-7, which is a combination of Figures 6-5 and 6-6. Both aggregate supply and aggregate demand would rise vertically as shown, as the prices of all traded goods, both exports and imports, rise in Switzerland. Both flows of Swiss goods and stocks of Swiss franc assets would be world-wide bargains attracting both purchasers and investors. Pressure would be concentrated initially on industries using indispensable foreign raw materials and components, and also on workers eating imported food. The labor market would also be apt to tighten for reasons other than the higher cost of living, with shortages developing and wages rising. These rises are included in the shift from S to S' in Figure 6-7.

There would also be problems on the financial side. To keep foreign exchange from falling and the Swiss franc from appreciating, the Swiss monetary authorities would have to buy at par all foreign currency presented in exchange for francs. To avoid inflationary creation of francs, the Swiss monetary authorities would have to engineer or at least tolerate a domestic money and credit "crunch" by cutting down on domestic demand to hold D and S at their original positions, without permitting the inflationary movements to D' and S' shown in the diagram.

In a flexible or floating rate regime, of course, these financial difficulties would be avoided, and the Swiss franc would float upward. But as in our Canadian illustration of the last section, this solution transfers pressure to the tradable-goods industries, including both exporters and competitors with imports. These industries, to remain competitive, must cut franc labor costs and profit margins. If they cannot, they will have difficulties initially in the world market and eventually even at home. ("If the dollar keeps on falling, Milwaukee beer will take over Munich and Wisconsin cheese will take over Geneva.'")

Figure 6-7.   Pressure on the Disinflating Country

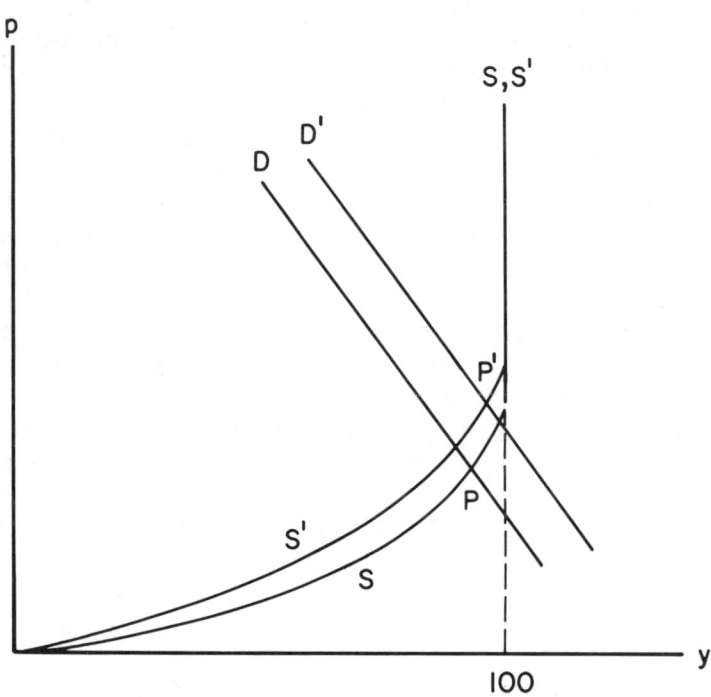

MYSTIFICATION?

Years of experience in the field of international macroeconomics have taught me all too well that there are many people who would prefer to turn to self-sufficiency, to higher protection, and to direct controls to avoid the strains and readjustments imposed by the international economy both on inflationary accommodation and disinflationary Puritanism. I can understand such reactions even when I cannot share them. In my opinion, protectionism and self-sufficiency sacrifice the domestic consumer to a few pressure groups in import-competing industries. As for direct controls, they are useful in surmounting short-term crises, but in the long run they eventually will be evaded, avoided, or distorted into corruption in anything less than a garrison state or a Gulag Archipelago.

APPENDIX: EXCHANGE STABILITY AND THE MARSHALL-LERNER CONDITION

Let x be the quantity of foreign exchange supplied or demanded per period, and $p(x)$ its price in domestic currency. (If there are several foreign trade partners, $p(x)$ is a trade-weighted average of the prices of their several currencies.) When domestic currency strengthens or foreign currency weakens, $p(x)$ falls, and vice versa when $p(x)$ rises.

We can agree, I am sure, that when $p(x)$ is sufficiently low but still positive, the demand for foreign exchange will exceed the supply, and that when $p(x)$ is sufficiently high but still finite, the supply of foreign exchange will exceed the demand. It is the intermediate range which causes our problem, for we can conceive easily of cases where a weakening dollar, for example, would affect the American balances of trade and payments in the "wrong" direction. One such case, ignoring capital movements, would arise from the American demand for foreign imports and the world demand for American exports being both completely inelastic. A falling dollar would then only increase the gap between exports and imports in dollar terms, and likewise between the demand and supply of foreign exchange.

This implies that the foreign exchange market is *stable* at extremely high or low values of $p(x)$ but that it may be *unstable* at one or more intermediate ranges. (By stability we mean that currency depreciation or weakening both results from and remedies a deficit balance under floating rates, while currency strengthening or appreciation both results from and remedies a surplus balance. By instability we mean that, while the causes of currency appreciation or depreciation are as in the stable case, the depreciation or appreciation exercise perverse effects, and that the floating rate system may accentuate surpluses or deficits instead of overcoming them.)

We illustrate an unstable exchange market in Figure 6-8. The demand for foreign exchange, like that for any asset, is drawn sloping downward. The supply function, however, results from the country's net exports, and is drawn reversing itself once in mid-passage. Three equilibria are shown, labeled (*P1, P2, P3*). Both *P1* and *P3* are stable, but *P2* is not. For a $p(x)$ even slight above *P2*, the rate will settle at *P3* instead of at *P2*. And

Figure 6-8.   Stability and Instability of the Foreign
Exchange Rate

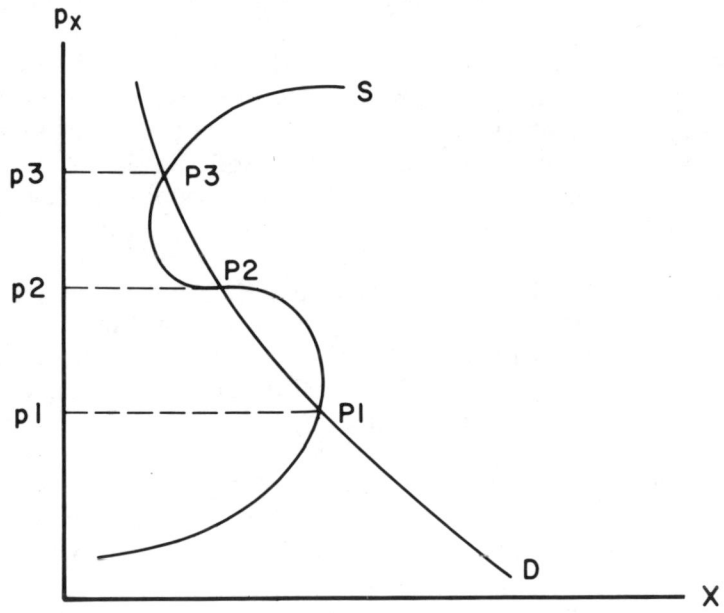

LEGEND

X – VOLUME OF FOREIGN EXCHANGE PER PERIOD

Px – PRICE OF A UNIT OF FOREIGN EXCHANGE (in Domestic Currency)

p_1, p_2, p_3 – EQUILIBRIUM VALUE OF p

P_1, P_3 – POINTS OF STABLE EQUILIBRIUM (at p_1, p_3)

P_2 – POINT OF UNSTABLE EQUILIBRIUM (at p_2)

furthermore, the measured supply-demand imbalance will increase rather than decrease during the early half of the adjustment process!

The Marshall–Lerner contribution to this analysis was the development of a brief algebraic condition for exchange stability in the simplified case where D and S are unaffected by income changes, where supply considerations can be ignored, and where capital movements are absent. This stability condition is that the sum of the domestic price elasticity of demand for all foreign imports taken together and the foreign price elasticity of demand for all domestic exports taken together should exceed unity. This is the Marshall–Lerner condition. When it is satisfied we can be confident that the exchange market will regulate itself as at *P1* or *P3* in Figure 6-8. Floating-rate optimists believe that this condition is met on nearly every case in the long run, and that points like *P2* are short run, pathological, or both. Floating-rate pessimists doubt this proposition, and fear that many par values on foreign exchange markets are in neighborhoods of unstable equilibria like *P2*.

For persons tolerant of quick changes of notation, I shall end this appendix by deriving the Marshall–Lerner condition in the simplified case which concerned them [4]. We define the trade balance B (in domestic currency) as exports X, for which payment is paid in domestic currency whose price is unity by definition, less imports M paid for in foreign currency whose weighted price is w.

$$B = X - wM.$$

When w changes, we have

$$\frac{dB}{dw} = \frac{dX}{dw} - (w\frac{dM}{dw} + M)$$

$$= \frac{X}{w} (\frac{w}{X} \frac{dX}{dw}) - M (\frac{w}{M} \frac{dM}{dw} + 1).$$

Interpreting the expressions in ordinary round brackets as elasticities of demand for exports and imports *(n, m)* respectively, we obtain

$$\frac{dB}{dw} = M(\frac{X}{wM} n + m - 1).$$

(The difference in the signs of the elasticity terms results from the fact that a rise in *w* *lowers* the foreign price of exports but *raises* the domestic price of imports.)

If trade is sufficiently close to balance that *x/(wM)* approximates unity, then

$$\frac{dB}{dw} = M(n + m - 1),$$

which means that the trade balance will move directly with the price of foreign exchange when the sum of the two demand elasticities exceeds unity.

NOTES

1. James Meade, *The Balance of Payments* (London: Oxford University Press, 1951).

2. The technical criterion applicable here is the so-called Marshall-Lerner condition. On this condition, see the appendix to the present paper.

3. Professor Abba Lerner's tract on *Flation* (Baltimore: Penguin Books, Inc., 1973) makes an interesting suggestion on wage restraint. He proposes money wage settlements equal to average productivity plus a cost of living allowance 1 percent below last period's inflation rate. This proposal would allow perceptible real wage increases when productivity is rising--3 percent per year, in Lerner's benchmark estimates. In the present American and British productivity stagnations, it eliminates real wage increases and may even impose decreases, thereby appearing as sacrificial on labor's part.

4. This particular proof I owe to the late Harry G. Johnson.

Chapter 7

THE INFLATIONARY EXPERIENCE: SOME LESSONS FROM ISRAEL†

Don Patinkin*

I would like on this occasion to make some informal remarks about the problem of inflation, based largely upon the experience of Israel. The price level in Israel has risen roughly one-hundred times in the last forty years. I have lived in Israel for thirty years, and prices have risen about twenty times in those thirty years. So, if learning by doing is a criterion, I should have learned a lot about inflation. However, the more I have experienced it, the more complex and mysterious inflation seems to be. What I find particularly difficult to explain are the changing rates of inflation. Even though Israel has had continuous inflation—not only since, but even before its existence as a state—the rates of inflation have varied enormously.

Israel witnessed a period of about seventeen years between 1954 and 1970 in which there was what at the time was considered to be fairly heavy inflation, but which in retrospect Israelis, and even Americans, would regard as moderate. As Table 7-1 shows, during this period Israel's average rate of inflation was four percent per year. In only six years in this

---

*Professor of Economics, The Hebrew University of Jerusalem.

†Editors' Note: This paper represents an edited transcription of remarks made March 28, 1979 by Professor Patinkin at the Florida State University Conference on Inflation held in honor of Abba P. Lerner.

seventeen year period did this rate exceed five percent, and it never became double-digit inflation. This period of relative stability came after the very serious inflation experienced in the early 1950s, and, as I will indicate in a moment, was followed by a period of even more serious inflation.

Inflation is usually associated with war or with development. As the table suggests, Israel is not a good example of that generalization. The period 1954 to 1970 was the one of most rapid economic development of Israel, and yet the one with the lowest rate of inflation. Since 1970 Israel has had increasing rates of inflation. Last year it was over 50 percent. The Yom Kippur war of 1973 did give a boost to the inflation rate, but the acceleration of the rate of inflation had started before the war. And in the years since this very high rate of inflation began, Israel has had very little real economic growth. Therefore, any correlation between inflation and growth has not been substantiated by the Israel experience: indeed, the correlation during the past few years has been negative.

It is interesting to note that the 1956 and 1967 wars took place without generating any serious inflation. Of course, those were relatively short wars, but still they involved very high rates of expenditure. I might add that the present prospects for peace will probably have an additional inflationary impact on the economy; for there are going to be tremendous expenditures in Israel in connection with the relocation of forces, military air fields, and so forth. So I certainly do not anticipate any lessening of the rate of inflation in the near future.

There are lessons that I have learned about living under inflation in Israel. Life goes on in the face of inflation. People continue to walk the streets calmly. They do not run with wheelbarrows full of money to the nearest stores; they do not hoard goods indefinitely. Economic laws are at work: it is true that people have a stronger preference for holding assets in a real form. For example, condominiums are the standard form of home ownership in Israel, with seventy percent of the working class in Israel owning their own apartments. Undoubtedly, there are many factors involved, but one factor underlying this practice is that condominium ownership provides a hedge against inflation. People do carry larger stocks, larger household inventories in terms of clothing, furniture, appliances and the like. People do not postpone purchases as much as they might, but there is still a large amount of stability in everyday life. There is no sense of panic. There have been times, during very

TABLE 7-1

PERCENTAGE CHANGE IN THE CONSUMER PRICE INDEX
AND REAL GROSS DOMESTIC PRODUCT
FOR ISRAEL, 1954-1978

Year	Consumer Price Index	Real Gross Domestic Product
1978	51.0	n.a.
1977	34.6	1.00
1976	31.5	.41
1975	39.2	1.28
1974	39.5	7.69
1973	20.6	12.06
1972	12.5	10.22
1971	12.0	7.95
1970	6.4	13.45
1969	2.2*	14.68*
1968	2.4	2.50
1967	1.6	2.65
1966	8.0	8.20
1965	7.6	10.21
1964	5.0	11.56
1963	6.4	10.38
1962	9.3	8.55
1961	7.5*	6.21
1960	3.0	6.05*
1959	1.0	12.68
1958	3.1	6.60
1957	1.0	9.53
1956	3.2	9.40
1955	2.2	n.a.
1954	3.4	22.49*

Source: Statistical Yearbook, United Nations, various issues
and Yearbook of National Accounts Statistics, United
Nations, various issues.

*Denotes a break in the series.
n.a. = not available.

rapid price increases, when there were some runs on stores; but in general, people become accustomed to the situation. Similarly, people in the United States now are living in a rather unexcited way even though the inflation environment is more intense. I remember visiting the United States in the 1960s when the country had started experiencing a 1 percent annual rate of inflation. There was a great hue and cry at the time whose intensity I could not understand. Now the United States is accommodating itself to its 12-13 percent rate of inflation, and I am not sure that the hue and cry is that much greater.

How do economists explain, or attempt to explain, inflation? One frequently heard explanation is simply that the price level has increased because the quantity of money has increased. There is no doubt that a strong correlation exists between the price level and the quantity of money. As statistics have verified in country after country, there is no prolonged inflationary process which has not been accompanied by a significant growth in the quantity of money.

In brief, inflation everywhere and anywhere is a monetary phenomenon. But one can also say that the price of potatoes everywhere and anywhere is a potato phenomenon. I think these are similar statements because the price level is the inverse of the purchasing power or value of money. And this is my way of saying that I have never been satisfied with this explanation of inflation because of its failure to explain why the quantity of money suddenly increases. Or to put the question in slightly technical terms, is the quantity of money an exogenous variable or is it an endogenous variable? Is the monetary increase something which comes from outside the system, or is it something generated by the system? Is it the result of the increase in the price level or is it the cause? We all know that statistical correlations do not determine causal relationships, and thus on the basis of a high correlation alone, we cannot say which variable is affecting which. Moreover, there is always a possibility that some third variable is affecting both of them simultaneously.

Let me put this question of causal relationship in another way: political leaders and ministers of finance have from time immemorial known how to print money. Why do they sometimes suddenly decide to print more? The statistical correlation between inflation and money supply growth does not answer that question, and consequently I have difficulty seeing the quantity of money as an economic explanation of the cause of inflation.

There is an explanation of the government's behavior that says that inflation is a tax on cash balances: inflation decreases the real value of the cash balances held by individuals, and this decrease is effectively a tax received by the government. This approach to inflation is also not a new one. A vivid and eloquent description and analysis of it can be found in Keynes' *Tract on Monetary Reform*, which was written immediately after World War I. In the *Tract* Keynes refers to inflation as a tax, and he even has the notion (which in recent years has been elaborated and refined) of the optimum rate of inflation. If a tax rate is too high people will not buy the taxed good, and consequently tax receipts will be too low. If the rate is very low, then receipts per unit will be low and so will be tax receipts. Thus, some optimum exists between these two extremes, and this is what Keynes said about inflation and the holding of real cash balances. Unlike the recent literature, he did not give any rules for finding the optimum; but he indicated that some optimum rate must exist.

Whatever the general validity of this as an explanation of inflation, it does not hold for the case of Israel: for in Israel every time the price level goes up, the government loses money--it does not gain. That results from the very special situation in which the Israeli government borrows by means of indexed loans, and lends from its development budget without indexing. Thus every increase in the price level increases the government's debt to the public, without affecting the public's debt to the government; and this fact more than offsets the nominal debt that government owes the public on money. Thus the government loses in real terms every time inflation occurs.

Of course, this anomaly could be rationalized by saying that the government decides to make expenditures in the form of subsidies to people to whom it is lending. This explanation is legitimate, but explanations of this type are tautological.

There is, though, one point that I do feel is correct. I do feel that inflations usually are connected with expanded government budgets. Correspondingly, a necessary, but not a sufficient, condition for lowering the rate of inflation is a reduction, or at least constancy, in this budget. Certainly I would say that this is true for Israel's case. I believe that the same is true for the United States. But, again, we must ask ourselves why is this pressure for government expenditures greater now than in other periods? Why have government expenditures been higher in these post-war decades than before? Perhaps the inflationary process is connected with the welfare state. However, the fact that widely varying rates of inflation arise in a given country in peacetime within a relatively short period of time makes it difficult to accept fluctuating government expenditures as the whole explanation of inflation.

Another explanation of inflation that is frequently advanced these days has to do with the price of oil. But again, explaining inflation in terms of the exogenous circumstance of the increased price of oil is not really an explanation, for at least two reasons.

First of all, the OPEC countries will explain that they are raising oil prices to keep pace with inflation in the Western countries. There is a recursive process here. Secondly, if a rise in the price of oil were the cause of inflation in the Western world, then it should have a uniform impact on the various countries of the Western world. Europe and the United States would have similiar impacts because they are both buying oil. An allowance would have to be made for the respective impor- tance of oil in the different economies, but after that adjust- ment the impacts should be the same. We know that it is not! The inflation response varies greatly between the various econo- mies of these countries.

I have not mentioned labor unions and wage demands. These are important parts of an inflationary process--particularly a prolonged inflationary process. However, there is an interaction between prices and wages. The distinction between cost infla- tion and demand inflation is one which may be relevant at certain points of an inflationary process, but in a prolonged process the two kinds of inflation become so intermingled that it is impossible to distinguish between them.

I mentioned indexation, and I would like to spend some time on the Israel experience with indexation as a possible response to inflationary pressures. Indexation in Israel started of necessity. In 1949-1951 the government had to borrow to finance its budget, but at the time there was very rapid inflation in Israel: the price level almost doubled in that period, and so no one was willing to buy nominally denominated government bonds. The government therefore began to issue, in the early 1950s, an indexed bond; it did not, however, index the loans it was making from its development budget.

This volume dedicated to Abba Lerner is a most appropriate place to relate a story about him and indexation, a story that very few people know, and that I happened to learn about from one of our graduate students in Jerusalem, Reuven Brenner, who was doing a doctorate on indexation. In 1955, the Israel government established a committee called the Lehman committee, named after its chairman, Ernst Lehman, who was a leading banker. Abba was then in Israel as a member of the Economic Advisory Staff, a group of foreign economists formed to advise the Israel government on problems of economic policy. The committee was asked to express its opinion on whether the loans that the government made should be indexed, and if so, how. After deliberations, it proposed that the government index all loans from the development budget with the exception of loans to agriculture. (Agriculture is a favored exception in every country!) The committee further proposed to apply the index linkage only to loans that exceeded two years in duration and to apply it to a maximum of 70 percent of the loan as the term of the loan increased to eight years or more. What was recommended, then, was not full indexation.

As might be guessed, Abba, whom we all know as a person who carries an argument to its logical conclusion, felt impelled to write a minority report. In this report he argued. "There is no economic justification for distinguishing between the length of the loan and the degree of indexation. All loans should be fully indexed regardless of their duration." Abba Lerner pointed out, quite rightly, that giving loans which were not indexed was tantamount to giving subsidies. I would like to emphasize that to give a subsidy is not necessarily bad; but to give an arbitrary one is. And failure to index a loan provides a subsidy to industry not in accordance with any principle, but instead arbitrarily, as a function of whatever the rate of inflation turns out to be: the higher the rate of inflation, the greater the subsidy. That is not rational. In any event, despite Abba's minority view, indexation in this limited way became characteristic of the development loans of the Israel development budget.

There was another mistake made in the indexation program: the linkage was not made to the cost-of-living index but to the exchange rate with the dollar. The rationale for this decision was that money for development was being borrowed by the Israel government from the United States, to which it would have to make repayment. Therefore, for the government to have a hedge against its obligation to repay, the proper linkage should be a dollar linkage. This decision proved to be very unfortunate. In 1962 the government suddenly devalued the Israel pound by 60 percent, and overnight people found that they owed 60 percent more because of linkage. A great hue and cry arose, and the government retreated. Indeed, there was such pressure on the government that loan indexation was more or less abandoned in the 1960s, and higher rates of interest were substituted. I should say that at the time this circumstance was not too damaging to the economy because this was the period of a fairly stable rate of inflation of 5-8 percent. A higher rate of interest would more or less take full account of the rate of inflation. Indexation is needed when there is an uncertain and fluctuating rate of inflation. With a constant inflation rate, the market itself will eventually make a roughly appropriate adjustment in the interest rate.

Indexation still remains in Israel, but it is a one-direction indexation. Government securities are indexed. A component of wage policy is also indexed. One might think that with higher rates of inflation, indexation would be even more important and even more valuable. In fact it has actually worked the opposite way. There is growing feeling in Israel that the indexation is making the rate of inflation much higher than it would otherwise be, because indexation has worked to prevent changes in the relative price structure, particularly in the relative price of foreign exchange. Under indexation, when a rapid increase in the foreign exchange rate occurs, the domestic price level rapidly rises to roughly the same extent, so that the Israel economy does not succeed in changing the relative prices of international goods as against domestic goods.

Another aspect of the situation is that industrialists contend that private securities cannot effectively compete with indexed government ones in an economy with roughly 50 percent inflation. This government indexed rate means that whoever buys the government security is assured of receiving a nominal rate of return of 50 percent. Industrialists claim that they cannot issue bonds or stocks that would compete effectively with such securities, and they often argue that it would be more profitable for them to sell their businesses and buy indexed bonds of the government instead. Part of this claim, of course, represents the kind of pressure that any group will exert in order to protect its economic interests. There is, however, an element of truth in the contention.

In general, there is growing disillusionment in Israel with indexation as a way of dealing with inflation, and the extent of indexation has been steadily decreasing. Indexation of government bonds, for example, began at a full 100 percent, it was then reduced to 90 percent, and now it has been further reduced to 70 percent. I might also note that the notion that indexation will make the government reluctant to engage in inflationary financing has not been substantiated by the Israel experience. Despite indexation, the rate of inflation has been higher in recent years than ever before. In part the government has reacted to this by decreasing the extent of indexation, as I have indicated. But the basic point is that if more money is needed to redeem bonds, then more money is printed. In sum, indexation has not really acted as an impediment to the inflationary process.

I do not believe that I have struck any cheerful notes in this paper, but this somberness is a reflection of the fact that economic thinking on inflation and on its solutions remains highly inconclusive. Inflation does have adverse effects on an economy in indirect ways, in generating uncertainty and a sense of malaise. However, as I pointed out in my opening remarks, an economy under inflation still continues to function, even if not as efficiently as it would if it did not have serious inflationary rates.

The natural question today is, "How does one reduce the rate of inflation?" Some people have schemes for this purpose. Abba Lerner has a scheme; Sidney Weintraub has a scheme; others have schemes. But I do not believe that inflation can be eliminated by any simple scheme. On the basis of the sad experience of seeing many different efforts at combating inflation fail, I have been forced to a position of skepticism. I do feel that it would be very important and very useful to Israel to reduce its rate of inflation. The same holds for the United States. But I do not see how one can easily stop the inflation process, or even lower it significantly. I believe that an anti-inflation program would have to be a combined effort, a combined and determined effort carried out along many different fronts. A necessary ingredient of that effort is a restraint on government spending. That is a necessary, although not a sufficient, step. But this action must be combined with wage policy and with other policies which at least will provide a period of adjustment during which people can be led to change their expectations about future inflation. I have not said too much about expectations here, but when an inflationary process continues for a long period, it generates self-perpetuating expectations which are very difficult to eliminate.

I am sorry that this chapter does not contain much hard wisdom, but the profession as a whole does not have much to say about how to extricate oneself without great difficulty from an inflationary process. So I would be very happy if the contributors to this volume could reach a consensus, not perhaps on how to eliminate inflation completely, but at least on how we can lessen the rate of inflation in the United States, Israel and other parts of the world.

※ *Part III*

THOUGHTS ON INFLATION CONTROL

Chapter 8

**AN EVOLUTIONARY APPROACH TO
INFLATION AND STAGFLATION**[1]

Mancur Olson *

WHY IS INFLATION SO CONTROVERSIAL?

It is puzzling that economists disagree so much more
about inflation and other macroeconomic and monetary issues
than they do about microeconomic matters.   Although many
laymen think economists disagree about everything, there is
something almost approaching consensus in economists' attitudes
on many abstract questions of microeconomic theory, such as the
necessary conditions for Pareto-optimal resource allocation, and
even upon many aspects of microeconomic policy, such as
tariffs, and the superiority for pollution control of effluent fees
to the usual regulatory standards.   By contrast, on inflation and
monetary and macroeonomic policy and theory there is profound
division, most notably between those economists who find much
of value in our legacy from Keynes and those of the monetarist
persuasion.

Why does this special divergence of views about monetary
and macroeconomic theory and policy exist?   The skills of the
participants in the debate, and the enthusiasm with which they
pursue their arguments and counter arguments make it unlikely
that the differences among the schools of thought about macroeconomics and inflation are due in any substantial way to logical
errors made by one side or another.   Although there are plenty of
logical errors that arise from time to time, the fact that they
can be demonstrated to be errors by rules of logic accepted by

*Professor of Economics, University of Maryland.

all sides, and the professional rewards for such unambiguous demonstrations, pretty well insure that a school of monetary or macroeconomic thought cannot thrive for very long if it rests basically on logical error.

The matter is not quite so clear cut when empirical inferences are at issue. It is possible, but in my observation rather rare, that schools of thought may differ principally because they rest on different empirical judgments. When so much hangs on the empirical evidence, the rewards to empirical researchers who can show which side is probably right are very great, so if it is possible for an investigation to settle the dispute the investigation will almost certainly be undertaken. However, as I have argued elsewhere [2], macroeconomic and monetary policies are like public goods in that they have indivisible consequences for whole nations at the least. The "social production functions" of public goods of vast domain are especially difficult to estimate, because experiments with the large units are so costly and the small number of these large units means that historical experience provides relatively few "natural" experiments. Thus, the empirical effects of various combinations of monetary and fiscal policy in different conditions are hard to determine. This difficulty can account for some continued divergence of schools of thought, but not a great deal, since the empirical differences are either resolved by empirical tests or clearly unresolvable with the available evidence, and in this latter case the agnostics are likely to overwhelm the sectarians.

SYNECDOCHE

In great degree, I believe, the persistence of profound disagreements among schools of thought in macro and monetary economics is due to the fact that the competing theories are partial or special theories, which their more doctrinaire exponents are anxious to treat as complete or general theories. There is no doubt that special or incomplete theories can be useful; indeed, no theory can be useful unless it abstracts from the unmanageable complexity of reality, so any useful theory must in some sense be incomplete. The problem in monetary and macroeconomics is that useful and extremely suggestive partial theories are believed by many of their more enthusiastic proponents to provide what is in essence *the* general truth; the theories are recognized to be simpler than the reality they are supposed to describe, but the matters from which they abstract are taken to be random, unimportant, exceptional, or outside of economics. The point that Keynes' *"General" Theory* is not so general as he claimed is by now a banality, although I shall attempt to show that the most important repsects in which Keynes' theory is "special" are altogether overlooked in the conventional arguments on this point. The monetarist argument, in my judgment, is at best also true only for a special case.

The special cases for which the Keynesian and monetarist doctrines respectively provide an essentially correct account are, of course, very different. Partisans, nourished by the important truth their paradigms contain, rush on to claim total victory, without waiting to ask whether there might not be some absolutely decisive feature of contemporary reality that they have overlooked. The partisans are likely to have given some thought to those features of reality that major opposing paradigms emphasize, for they have often debated these paradigms and thus they will normally have more or less sufficient reasons for excluding any assumption of the opposing theory that they choose to exclude. The most serious problems arise from decisive features of reality that are ignored in all of the known theories. There may be some fact, like the dog that didn't bark, that hasn't been noticed, but when noticed forces us to look at all the stylized facts in a different way than any of the prior theories have led us to do.

There is evidence that the leading aggregative economic theories are crucially incomplete in the fact that none of them led economists to expect "stagflation," or even gave them a generally accepted explanation of it. The simultaneous existence of inflation and recession, and even sometimes a tendency for prices to rise faster when real output falls in a recession than it did in the immediately preceding expansion, [3] was not predicted by either Keynesian or monetary economists, and must surely be puzzling in terms of any theory which (like these two) purports to explain changes in the price level or real output entirely in terms of changes in demand.

As might be expected from the fact that there are people of talent as well as doctrinal loyalty in both the Keynesian and Monetarist camps, quite a number of models and arguments have been constructed to explain aspects of the stagflation paradox in ways which are consistent with one or another of the aggregative orthodoxies. Many of these models or arguments are interesting and some contain significant elements of truth. Indeed, the macro and monetary economists who have worked on explaining the paradox of stagflation in general terms should be singled out for praise, for they have devoted their attentions to the central anomaly of recent economic experience and thus have been far more relevant than the majority of their co-workers have been. Yet, it remains true that these explanations are not only after-the-fact explanations, but essentially also *ad hoc* explanations as well; they tend to be consistent with the recent experience that led the economist to formulate them, and of course also with one or the other of the aggregative doctrines, but these models rarely if ever explain much beyond the experience from which they were derived. Indeed, many of these models are mute, even about dramatic features of macro and monetary history in the periods before stagflation set in.

The "rational expectations" arguments, suggestive as they may sometimes be, are only rarely related by their exponents to the experience of the great depression in the interwar years. If the level of real output is not sensitive to changes in fiscal policy or the stock of money, except when such changes arise through successful trickery that generates false expectations, why did the depression that began in the United States in 1929 and ended only with World War II involve such an enormous and prolonged reduction in employment and real output? Consider also the case of Great Britain in the interwar period. Britain then as now used a system for measuring unemployment that, by comparison with current United States practice, understates the degree of unemployment; yet from shortly after World War I until World War II Great Britain never recorded less than ten percent unemployment. This interwar experience could be explained on an expectations hypothesis only if people, in the midst of the greatest depression ever, expected an inflation so dramatic it would justify setting various wages and prices far above the levels that would clear current markets. This is, to put it mildly, doubtful, and it is even more doubtful that most people would have persisted in such widely erroneous expectations for a dozen years in the case of the United States, or twenty years in that of Great Britain. Neither is it credible that, when unemployment and welfare arrangements were so much less generous than today, and when most workers were the only source of support for their families, the "natural rate" of unemployment could leave a tenth to a fourth of the work force unemployed. Monetarist explanations of the current stagflation must rank as *ad hoc* explanations at best if they do not encompass the great depression as well as recent stagflation.

Those explanations of stagflation that rest on Keynesian foundations are also far from sufficient. Some Keynesian accounts of recent experience refer to negatively-sloped Phillips curves and perhaps also to shifts in such curves. There is no need to invoke the Monetarists or other criticisms of the Phillips curve notion to show that such accounts are inherently inadequate, for the simple reason that neither Keynesian theory nor neoclassical microeconomic theory provides any reason why there should be a negatively sloped Phillips curve; as others have said, the Phillips curve is a finding in search of a theory.

A Keynesian-type explanation of stagflation is really not an explanation at all unless it includes a general theoretical explanation of why a Phillips curve should have this or that slope, and why the curve shifts, if it is alleged to shift. Any Phillips curve relationship must, in other words, be derived from the interests and constraints faced by individual decision-makers. The fact that Phillips curve-type accounts of some recent experience are not explained in terms of individual behavior reminds us that even Keynes' account of the unemployment equilibrium assumes "sticky" or "rigid" wages and prices, and that this "stickiness" is not itself adequately explained. Thus the Keynesian theory, far from being general, is incomplete even for the case of depressions, until a satisfactory explanation of sticky wages and prices has been provided.

COST-PUSH CONFUSIONS

The fact that Keynesian and monetarist models did not even alert people to the possibility that inflation and unemployment would increase together helps explain the prevalence, particularly among laymen, of "cost-push" explanations of inflation. But as others have shown before, the usual cost-push arguments are manifestly unsatisfactory. These accounts ascribe higher prices or wages to the monopoly power of big business or big unions, but they usually offer no explanation of why there should be continuing inflation, or why there should be more inflation in one period than another. The typical cost-push argument does not explain why an organization with monopoly power would not choose whatever price or wage it found most advantageous as soon as it obtained the monopoly power, after which point it would have no more reason to increase prices or wages than a pure competitor. In the absence of some adequate explanation of why organizations with monopoly power didn't take advantage of that power when they first acquired it, or some explanation of why monopoly power should increase over time in a way consistent with the history of inflation or stagflation, the cost-push arguments are obviously inadequate. As many others have pointed out, they must also be accompanied by some account of why monetary or fiscal authorities would provide increased demand after the alleged cost-push had increased wages and prices, so that the cost-push would culminate in inflation rather than in unemployed resources.

There is further evidence of the incompleteness of the Keynesian and Monetarist theories (and also a hint about how to improve them) in the association between rates of real economic growth in different developed countries, and the country's success in combating inflation and unemployment, and also in the historical evolution of the macroeconomic problem. Let us look first, although only very briefly and unsystematically, at the relationship across developed countries.

INTERNATIONAL COMPARISONS

Since World War II, the two developed countries whose growth has been most surprising are Japan and West Germany. Although the predictions about their economic futures just after they were defeated in World War II were bleak, these two nations have grown exceptionally rapidly, after they had rebuilt their economies and recovered their pre-war living standards no less than before. The major developed democracy with the slowest rate of growth since World War II is, of course, the United Kingdom, although the United States, Canada, Australia, and New Zealand have experienced rates of growth that are about as slow.

Admittedly, we have mentioned only extreme cases, but it is nonetheless instructive to note how differently the fast-growing and slow-growing nations have fared in dealing with the only really serious disruption of macroeconomic stability in the developed democracies since World War II, the inflation-stagflation of the 1970s. Obviously, there is a problem in measuring the extent to which a nation has achieved macroeconomic stability, since both the inflation rate and the extent of unemployed resources need to be taken into account, and it isn't clear how heavily each of these should be weighted, or how much the weightings should be changed as nations come to have an unusually bad performance by one of these measures and an unusually good performance by the other. In the extreme cases I have chosen to focus on, however, we can get around this weighting problem rather readily by noting that, broadly speaking, West Germany and Japan have done far better than the United Kingdom, and often also better than the United States, and the other slowly growing countries I mentioned, in dealing with *both* inflation and unemployment. From 1972–77 the annual average rate of inflation in the United Kingdom was 14.8 percent, whereas in West Germany it was 5.6 percent and in Japan 11.6 percent. If we look at the number of unemployed resulting from this inflation, we do not by any means get a Phillips curve type of relationship; Britain has 1.38 million unemployed, Germany, .99 million, and Japan (a much more populous society) 1.24 million unemployed [4]. West Germany and Japan, moreover, have had to rely totally on imported oil.

To be sure, many factors are involved (such as the special role of guest workers who can be sent home when unemployed in West Germany), and only polar cases have been considered, so no conclusions are yet in order. There is also no lack of explanations in the prevailing orthodoxies. Some monetarists will say that monetary expansion and inflation generates inflationary expectations that are built into wage and price levels, so that when the inflation slows down there is more unemployment than there would otherwise have been—inflation causes recession. Some Keynesians will say that the greater growth of productivity in the rapidly growing countries makes it easier for them to keep both stable prices and full employment, since for any given wage level (and wages are sticky) there can be lower prices with higher productivity, and the lower labor cost per unit of labor will also induce employers to take on more labor and lower the unemployment rate. Some Marxists will say that the social tensions or class conflicts that give rise to inflation are easier to resolve when growth makes it possible to give more to everyone.

Clearly nothing of theoretical importance has been established, nor could it be even with a systematic and complete assessment of the relative performances of all the developed countries—there are special circumstances that may be decisive in each of them. Yet, in combination with the temporal pattern we shall turn to next, there is perhaps a hint that certain structural differences that favor rapid growth also favor macroeconomic stability. This hint, as we shall later see, becomes stronger when we note how very much more concern about "incomes policies," "social contacts," and "inflationary wage settlements" there is in Great Britain (and to some extent also in

Australia, Canada, New Zealand, and the United States) than in Japan and West Germany.

RECENT HISTORICAL COMPARISONS

Historical differences in macroeconomic problems, and differences in macroeconomic problems across societies of widely different levels of economic development, have not been examined as often as one might wish. Perhaps one reason is that both the Keynesian and monetarist perspectives, at least as they are usually presented, do not claim to rest on the special institutional conditions or other factors that might distinguish the advanced capitalistic countries in, say, the last half century, from the societies in earlier times or from various developing nations. It is of course well known that neither monetarist nor Keynesian models are intended to apply to barter or subsistence economies, but rather to economies where goods can freely be exchanged for money. Monetarists, and for that matter Keynesians, mindful of the significant role that money plays in Keynes' model, are obviously also interested in banking and in other financial and credit institutions. Keynesians will mention and monetarists will emphasize, the instability of United States, and even the world banking systems in the twenties and early thirties, and quite rightly relate these with greater or lesser emphasis to the onset of the great depression. There are still other institutional differences that are occasionally mentioned, such as the Keynesian references to the growth of automatic stabilizers. But on the whole the typical presentations of both Keynesians' and monetarists' doctrines do not say much about the institutional or other conditions in which the theory is supposed to apply, and instead emphasize the generality of the theory that is espoused. Keynes could readily have used various assumptions of his theory, such as the assumption that savers and investors are in substantial degree different people who may have inconsistent intentions, or the assumption of sticky wages, as a basis for restricting its application to certain societies and historical periods. Unfortunately Keynes did not, at any event with any regularity, do this. Indeed, he went so far as to justify the mercantilism in Europe in the sixteenth, seventeenth, and eighteenth centuries, largely on the ground that export surpluses from mercantilistic trade restrictions and export subsidies countered unemployment. The *General Theory*, of course, also carried indefinitely forward in time, perhaps even until "euthan asia of the rentier." Keynes was not much more expansive than the monetarists who keep repeating that "inflation is always and everywhere a monetary phenomenon."

There are certainly *some* features of macroeconomic and monetary history that are consistent with the supposedly eternal generality of both major theories. The association of hyper-inflations and vast increases in the money supply certainly holds across diverse societies and historical periods; the experience especially of the Confederacy in the U.S. Civil War, with Assignats in the French Revolution, and many triple or four digit inflation rates in Latin American countries at diverse levels of economic development, suggest that the monetarist connection between the money supply and nominal income holds at least to some degree in a wide variety of conditions. There is probably also a rough association over historical epochs between smaller changes in the quantity of money and less dramatic changes in the price level, as in the rising prices in Europe after the discovery of gold in sixteenth century Latin America. The quantity theory of money goes back, after all, at least to David Hume.

In a similar way, there is also a broad association over different historical periods between wars, deficit spending, and investment booms, and changes in at least money income. This is entirely in keeping with Keynes' model. Since money can also play a quite significant role in a Keynesian or IS-LM model, the broad connection between monetary changes and nominal income is also compatible with a Keynesian framework, unless of course the connections were so precise and regular that they implied there was never any case for anything beyond the quantity theory of money.

When we get to the monetarist assumption that the level of employment of resources, whatever the change in the price level, tends to the "natural" or full employment rate, and the Keynesian postulate that short-term or cyclical fluctuations in both the level of real output and the price level are due in general to changes in aggregate effective demand, the situation is no longer so simple or insensitive to historical change. Let us look first merely at changes in the United States over the relatively brief period since World War II. Since monetarists have in general been more resistant than Keynesians to sugges-tions that structural and institutional changes were among the causal factors in post-war inflationary experience, it may be expedient to take our facts initially from a leading monetarist writer, Phillip Cagan.

Cagan examined data on the changes in prices and in output for the United States since 1890. He not surprisingly found that the tendency for prices to fall during recessions has declined over time. He observes that

> ". . . the change in rates of change [of prices] from each expansion to the ensuing recession became less negative and, in the last two cycles, the change became positive-- that is, the rate of price increase in the recession exceeded that in the expansion, perverse cyclical behavior not exhibited before. The distinctive feature of the postwar inflations has not been that prices rose faster in periods of cyclical expansion--many previous expansions had much higher rates--but that they declined hardly at all, or even rose, in recessions. . . . The startling failure of the 1970 recession to curb the inflation was not a new phenomenon. . . but simply a further step in a *progressive* post-war development . . .the phenomenon of rising prices in slack markets is quite common . . . .
>
> Part of the smaller amplitude of cyclical fluctuation in prices reflects the reduced severity of business recessions since World War II, for which some credit goes to the contribution of economic research to improved stabilization techniques. Nonetheless, in addition to the smaller cyclical contractions in aggregate expenditures, the response of prices to a given amplitude of contraction has declined, so that now proportionately more of the contraction in expenditure falls on output. [5]

Although the finding that what is loosely called stagflation has emerged recently is, of course, commonplace, there are two features of Cagan's observations that deserve to be emphasized. The first is his insistence that there has been a *progressive* or *gradual* emergence of this problem. This is certainly correct-- the puzzling experience of the seventies was foreshadowed for example in the fifties, when the "cost-push" arguments first appeared. Yet, nothing like this was evident early in the century or in previous centuries. This suggests that we should look not simply at the Vietnam war and rising oil and food prices to analyze the current inflationary situation, but also be alert for gradual and cumulative changes in American society or policy that may be implicated in some way in the current inflationary problem.

A second feature of Cagan's observations that should be underlined is the point that, because of the changing behavior of prices, over time an *increasing* proportion of the effect of any reduction in aggregate demand shows up as a reduction in real output. There are, in other words, apparently some *gradual* developments which are bringing at least the more discerning monetarists and Keynesians closer together: both are noting the significant and apparently increasing extent to which the level of real output can vary with changes in the level of aggregate demand.

LONGER HISTORICAL COMPARISONS

The gradual changes that Cagan and others identified in modern experience are, as is often pointed out, also found in many other countries. More importantly, they are also evident, and evident in a more dramatic way, when we take a really long range historical perspective. Although the reliable data that are needed to make definitive judgments about macroeconomic and monetary history in prior centuries are lacking, the qualitative evidence and the scattered data that do exist are sufficient to have generated almost a consensus among economic historians about certain broad outlines of historical experience. These broad outlines, well known as they are, somehow have not been taken into account in either the Keynesian or the monetarist theories.

One of the most prominent, if not the most prominent trends in aggregative economic history, is the tendency for reductions in aggregate demand, whether due to monetary developments, fiscal choices, investment behavior, or whatever, to have an increased effect on the level of real output as time goes on. Although there apparently have been fluctuations in the price level about as long as there has been a money economy, and certainly for the last five centuries, substantial drops in the level of real national output for monetary or macroeconomic reasons are a relatively recent phenomenon. There were, of course, crop failures and other such sources of fluctuation in the real output of societies from the earliest times, and individual towns, communities, and industries could suffer depressions, but at the aggregative and national level a drop in aggregate demand would result mainly in a fall in the price level, rather than a reduction in real output. Although things were beginning to change somewhat in the latter part of the nineteenth century, the years from the peak of inflation of the Napoleonic Wars in 1812 to the low point in 1896 will nonetheless serve to illustrate the point dramatically. Over that period in Great Britain, then the most advanced and important country in the international economy, the price level fell by more than half. Experience in the United States and other countries was not greatly different. Yet during that period the industrial revolution was completed in Britain and spread to most of Western Europe and North America. Broadly speaking, the longest and most widespread period of peaceful growth in per capita income that the world has ever seen took place in a period in which the price level was more often than not falling. As the nineteenth century wore on, the bottom years of the cycle probably brought increasing unemployment, but by comparison with twentieth century experience the downswings in the cycle brought relatively small reductions in real output.

There were, of course, many "panics" and "crises" even in the early nineteenth century. It was naturally when the price level fell that those who had borrowed money tended to have the hardest time paying it back—they were paying a higher real interest rate than they would have paid had the price level not fallen. As the Populist movement in nineteenth century in the United States reminds us, those who had borrowed money when prices were higher certainly didn't like the deflation. When prices fell and some firms couldn't pay their debts, there might, of course, be a "panic," particularly in view of the unstable banking system, especially in the United States, which often led to bank failures. These panics and crises naturally depressed expectations and led to some reductions in employment and real output, but in terms of the experience of the 1930s, or our sense of what would result from comparable falls in the price level today, the effects were relatively minor and brief. The big picture is that, although the price level fell substantially, real output and employment increased by unprecedented amounts.

The difference between the character of the macroeconomic experience between the nineteenth and twentieth century is evident even in the language of daily life. Although some writers have exaggerated the newness of the term, the fact remains that "unemployment" is a term that came into common use only late in the 19th century. The *Oxford English Dictionary* states that the word "unemployment" has been in common use since only about 1895, but F.P. Thompson points out that the word can occasionally be found in Owenite and Radical writings as early as the 1820 and 1830s [6]. Early observers of unemployment tended to use such circumlocutions as "want of employment" or "involuntary idleness." The usual German word for unemployment, "arbeitslosigkeit," was also rarely used before the 1890s. The usage of the French word "chomage" goes back to the Middle Ages, but this word also has connotations of leisure, as in the expression "un jour chome" for a day off [7]. If the falling price level in the early nineteenth century had led to widespread and continuing unemployment of labor or other resources, some word to describe such an important if not tragic state of affairs would surely have come quickly into common usage in the languages of all the relevant countries.

The extent to which a reduction in aggregate demand is reflected in unemployment of resources and reductions in real output must be distinguished from the magnitude of fluctuations in aggregate demand. The interwar period was so disastrous, not only because reductions in aggregate demand were reflected in such substantial degree in reduced employment and output, but also because the drop in demand was so very great. The years since World War II, as Cagan pointed out, have by historical standards been relatively stable, in part because of what economists and governments have learned about stabilization policy. But the evidence cited shows that, because of increasing inflexibility of prices, our stagflationary economy is unprecedentedly liable to suffer unemployment and loss of output when aggregate demand falls off.

Obviously, something is accumulating or progressing over time, such as changing policies, structures, or institutions, which is changing the character of the macroeconomic problem. We know, both from the tendency for real output to vary more with changes in aggregate demand, and from direct observation of the prices themselves, that stickier prices and wages are crucial to the change that is taking place. But we do not *explain* the change by referring to sticky prices, any more than we explain anything by referring to *ad hoc* assumptions like "rigid wages" or merely descriptive concepts like Phillips curves. The *cause* of the fact that most wages and prices were less flexible in the interwar years than in the nineteenth century, and still less flexible in these stagflationary times, must be found. That cause, in turn, must play a leading role in our macroeconomic theory.

THE "POLITICAL ECONOMY" MODEL

I am, of course, partial to the explanation of increasing sticki-ness of wages that derives from my general model on "The Political Economy of Comparative Growth Rates." But that partiality should not concern the reader unless he knows of some *other* theory that also fits the facts at issue. If an alternative explanation is or has been found, the judgment about the relative suitability of the different theories then arises. Scientific judgments must then be made in terms of such criteria as how many correct predictions about *other* matters (e.g., growth rates) each theory makes, how parsimonious each theory is, and so on. But any such judgments are matters for other occasions and other economists. The task now is to spell out the implications of the Political Economy of Comparative Growth Rates model for wage and price stickiness. Since that model is described in detail elsewhere, I shall merely refer to its main features here.

The political economy model begins with all of those organi-zations or collusions of firms or individuals which attempt to further the interests of their members, either through combined action in the market place or through lobbying government. All such organizations provide what is, analytically speaking, a public or collective good for the group whose interests they serve, even if other groups are harmed by their actions. Indivi-dual voluntary action is for familiar reasons unlikely to provide group-optimal amounts of a collective good. Other things equal, the larger the set of individuals who benefit from a collective good, the less likely that an individual in the group will act to provide any of the collective good, since the "external economy" or benefit to others will be relatively greater. It follows that optimal group action will at the least usually require extensive and time-consuming bargains, if it occurs, and only reasonably small groups will be able to cooperate in this way. Larger groups will require coercive power to support any organizations, just as the state requires compulsory taxation, or some privileged or lucky situation which makes it possible for them to bribe individuals to support a collective effort through some sort of tied sale. The most important large common (special) interest organizations in American society, at least, do have either coercive power or other selective incentives. Since the logic of the present argument is set out in *The Logic of Collective Action*, [8] no more will be said about it here.

This model of collective action, in combination with the straightforward microeconomic theory of markets, together lead to the following five working hypotheses:

WH1— Since some groups, such as consumers, taxpayers, the unemployed, and the poor, will never organize, because they are large and without selective incentives, the society has not and will not reach the point where representatives of all its groups can meet together and bargain for a more efficient "core" allocation.

WH2— Since selective incentives are hard to obtain, collective action is problematical and will occur only in relatively favorable conditions for those groups that have the possibility of organizing. *Societies will accumulate more such organizations over time* as additional groups enjoy unusually favorable conditions.

WH3— At least when they are not large in relation to the whole society, such groups will on balance reduce both economic efficiency and growth. They will often do this partly through the market, by blocking entry and setting supra-competitive prices, and often through lobbying for special government policies that favor them while reducing economic efficiency.

WH4— If such groups encompass a large part of the labor force, or the owners of a large part of the capital stock, their own members will bear a large enough share of the costs of any anti-social action that this will tend to countervail adverse effects on efficiency and growth.

WH5— The accumulation of common-interest organizations or collusion over time, and the growth of the role of government intervention in markets that it encourages, reduces the frequency of change of the variables that the common-interest organizations influence or control, since these groups make decisions either through complex multi-lateral bargains requiring consensus, or by time-consuming constitutional procedures.

The model leads to the prediction that countries like Germany and Japan that have had totalitarian government and occupying armies that destroy common-interest organizations, or reconstitute them on a more encompassing basis, will have relatively high levels of economic efficiency and growth. Those societies, such as Great Britain, that have had stable freedom of organization and security from invasion the longest will tend to grow more slowly. Societies with very encompassing organizations, like Sweden, will sometimes do better than similar societies with less inclusive organizations. Recently settled states of the United States will have had less time to accumulate common-interest organizations, as will those states which were defeated in the Civil War, and both new states and ex-Confederate states will tend to grow more rapidly than the states in the Northeast and older Middle West, which have had a longer time to accumulate common-interest organizations.

STICKY WAGES

The way in which the argument that has just be adumbrated would fill the hiatus in macroeconomic theory is presumably obvious. It may, nonetheless, be well to illustrate the applicability of the model by looking at one area—wage determination—and its relationship to the familiar debate about whether there can be a negatively sloped Phillips curve in the long run. It is, of course, a mistake to suppose that all wages are unusually sticky or that only wages are sticky. The argument I have made emphasizes the degree of collusion and organization of common-interests, and although this is usually relatively high in the labor market, there is no hard and fast connection. Still, wage stickiness should be a good and classic example of the class of phenomena with which the model deals and should also help us understand how inflation is affected.

It is commonly argued or observed that many wages are rigid downward, in the sense that they do not fall for a considerable time even when it would appear a reduction in wages might be widely advantageous. It is also often noticed that when there is sudden or unexpected inflation, wages will also rise more slowly than many prices. Thus the primary need is for a model of the situation which recognizes that there are various negotiated or partly politically determined wage levels which may *eventually* either fall or rise, if the changes in demand or cost conditions making a wage change advantageous are strong and prolonged enough, and which in a basic way treats the lags and complexities in the negotiating or decision-making processes with natural symmetry. Yet it is also faithful to the pervasive perception that there is a special difficulty or delay in cutting the money wage. This perception, it must be emphasized, is not the generalized observation that we live in an inflationary world, but instead a vast number of occasions where the demand for a given category of labor falls, or something else happens which should make the equilibrium wage go down. Yet the money wage remains unchanged for at least a surprising length of time.

Where a wage is negotiated by formal collective bargaining, or by a process as openly political as that which determines the minimum wage, all three of the following conditions will normally apply: (1) the monopoly power or political clout that is behind the collective bargaining or political wage setting will tend toward a supra-competitive wage; (2) money wage levels (in the absence of indexing) will be changed only at intervals, such as that given by a contract of two or three years' duration, except perhaps when there are dramatic changes in conditions, and (3) a privileged position will almost always be given to the status quo money wage, in that it will be the social choice unless and until there is mutual agreement on a new contract or the "constitutional" processes for deciding on changes have been completed, and the bargaining or constitutional processes for making changes often take significant amounts of time.

When the situation has been fully and properly spelled out, the solution is amazingly simple. If demand or cost conditions change in such a way as to create pressures for a lower money wage, the fact that the status quo has priority until a time for making changes has arrived, and a new bargain or political decision has been made, insures that for what may be a considerable period both the money wage and real wage will be at above equilibrium levels. Abstracting from possible "second best" problems, there then will be a smaller level of real output in the economy than could be attained. The employers will have an incentive to hire fewer workers, and there will be unemployment or crowding of labor into any sectors where wages can change instantaneously. The supra-competitive real wage that existed in the old equilibrium is now even farther above the Pareto-optimal level.

The other relevant possibility is that demand or cost conditions will change in such a way as to create pressures for a higher money wage. The fact that the status quo has priority insures that for what may be a considerable period the money wage and the real wage are lower than the new situation, in combination with the monopoly power or political clout behind the wage setting practice, will warrant in the long run. Until the change in the money wage can occur, the employers will chose to hire more workers than otherwise, thereby tending to raise the level of employment, and during the transition period the effect of the monopoly or lobbying power will not be fully evident. Thus the inflation, by reducing real wages for a time, temporarily raises the level of employment and probably reduces other excess burdens of supra-competitive wages as well.

The considerations I have mentioned will alone account for a short-run Phillips curve. Unexpected inflation temporarily reduces the degree of monopoly and the effect of unemployment on wage (and price) rigidities; deflation or less than expected rates of inflation temporarily increases the degree of monopoly and the social costs of the rigidities.

Now let me get to the closely related point about what might be called the "eternal Phillips phenomenon." It's a reasonable first approximation to say that monetary policy can be changed in a matter of days (if not less). Some of the effects of monetary changes will be evident promptly, as soon as the change in monetary policy is noticed, although some of the effects may appear only after a considerable lag. By contrast, the minimum wage laws, collectively bargained wages, public utility prices, and legislation abolishing or creating monopolies can be changed only over a period of many months or even many years. Given that the administration can marginally change the rate at which appropriated monies are spent, the lags in fiscal policy are probably somewhere in between. But fiscal policy probably has rather prompt effects. (There is also a difference in the division of powers, with the executive branch of at least many countries given complete control over monetary policy, only partial control over policy on stationary prices and monopoly policy, and almost no control over collective bargaining.) It is further normally true that at least in the short run the social cost of the real output lost from recession exceeds the social cost of the less-than-optimal-size of real money balances and other subtle costs of inflation, unless the inflation has reached very high levels indeed. It follows that the quickest way, and sometimes the only way, an administration can raise the level of employment and real output and reduce the costs of monopoly power is through inflation. Monetary and fiscal policy can be changed faster than "rigid" wages and prices can be changed, so it won't be possible for the organized interests to maintain the real wages or prices in the short run. A somewhat inflationary policy in the short run is accordingly advantageous for society in the short run.

Moreover, even in the long run, and even with rational expectations, the Phillips curve arising from the foregoing aspects of reality will *never* become vertical. Even if the public knows what the government is doing, the fact that the crucial wage can't change as fast as monetary policy at least means that the government can always generate more real output and a lesser degree of monopoly by taking advantage of the possibility of lowering real wages during the crucial lag period. The only possibility that could make the Phillips curve vertical, even in the longest run, is institutional change great enough to do away with the fundamental features of reality described above: the priority for the status quo and the lag in adjustment would themselves have to be done away with. It is by no means certain that the coalitions that give rise to the political or monopoly power behind the whole process could ever acquire the capacity for immediate decision-making, or would want to. Even if indexing is used, a lag in the collection and publication of the cost-of-living index, or any stable imperfection in it known to the government, or any sticky-wage area to which the index did not apply, would permit an eternally non-vertical Phillips pheno-menon.

STICKY PRICES

If the foregoing theory and the argument about wages is correct, it would imply that we could get some idea about which product prices would change most slowly. They would presumably be those product prices that are set or greatly influenced by common-interest organizations directly and/or by governments. In general, if my collective action model is correct, the more concentrated industries are more likely to be organized. Once again Phillip Cagan has performed the signal service of putting forth the facts which I need to emphasize, while retaining his unflinchingly monetarist perspective. As Cagan puts it:

> Why do prices not clear markets in the short run? While manufacturing prices have at times fallen precipitously, as in the business contractions of 1920-21 and 1929-33,

usually they do not. To be sure, the available data do not record the secret discounting and shading of prices in slack markets, and actual transaction prices undoubtedly undergo larger fluctuations than the reported quotations suggest.   The difference between reported and actual prices [will be] discussed further. It is not important enough, however, to invalidate the observed insensitivity of most prices to shifts in demand. . . .

It turns out that the concentrated industries (defined as industries in which the four largest firms account for a high percentage of sales) do display less amplitude of cyclical price changes. . .concentrated industries are more likely to be characterized by some discretionary price setting by big firms, as distinct from the highly competitive markets for many agricultural products and raw materials, which are characterized by market deter-mined prices. . .The importance of price setting is that firms in industries where it is the rule appear to coordi-nate price changes with each other so far as possible. The various methods of coordination require these firms to disregard short-run shifts in demand and to concentrate instead on changes in cost. As a consequence, their prices exhibit smaller fluctuations over the business cycle and less sensitivity to accelerations and retardations of general inflation.   They appear to be less flexible, and they impede the propogation of inflationary pressures through the economy.   Their lags of adjustment are evident in an inflationary upswing by the fact that basic commodity prices move earlier and faster. As inflation-ary pressures wane, they make catch-up increases that present the paradox of rising demand at a time when demand is slackening.   On this interpretation inflexible prices do not initiate inflation; but they play a crucial role in transmitting it and delaying the success of policies to curb it. [9]

The reality that Cagan describes, although observed with differ-ent glasses than I use, is exactly as the model offered here would predict.

TOWARD A GENERAL MACRO THEORY

If the argument offered here is correct, Keynes' brilliant model should not be viewed as a general theory. Keynes was writing in Great Britain in the twenties and thirties. The society in which he wrote had accumulated far more common-interest organizations than any other society *at that time*. The pattern of demands the British economy faced were far different than before the War, and the industries in which Britain had comparative advantage had changed somewhat too. These considerations entailed that Britain needed a new structure of relative wages and prices, and a considerable reallocation of resources. In the absence of price and especially wage flexibility there was a great deal of unemployment of resources. For a time this problem was exacerbated by Churchill's over-valuation of the pound. Still, as the late Harry Johnson has trenchantly argued, if the relevant wages and prices had fallen enough, British resources would have been fully employed. But the British institutional structure had been developing for a long time, and the relevant wages and prices did not fall in the short-run, and some not even in the medium term. In a sufficiently long-run, these wages and prices would have adjusted, but (to borrow a phrase from Keynes) in the long-run we are all dead. Thus Keynes's general theory is in fact an ingenious and invaluable, but by no means general theory. Had Britain emerged from World War I with the clean institutional slate which Germany had after World War II, Keynes would perhaps not have had an occasion to write the book. Had the United States not also had a modest period of stability and institutional accumulation (especially of business—note the Smoot-Hawley tariff), Keynes might not have had such a profound impact upon the United States. From this perspective it is no accident that post-war German opinion has not been very susceptible to Keynes.

Though Keynes *recognized* that inflexible wages and prices often (he thought always) had profound macroeconomic significance, and in that respect was far ahead of many monetarists even in our own day, he did not take the trouble to *explain* the inflexibility. Without any explanation of these inflexibilities, Keynes' followers in the era of stagflation have often supposed that the "rigid" wages and prices would not be affected by the increases in aggregate demand—they assumed the fixed wages and prices were simply given, and would not be affected by expansionary fiscal policies, whereas they were only inflexible, and would eventually change in predictable and rational ways. There is no need to dwell on the costs of this mistake, for the monetarists point it out repeatedly.

But the monetarists, although they never make the mistake of acting as though prices and wages would never change, have been no more thoughtful about the political economy of these processes than the Keynesians. If the monetarists had thought seriously about the institutional accumulation I have described (or even taken note of their own warnings about the growing role of government in wage and price determination), they would not have been so long attached to the idea that the economy is almost always at or quickly heading toward the full employment level of output: they would not have analyzed the American economy of the 1970s in a way that (at best) was appropriate to the early nineteenth century. If Milton Friedman had thought more about the gradual accumulation of common-interest organizations in stable societies, he might instead have said that, if there is a natural rate of unemployment at all, it is naturally (except in catastrophies) always increasing.

NOTES

1.   The author thanks the National Science Foundation and Resources for the Future for support of his research. He is especially thankful to Brian Cushing, Douglas Kinney, and Howell Zee for assisting him on the research on this topic and to Moses Abramovitz, Dudley Dillard, Paul Meyer, Michael Parkin, and Donald Whitehead for helpful suggestions. Special thanks are due to the editors for agreeing in advance that portions of this paper may be used in other publications.

2.   In "Beyond the Measuring Rod of Money" (manuscript, forthcoming) and (less satisfactorily) in "Evaluating Performance in the Public Sector," *The Measurement of Economic and Social Performance*, Studies in Income and Wealth Vol. 38, National Bureau of Economic Research, Milton Moss, ed. (New York: Columbia University Press, 1973), 355-84.

3.   Philip Cagan, *The Hydra-Headed Monster: The Problem of Inflation in the United States* (Washington: American Enterprise Institute, 1974), p. 3.

4.   These data are borrowed from Patrick Minford of the University of Liverpool; see his forthcoming paper on "The Problem of Inflation" (Table II). It is important to emphasize that the lesson that Minford draws is not the same as the one

that will be offered in this paper; Minford is arguing for the superiority of the monetarist model.

5. Phillip Cagan, op. cit. This quotation and the following one are from scattered sections of Cagan's essay, and leave out most of Cagan's own explanations of the facts he states. The selective quotations do, however, provide a fair summary of those facts in Cagan's account that bear most directly on the present argument. The italics are mine. I am thankful to Thomas Mayer for calling Cagan's argument to my attention.

6. E. P. Thompson, *The Making of the English Working Class*, p. 776, fn. 2. I am grateful to Peter Murrell for this reference. The word "unemployed" goes much further back, and was used, for example, to describe fallow land; note this passage from *Paradise Lost*: "Other creatures all day long rove idle unimploid and less need rest (iv, 617).

7. See John A. Garraty, *Unemployment in History* (New York: Harper and Row, Colophon edition, 1979) p. 4.

8. Cambridge, Mass.: Harvard Economic Series, Harvard University Press, 1965, 1971.

9. Phillip Cagan, op. cit.

✳ *Chapter 9*

THE ANTIINFLATION VALUE OF DIRECT CONTROLS

*Charles E. Rockwood**

INTRODUCTION

Most economists continue to recommend near exclusive reliance upon monetary and fiscal policy for inflation control. This is despite the fact that the United States has been increasingly less successful in dealing with the inflation–unemployment dilemma. The second most frequently recommended policy remedy, to be used in conjunction with monetary and fiscal policy, is restructuring the economy: to make it more competitive, to increase the private cost of unemployment, to improve job mobility, or whatever. A distant third recommendation in this broad listing of possible stagflation remedies is direct control of prices and wages to supplement price stabilizing monetary and fiscal policy. Lack of attention to this latter policy option is regrettable both because direct controls, reasonably structured and properly introduced, offer definite hope of making a measurable contribution to the antiinflation fight, and because the alternatives to direct controls are so imperfect.

This chapter argues first that alternatives to direct controls are highly unsatisfactory, and second that direct controls, for a time, can influence price and wage behavior favorably. A third task of the chapter is consideration of some of the broad problems associated with implementation and management of any well designed controls program.

*Professor of Economics, Florida State University.

Discussion in this chapter thus is devoted to arguing the case for direct controls on prices and wages as a temporary supplement to monetary and fiscal policy for inflation control. Less attention is devoted to the specific wage-price control program. That topic is addressed by both Abba Lerner and Sidney Weintraub elsewhere in this volume. The position taken here is that a number of superficially quite similar direct-control proposals have essentially similar problems of design, management-implementation, and potential success.

ALTERNATIVES TO DIRECT CONTROLS

The bulwark of the United States defense against inflation has been restrictive monetary and fiscal policy largely unsupported by other government antiinflation programs. The approach has not been effective and our inability to reconcile the objectives of reasonable price stability and relatively full employment has become one of the most fundamental of the economic crises of our age.

In the absence of an innovative solution, perhaps direct controls, the inflation-unemployment dilemma will surely continue, and continue to lead to perennial dissatisfaction with the economic performance of this and other nations. It will continue to lead to suboptimization of economic goals by encouraging destabilizing shifts in monetary and fiscal policy as first one policy mix and then another is emphasized, in a manner akin to what Henry Wallich once called drag racing the monetary system—first the accelerator, then the brakes. Inability to reconcile the objectives of reasonable price stability and relatively full employment will continue to lead still further to a wide variety of frequently undesirable policy experiments in which a primary motive force is the need to reduce abnormal unemployment during a period of monetary and fiscal contraction even if the unemployment reduction program is very inefficient.

A part of the problem in dealing with the inflation-unemployment dilemma is the notion that labor and product markets will respond to macro market signals or can be restructured until they do. The argument that the supply of labor responds to fluctuations in the real wage and that product price movements are directly related to shifts in demand suggests conservative monetary and fiscal policy as the principal antiinflation remedy, with unemployment tending, over time, to settle at the natural rate. The argument that if actual markets do not conform reasonably well to the market behavior model, then they should be restructured until they do suggests micro approaches to the macro problem of inflation and unemployment—more vigorous antitrust policy, restructuring of a variety of social programs to provide greater economic incentives for work and for production, and the like.

THE MONETARY AND FISCAL POLICY ALTERNATIVE

The well-known difficulty with placing near exclusive reliance upon monetary and fiscal policy is that the United States economy has not been responding well to contractionary macro market signals, at least in the short period. Episodes of monetary and fiscal restraint in the recent past reveal all too clearly how effective many product and labor markets can be in pursuing independent pricing policies. The overwhelming evidence is that the short-run Phillips curve is very flat on the contraction side.

Whether the monetarists are correct in arguing that we have not tried hard enough, that we need to hold to the monetary anti-inflation remedy more resolutely, is a proposition that may never receive a thorough test for political reasons. Perhaps the proposition should never be tested for economic reasons as well.

Both the Ford and Carter administrations have sought to test the "try harder" approach by pursuing a policy of gradualism. But even gradualism is expensive. Arthur Okun has concluded that each $200 billion reduction in real output, under a period of gradual restraint, would produce a reduction of only between .6 and 1.8 points in the basic inflation rate for the 1980s [1]. Extension of this analysis suggests that reducing the inflation rate from somewhere around 8 percent to a near zero rate by torturing the economy on the rack of gradualism could cost between $2.6 and $8 trillion over the decade. The estimate is between 1.2 and 3.6 times the current annual production of goods and services.

It has been argued that a policy of gradualism would teach economic decisionmakers to anticipate events. Thus it would minimize the probable output loss associated with return to near price stability. But a policy of gradualism that was not resolutely adhered to also could teach decisionmakers not to anticipate inflation reduction. A wavering policy thus could be expensive in terms of output foregone, without producing a noticeable moderation in wage and price increases. This seems most nearly akin to our experiences of the last decade or so.

The conclusion seems inescapable, standing alone monetary and fiscal policy is an extremely expensive means of inflation control in the short period.   The frightening possibility also exists that it would be extremely expensive over a longer period. To some this suggests the need for a restructuring of the economy, to soften the trade-off between inflation reduction and increased unemployment. The difficulty with the restructuring approach is that the kinds of economic change needed are so sweeping as probably to be beyond our grasp.

THE ECONOMIC RESTRUCTURING ALTERNATIVE

The task of making the economy more responsive to monetary and fiscal policy signals might be likened to making the economy more competitive. This analogy applies both because the latter will enhance the former and because the magnitude of the structural change needed is so enormous in both cases. Realistically, perhaps all that can be hoped for as a consequence of intensive restructuring efforts is that the economy does not become *less responsive* to monetary and fiscal policy than it is at present. Recent trends seem to be toward a flatter short-run Phillips curve on the contraction side. Just to counter this trend may be all that could be hoped for.

A number of economists have made specific suggestions for reducing the natural rate of unemployment below its current approximate rate of 5.4 percent [2]. Most of these suggestions do not appear to deal specifically with the trade-off problem. Rather, they deal with how to increase the incentive for hiring workers and/or decrease the incentive for being unemployed. But, reducing the natural rate of unemployment may have little to do with the shape of the short-run Phillips curve.

Of course, if the natural rate of unemployment is reduced at the same time monetary and fiscal stringency is imposed, the illusion may be presented that the trade-off between inflation reduction and additional unemployment has been softened. Actually, a productivity gain will have been devoured by the inflation control program. Politically, it may be helpful to hide the true cost of restrictive monetary and fiscal policy in this way, but the economic cost is not likely to be much reduced.

Furthermore, if the natural rate of unemployment is temporarily reduced, through unanticipated gains in productivity which make the natural rate of unemployment compatible with higher-than-natural wage gains, higher wage settlements may be fostered in the future. Future inflation control then will become more, rather than less, difficult. A present inflation problem will be alleviated, a future problem intensified.

Proposals to increase the private cost of unemployment for workers and employers; to improve the marketable job skills of the unemployed, by providing assistance in skill development or geographical availability; or to reduce the need for skill and geographical mobility, by encouraging employers to adapt their needs to the types and locations of available workers, are all highly desirable policy activities. Probably none of these activities will greatly affect the shape of the short-run Phillips curve.

ANTIINFLATIONARY VALUE OF DIRECT CONTROLS

The proposals outlined thus far for dealing with the inflation-unemployment dilemma offer little hope of moderating the high economic cost of "traditional" antiinflation programs. The illusion of cost reduction may be present, but likely not the fact. It thus behooves the prudent policy maker to consider a more eclectic program. That eclecticism leads inevitably to the consideration of direct controls on wages and prices.

The most commonly cited objection to direct controls as an antiinflationary device is that they simply do not work. Evaluation of the historical record of wage and price controls in order to assess this contention is a very difficult undertaking, as it requires that control periods be compared with the probable alternative. Because of the complexity of the comparison between the actual and the hypothetical, it is not surprising that the collective judgment of students of the problem is mixed. However, it seems fair to say that the evidence points to the conclusion that controls sometimes have been effective, although not always. Some illustrative studies make this point quite clearly.

Otto Eckstein and James A. Girola analyzed all five twentieth-century control episodes in the United States (World War I, World War II, the Korean war, the Kennedy-Johnson guidepost era, and the Nixon control episode) in terms of single wage and price equations as well as interim-period equations [3]. In this analysis Eckstein and Girola found price controls had a highly significant retarding effect on price movements during World War I, World War II, and the Nixon control period. These results lead to the provisional conclusion that price controls can work. The conclusion needs to be tempered, however, by the knowledge that the NRA Codes of the 1930s, which were intended as a form of cartel raising, surprisingly appear in the Eckstein-Girola analysis to influence prices downward rather than upward. This strange result casts some doubt on the validity of the Eckstein-Girola long-term approach. Also, the shock of the Nixon decontrol period is revealed in the Eckstein-Girola analysis as having lifted prices up more than otherwise would have been expected. Still, by their analysis, price controls usually have had a price restraining impact.

By contrast with the price control case, Eckstein and Girola found direct controls on wages did *not* have a statistically significant restraining effect during any control period and that wages during World War I moved up more than might have been expected in light of associated price trends and other elements of the macro environment.

Since Eckstein and Girola found price movements highly significant in their wage equations, what they may have revealed is that direct controls on both wages and prices sometimes work but that price controls appear to be the more effective.

A perhaps more orthodox method of evaluating the influence of wage and price controls, which involves fewer data and structural shift problems than the Eckstein-Girola study, is to develop wage and price equations for short periods rather than for almost a century. Individual control episodes then are reviewed in light of their influence on shorter wage and price movements. This literature, which is too extensive to review fully, also seems to point to some restraining impact from the imposition of direct controls. Two studies are presented as illustrative of this argument.

Bradley Askin and John Kraft, in a study for the Price Commission [4], reviewed the impact of Nixon era controls using three wage and price models and simulating results for a common data set. The first model simulated was a slightly revised form of a distributed lag adjustment model developed by Robert J. Gordon [5]. The second model was an imposed adjustment model of a form originally set forth by Otto Eckstein and Roger Brinner [6]. It is similar in many respects to the Eckstein and Girola analyzed above as well as to the work of Gordon. The third model was a modified version of a current period adjustment model originally developed by Calvin Siebert and Mahmood Zaidi for the manufacturing sector [7].

The simulations undertaken by Askin and Kraft yield somewhat different results. All three simulations produce the conclusion that the rate of price inflation was reduced during the Nixon wage-price freeze and during the Nixon Phase II control period. However, there was some difference in the estimated amount of price restraint.

The Askin and Kraft simulations were inconclusive in their evaluation of the impact of the Nixon Phase I and Phase II controls on wage movements. The modified Gordon model indicated the rate of increase in the wage-level was reduced by the early phases of Nixon's controls program. The other two models indicated that the rate of increase in the wage-level actually was accelerated by the Nixon controls.

The effect of the Nixon decontrol period was not systematically investigated by Askin and Kraft. However, their study suggested that gains made during the Phase I and II control periods may well have been lost during the decontrol phase.

The effect of the Kennedy-Johnson guidepost era on wage movements was examined by George L. Perry [8]. In this work Perry evaluated the guideposts using a wage equation which he had developed a few years earlier [9]. In his analysis Perry found that the rate of change in wages was below the predicted rate for fifteen consecutive quarters (1962 IV-1966 I) that corresponded almost exactly with the guidepost period.

In speculating about why the guideposts seemed to have succeeded, Perry examined wage trends in selected "visible" industries that he thought likely to be highly susceptible to controls as opposed to "invisible" industries that he thought were not likely to be very susceptible to controls. Comparison of the relative rates of change in wages between the two classes of industries, with few exceptions, supported the hypothesis that the guideposts seemed most effective in the visible industries. Perry then concluded that the guideposts probably held down the overall rate of wage change, but did so at the expense of a distortion in the structure of wages. The Perry conclusion did not go unchallenged [10]. Nevertheless, it remains at least weak evidence that the Kennedy-Johnson guideposts had some controlling influence over wage movements.

In summary, enormous difficulties stand in the way of evaluating the influence of direct controls on wages and price. Nonetheless, such evidence as is available supports the conclusion that for a time direct controls can restrain wage and price movements.

EFFECTIVE DURATION OF CONTROLS

The argument that wage and price controls cannot work at all fails to stand up to empirical examination. Controls do appear to work sometimes. By contrast, the argument that direct controls tend to break down over time is amply supported by the empirical evidence. Thus, the best, if not the only, use for direct controls as an antiinflation instrument would appear to be over the short term. Properly designed and implemented, controls might be used in the short term to help break the "psychology" of inflation. But the prospect is very dim for successful implementation of a long-term, continuous program of direct controls.

The two principal reasons why direct controls tend to break down over time regardless of structure are: (1) The longer the control episode, the more control prices are likely to diverge from the market equilibrium prices that would have occurred without controls. (2) As experience with controls is gained, the methods by which the controls might be circumvented become better known. Both market pressure for control deviation and knowledge of how to defeat the control system build over time.

The breakdown process can be accelerated or retarded by the structure of the controls, the manner of their enforcement, and the monetary and fiscal environment within which the control system is placed. The monetary and fiscal environment is especially important. For wage–price controls to be at all effective, monetary and fiscal policy and wage–price policy should be complementary rather than conflicting. If this is not the case, disaster is sure to overtake the controls program.

The problem of expansionary monetary and fiscal policy torquing a controls program until it breaks is perhaps exemplified by the Nixon control program in its latter stages. Especially toward the end of that program, a too liberal monetary and fiscal policy no doubt hastened the breakdown of controls (during Phase III) and added to the decontrol jump in prices and wages (during Phase IV). All or most of the gains in wage and price restraint made earlier were lost.

Another example of monetary and fiscal policy being out of tune with wage–price policy is the Australian wage control experience in the 1950s. During this period the Australian money supply rose at a rate approximately double that of their National Income. The not unexpected result was that the rate of growth in wages paid greatly outstripped the rate of change in legally allowable wage rates. The economy then experienced wage drift as employers upgraded their workers into higher pay categories, increased the amount of overtime premiums, paid their workers secret bonuses, and the like [11].

Evidence as to exactly how long wage-price controls might remain effective is unclear and remains subject to numerous program design and implementation factors, as well as to the degree of compatibility between the controls and the prevailing monetary and fiscal policy environment. As one benchmark, the control episodes which Eckstein and Girola identify as successful (World War I, World War II, and the Nixon control period) were, two years, four years, and one and one half years in duration.

ENFORCEMENT AND CONTROL BREAKDOWN

When controls begin to break down, because of monetary and fiscal pressures which run counter to the control objectives or for some other reason, the suggestion often is made that stronger penalties for noncompliance are needed. Accounts of how controls are circumvented become widely known, and a move to favor greater enforcement activity sometimes is the result.

One cannot imagine a well-structured control program without some coercive aspects. The enforcement regime, its fairness and its efficiency, is important to the success of any control mechanism. These points are obvious. But it also is evident that even the strongest of enforcement powers will not be effective (1) when the monetary and fiscal environment is at odds with the control objectives or (2) when the structure of the controls is inappropriate in some other way to the economic context in which they are being employed. Two examples of very tightly controlled economies that nevertheless experienced control breakdown illustrate this point.

The first example is drawn from the fourth century A.D. when, in the face of runaway prices, the Roman Emperor Diocletian took the drastic step—unprecedented in Roman history—of establishing a list of maximum prices and wages for a wide variety of goods and services [12]. But Diocletian did not at the same time restrict the process of monetary expansion taking place through debasement of the coinage. As a result, and in spite of the fact that violation of the maximum price edict was a capital offense, the control program was not effective. As a contemporary critic of Diocletian explained: [13]

> ... when by various iniquities he [Diocletian] brought about enormously high prices, he attempted to legislate the prices of commodities. Then much blood was spilled ... nothing appeared on the market because of fear, and prices soared much higher. In the end, after many people had lost their lives, it became absolutely necessary to repeal the law.

The second example of control breakdown in a fairly tightly controlled economy is drawn from the Soviet economy of the 1930s, where there was considerable evidence of an economy responding to wage inflation pressures through wage drift [14]. This circumstance occurred in spite of the fact that wages were set by law and factor input proportions were fixed, as were their prices. However, labor was free to move within the manufacturing sector, and as a result workers moved from job to job as managers raided each other for workers. In response to secret wage concessions (upgrading of a worker's skills, unofficial bonuses, and so forth), worker mobility for one period ran as high as an average of one and one-half times per year for major firms in the manufacturing sector. Substantial wage drift was the result.

COST OF DIRECT CONTROLS

Some who might concede that direct controls, given the proper macro setting, enforcement regime, and the like, will work at least for a period to reduce inflation nonetheless object to controls because of their cost. The bureaucratic cost of controls administration is one element of this objection. The cost of repressed inflation--an imperfect product mix and increased transactions costs--exemplified by shortages, quality deterioration, rationing, and queuing--is another element of this objection.

There is no doubt that the cost of controls can be large. Not might there be a large governmental staff to promulgate, administer, and perhaps enforce controls, but the public at large could be forced to spend a considerable amount of time reacting to and learning to live with the control system established. Critics of controls point to these costs and to questions about whether controls work at all as the prime reasons for their opposition to direct controls.

It may well be that if the best way to reduce the inflation rate is a governmental program which includes direct control of prices and wages, then inflation may not be as economically harmful as its remedy. Others before us have concluded that the cure is worse than the disease, which presumably accounts in part for the wide prevalence of inflation throughout the world. But if the decision has been made to reduce the inflation rate by the best means available, and if real GNP does not decline as much as expected, then the cost of the controls by definition would seem to have been exceeded by their benefit.

From this perspective effort devoted to an enumeration of the cost of controls is largely beside the point. In particular, citation by example is apt to give a false impression of the true administrative and repressed inflation costs of controls. However, if the issue is not whether to have a controls program but rather what type of controls program to have, then the question of cost becomes very important. How a controls program is structured and administered obviously has much to do both with its effectiveness and with its cost. In the context of this kind of necessity for choice, the innovative control proposals of Abba Lerner, of Sidney Weintraub, and of many others are truly valuable contributions.

It is evident that control programs differ in effectiveness, as witnessed by the econometric and testimentary evidence. Presumably this variability is largely the result of differences in repressed inflation costs, a function both of time and of the economic wisdom of the regulatory regime. It also is evident that control programs differ considerably as to bureaucratic cost.

Aside from a program of largely voluntary controls, such as President Ford's WIN (Whip Inflation Now) program, which might not be very effective but also might not require much administration, the least expensive control program to administer which we have tried in this country probably was the ninety-day wage-price freeze imposed under President Nixon. This phase of the program was of short duration and did not involve elaborate rules or administrative structure. For government personnel, the program is estimated to have utilized the services of forty-five persons hired by the Cost of Living Council, 300 persons already working for the Office of Economic Preparedness and about 2,000 persons from the 360 Field Offices of the Internal Revenue Service. In addition, the 2,850 field offices of the Agricultural Stabilization and Conservation Service were called upon to serve as information centers. But the employees of this agency also continued their other duties [15]. It is clear the program did not require a large number of government administrators. Neither did the program seem to require enormous compliance efforts, although they were not trivial.

The Cost of Living Council promulgated about seventy-five rulings explaining the freeze order. For example, raw agricultural products were excluded from the freeze, as were imports and exports, business profits and some other items. State and municipal governments, however, were subject to the freeze as were armed forces longevity pay increases, prices charged at military commissaries, workers with substandard income, dues payments to clubs and associations, dividends to stockholders, interest rates, and so on. Obviously, the private and interestingly enough the government sector had to learn and attempt to abide by these rulings. Part of the effort to do so yielded approximately 800,000 inquiries to the Internal Revenue Service. However, the program resulted in only 46,387 complaints about noncompliance during the ninety days the freeze was in effect, which was approximately 172 complaints per million of population. In ninety-two percent of these complaints, no violations were found. Most of the remaining cases were resolved by a relatively quick and informal process. Only forty-five cases went to court. The Justice Department initiated eight of these cases and won most of them. The government was itself sued in the remaining thirty-seven cases and again fared well in the courts [16].

World War II controls on wages and prices are an example of a much more thoroughgoing and more expensive control program. Under the spirit of cooperation that prevailed at the time, no doubt virtually every government, private agency and institution participated in the wage and price control program in some degree. However, official responsibility for wage regulation resided in the National War Labor Board (January 12, 1942-December 31, 1945) and for price regulation in the Office of Price Administration.

The National War Labor Board worked under a program of voluntary cooperation in which parties to wage bargaining almost without exception subscribed to a no-strike, no-lockout pledge.

In its administration of the program, the War Labor Board and its regional agencies acted upon 463,000 applications for permission to make particular types of wage adjustments, involving about 26 million workers. In addition, about 70,000 cases of alleged or admitted violations were processed, but there were only about 100 recorded cases of outright dispute of the board's authority. The wartime wage regulation program was sufficiently well managed that civilian labor did not have to be conscripted, although some labor shortages did develop. The number of work stoppages due to labor disputes was much below both prewar and post-war experiences [17].

The paid staff of the WLB, including those in the field offices, at its peak consisted of only 2,613 full-time employees. However, the board and staff were greatly burdened with work and used the facilities of other agencies: the Wage and Hour Division of the Department of Labor, the Bureau of Labor Statistics, the U.S. Conciliation Service, and the Bureau of the Budget. In addition to soliciting the help of these agencies, the WLB called upon several thousand industry and public representatives to serve on the Regional War Labor Boards, on dispute panels, on the National War and Labor Board, and on the tripartite commissions established in various industries. These part-time representatives were paid on a per diem basis [18].

The cost of the World War II Office of Price Administration (OPA) is difficult to estimate. A really thorough review of the agency and its activities seems never to have been made. The agency was large, and it underwent a number of organizational changes during the war. Its activities were quite broad. Principally OPA (1) set prices at all levels, (2) arranged subsidies for firms whose output was essential to the war effort but which could not survive under OPA established prices and WLB established wage rates, and (3) administered the wartime rationing program.

The ration division of OPA utilized decentralized control. By the fall of 1943, there were eight regional offices and ninety-three district offices, with a total employment approaching 3,500 persons. These offices supported a system of local boards that in August of 1944 numbered 5,520 and were staffed with 98,641 volunteer board members, who devoted about 12 hours per month of their time. Their personnel also included 35,110 full-time paid staff, 667 part-time paid staff, 29,828 clerical volunteers, and 19,746 peak-load volunteers. In all, nearly 200,000 persons were involved [19].

OPA also operated through the commercial banking system. The overwhelming majority of the nation's 15,000 commercial banks opened accounts with wholesalers and retailers dealing in rationed commodities, issued tokens, changed tokens for coupons, and the like.   Affected were 200,000 sugar retailers, wholesalers, and refiners; 200,000 coffee retailers, wholesalers, and roasters; 200,000 retailers and wholesalers of processed foods; an almost equal number of sellers of meats, fats, canned fish, cheese, and canned milk; and 30,000 gasoline retailers. Shoe retailers, fuel oil distributors, bicycle distributors, and shoe distributors were also affected [20].

The extent of other OPA activity is harder to determine. For example, the OPA price control division used the same decentralized structure and offices as did the ration division. But it is estimated that the budget of the Price Department, including the accounting and enforcement divisions, never exceeded one-third of the OPA budget; that is, about $250 million was spent on wartime price control, of which roughly 10 percent went for salaries for 5,705 persons. These itemized costs are, of course, the price division administrative costs and were only a small part of the total expenditure for wartime price control. Specifically, the Commodity Credit Corporation, the Reconstruction Finance Corporation, and other agencies working with OPA also expended some $4.5 billion in the subsidy program [21].

In total, World War II controls (OPA and WLB combined) appear to have cost in government administrative and direct subsidy expenses about one-half of one percent of GNP.

CONCLUSIONS

The form of any direct controls program selected is very important. It bears both upon the probable success of a controls program and upon its cost. The exploratory work of Abba Lerner and others devoted to consideration of a variety of controls alternatives thus is extremely valuable. At issue ought to be how to structure controls, Kennedy-Johnson guideposts, Weintraub's Tax Incentive Plan, the Lerner-Colander Market Anti-Inflation Plan, or whatever, when to introduce the controls program selected, how the enforcement regime should be structured, when the controls program should be lifted, and a host of related questions.

Perhaps even more important to the consideration of controls is the macro setting in which they are to be imposed. If the macro setting is supportive, controls seem likely to help. If not, they easily will be defeated no matter how well structured they might be. Ideally, it would seem that restrictive monetary and fiscal policy should be imposed first. Controls should be phased in when the macro policy is expected to begin to take strong effect. In this way business and labor would be required to price in a manner consistent with a disinflationary macro environment. Controls then would require price setters to do what in retrospect the economic environment would have suggested. When this happens there is at least the possibility that imposition of direct controls will allow the monetary and fiscal policy authorities to hold resolutely to their antiinflation goals because unemployment will not rise to an extraordinary degree. The goal of the control program, then, should not be to reduce unemployment at the same time that restrictive monetary and fiscal policy is imposed. Rather the goal should be to prevent unemployment from rising as much as it otherwise might. If the full harshness of Okun's Law can be avoided, then perhaps genuine monetary and fiscal restraint will be politically acceptable.

Evidence seems reasonably strong in support of the conclusion that there is no practical alternative to direct controls, balanced by appropriate restrictive monetary and fiscal policy, as an antiinflationary device. At least weak evidence can be found to suggest that direct controls might make a modest, but nonetheless critical, contribution. Consequently, the pessimism with which the profession in general regards direct controls seems unwarranted.

NOTES

1. Arthur M. Okun, "Efficient Disinflationary Policies," *American Economic Review* 68 (May 1978): 348-357.

2. Robert J. Gordon, "Structural Unemployment and the Productivity of Women," in *Stabilization of Domestic and International Economy*, eds. K. Brunner and A. Meltzer, vol. 5, Supplementary Series, *Journal of Monetary Economics* (1977): 189-191.

3. Otto Eckstein and James A. Girola, "Long-Term Properties of the Price-Wage Mechanism in the United States," *Review of Economics and Statistics* 60 (August 1978): 323-333.

4. A. Bradley Askin and John Kraft, *Econometric Wage and Price Models* (Lexington, Mass.: Lexington Books, 1974).

5.   Robert J. Gordon, "Wage–Price Controls and the Shifting Phillips Curve," *Brookings Papers on Economic Activity*, No. 1 (1971): 105-166.

6.   Otto Eckstein and Roger Brinner, *The Inflation Process in the United States*, U.S., Joint Economic Committee, 92nd Congress, 2nd Session, 1972.

7.   Calvin Siebert and Mahmood Zaidi, "The Short-Run Wage-Price Mechanism in U.S. Manufacturing," *Western Economic Journal* 9 (September 1971): 278-288.

8.   George L. Perry, "Wages and the Guideposts," *American Economic Review* 57 (September 1967): 897-904.

9.   George L. Perry, *Unemployment, Money Wage Rates and Inflation* (Cambridge, Mass.: MIT Press, 1966).

10.   Paul S. Anderson, "Wages and the Guideposts: Comment," *American Economic Review* 59 (June 1969): 351-354; Michael L. Wachter, "Wages and the Guideposts: Comment," *American Economic Review* 59 (June 1969):   354-358; Adrian W. Throop, "Wages and the Guideposts: Comment," *American Economic Review* 59 (June 1969):   358-365; and George L. Perry, "Wages and the Guideposts: Reply," *American Economic Review* 59 (June 1969): 365-370.

11.   Charles E. Rockwood, "National Wage Fixing Arrangements in Australia," *Southern Journal of Business* 2 (October 1967): 26-37.

12.   "The Edict on Maximum Prices," *Transactions of the American Philological Association*.

13.   Naphtali Lewis and Meyer Reinhold, *Roman Civilization: Sourcebook II: The Empire* (New York: Harper and Row, 1966), pp. 458-460.

14.   Franklyn D. Holzman, "Soviet Inflationary Pressures, 1928-1957: Causes and Cures," *Quarterly Journal of Economics* 74 (May 1960): 167-188.

15.   Arnold R. Weber, *In Pursuit of Price Stability: The Wage-Price Freeze of 1971* (Washington, D.C.:   The Brookings Institution, 1973).

16.   Ibid.

17.   U.S. Government, National War Labor Board, *Termination Report* (Washington, D.C.: U.S. Government Printing Office, 1946).

18.   Ibid.

19.   U.S. Government, Office of Temporary Controls, Office of Price Administration, *Field Administration of Wartime Rationing*, by Emmette S. Redford (Washington, D.C.: U.S. Government Printing Office, 1947).

20. U.S. Government, Office of Temporary Controls, Office of Price Administration, *A History of Ration Banking,* by Joseph Alexander Kershaw (Washington, D.C.: U.S. Government Printing Office, 1947).

21. U.S. Government, Office of Temporary Controls, Office of Price Administration, *Problems in Price Control,* by Virgil B. Zimmerman (Washington, D.C.: U.S. Government Printing Office, 1947).

✳ *Chapter 10*

OBSTACLES TO CURTAILING INFLATION

Edmund S. Phelps[*]

PRELIMINARIES

In this chapter I shall attempt to sort out the real from the imagined problems associated with stopping, or at least with curtailing to the optimum level, the rate of inflation. It will be my conclusion—a hopeful hypothesis though not a provable verity—that there do exist ways, the way of Abba Lerner and David Colander and the way of mandatory controls, that if perfectly implemented would curb inflation without causing a temporary economic slump in the process. But there is a question, at least in my mind, whether we have the wit to use any of these methods with a high degree of success.

A great many of the discussions of the inflation problem, both in Europe and in America, proceed on the assumption that wage setting throughout the economy is periodic and synchronous—as if all wages were set on January 1 of every year, or every other year, for example. This assumption is sometimes adopted because it is believed to be close to the truth, and perhaps it is true enough of some European economies. The assumption is more often adopted on the belief that the more general and the more realistic assumption of non-synchronous wage-setting is "not of the essence" for the problem at hand. While the assumption of periodic and synchronous wage-setting is certainly not a realistic description of the determination of

---

[*]Professor of Economics, New York University.

wages in the American economy, let us begin with that assumption in order to appraise the various positions on disinflation that have been reached on the basis of that assumption.

SYNCHRONOUS WAGE-SETTING

In one school of thought the problem of stopping inflation is a test of nerve, a matter of strategic courage, for the central bank. Inflation control involves game-theoretic considerations much like, or at least reminiscent of, those that Thomas Schelling and others brought to nuclear deterrence. There is, nevertheless, a certain schism within that broad school of thought. Some members of this school hold that if, like the lion in the *Wizard of Oz*, the central bank will just cast away its self-doubt and display courage, then its actions will meet with early success at little cost. Other members of this school insist that the cost of success would be very great if the bank had the needed courage to stay the course, so great that success (total success at any rate) would require more courage than the bank has; so it would be better for the bank in the wisdom of self-knowledge not to embark on a vain display of courage in the first place.

Some discussions of the central bank's problem are conducted as though the bank were locked in combat with some economy-wide labor union. The situation is viewed as a two-person non-cooperative game of the non-zero-sum type. The pay-off matrix of Figure 10-1 illustrates the game [1]. Labor, playing the columns, moves at the beginning of each period, simultaneously with the Bank and without knowledge of what the Bank has decided to do; the Bank plays the rows with similar ignorance of what Labor has decided. Although it is not at all necessary to the argument that follows, let us for the sake of definiteness adopt the Natural Rate hypothesis according to which the same "full-employment" level of unemployment can be secured with the expectation of steadily rising money-wage rates and money supply as can be achieved with the expectation of constant money-wage rates and constant money supply (correcting for velocity). Let us also suppose until further notice that the demand for real cash balances is independent of the money rate of interest at least over the relevant neighborhood—the old-fashioned Quantity Theory of money. Then full employment requires a certain ratio of the money supply to the average money-wage rate (given the wage-rate structure), which ratio is independent of expectations about the rate of inflation. A smaller ratio of money to the wage will yield a deficiency of aggregate demand and thus a lesser amount of employment; a larger ratio will yield a level of employment in excess of the "full-employment" or normal level of employment.

Figure 10-1. The Wage Game I

LABOR

	END WAGE GROWTH	MAINTAIN WAGE GROWTH
END MONEY GROWTH	I 4 , 2	II 1 , 1
MAINTAIN MONEY GROWTH	III 2 , 3	IV 3 , 4

BANK

Our hypothetical economy has been experiencing full employment with inflation, and in the absence of some kind of monetary-policy shift or some fortuitous shift of wage policy by Labor, the economy will land once more in cell IV of the pay-off matrix in the current period. But the Bank prefers full employment via cell I to full employment through cell IV; this is shown by the first numbers in those two cells which are the Bank's utility indicators, the second numbers being Labor's utility indicators. The Bank would therefore like to put an end to its increases of the money supply, to play Row 1, if in so doing it will convince

Labor to expect that the Bank will go on playing Row 1 in the future; for once convinced of the Bank's resolve to go on playing Row 1, Labor would opt for full employment in cell I in order to avoid underemployment in cell II.

However, according to the payoff matrix, Labor would prefer to go on increasing wages as usual, to continue playing Column 2. Labor prefers full employment via cell IV to cell I, and if it can convince the Bank of its determination to go on playing Column 2 the Bank will resignedly opt for full employment in cell IV in order to avoid under-employment in the hated cell II.

It follows that the economy may suffer a disequilibrium outcome: Labor goes ahead with a wage increase in the hope that the Bank is going to raise the money supply, and the Bank withholds an increase of the money supply in the hope that Labor will have restrained wages—that is, the underemployment outcome of cell II. That situation could lead to an indefinitely persisting impasse in which each side grows more confident with every play that the other side will surrender on the current move: the Bank more hopeful than ever that Labor will now rescind the offending wage increase, in which event the Bank will have won, and Labor ever more hopeful that the Bank will now lift the destructive embargo on increased money, in which case the Bank's credibility will have vanished and it is safe to conclude that inflation will resume. Alternatively, the situation could lead eventually to the total victory of one side or the other.

So far I have given no reason why Labor might prefer inflationary full employment in cell IV to full employment in cell I, a preference on which the above argument depends. An oft-cited reason is that the labor union wants always to appear (to its members) to deserve the credit for the maintenance—in the presence of productivity growth, the improvement—of real wage rates. Like the wizard in Oz, the union depends mostly on image, even for its real power. Another reason is that something may go wrong to prevent money prices from subsiding *pari passu* with money wage rates with the consequence that, rightly or wrongly, the union will receive the blame of its members; the union's defense would have to depend on counterfactual theorizing not subject to direct test.

But there is, I think, a quite different reason why Labor might prefer to stick to its inflationary course—in the hope, of course, that the Bank will be induced sooner or later to resume ratifying or validating the upward march of money wages. A hypothesis of the new pay-off matrix in Figure 10-2 is that the Bank prefers the overemployment outcome of cell III to the (inflationless) full-employment outcome of cell I.   Labor may fear that if it abandons playing its accustomed Column 2, on the fond wish that the Bank will move to Row 1 as it seems to have said it wants and intends to do, the Bank will disappoint it by sticking to Row 2 in order to achieve the outcome of cell III-- that being even better than cell I for the Bank.   What I am arguing, then, is that the economy might be stuck in the inflationary cell IV even though it is the implication of Figure 10-2, unlike Figure 10-1, that *both* parties prefer full employ- ment in the noninflationary cell I to full employment in the inflation-ridden cell IV.   It supports that argument to observe that cell IV is a Nash equilibrium [2] , as it is in Figure 10-1 as well, since neither party is motivated to cause a departure from cell IV if it takes as given the move of the other party which corresponds to that cell IV.   Nevertheless, it could be argued that the appropriate concept of equilibrium makes cell I the relevant game-equilibrium outcome, not cell IV.   If Labor switched to Column 1, the Bank might "reason one step ahead" to the conclusion that if it were then to stick to Row 2 Labor would revert to Column 2, and so the Bank would accede to cell I after all and Labor may as well make the switch.   On the other hand, this more sophisticated concept of game equilibrium loses force if the repeated game will soon come to an end, to be followed perhaps by another repeated game, as the Bank passes into new political hands.   Then it may be reasonable for Labor to suspect that the outgoing player for the Bank would succumb to the temptation of cell III if Labor were to announce its intention to switch to Column 1.

The message of these game models, therefore, is that disin- flation without an intervening or eventual resumption of the inflation is problematic either because the trade union does not prefer noninflationary full employment to inflationary full em- ployment or because, while preferring the former to the latter, it distrusts the willingness of the monetary authorities steadfast- ly to cooperate by foregoing the occasional opportunity for a short-run gain.   It must be doubted, however, that this message has any applicability to the American economy, whatever light it may shed on some European economies.   In the United States unionized jobs have shrunk to nearly a fifth of the total, and the unions here do not coordinate among themselves to establish a concerted or monolithic wage policy.   Yet game-theoretic considerations still arise for the wage determinations of union-, firm-, and person-setting wages.

Figure 10-2.   The Wage Game II

LABOR

	END WAGE GROWTH	MAINTAIN WAGE GROWTH
END MONEY GROWTH	I 3, 4	II 1, 1
MAINTAIN MONEY GROWTH	III 4, 2	IV 2, 3

BANK (left side label)

Still adopting the convenient though unrealistic assumption that all wages as well as the money supply are set periodically and synchronously, let us now suppose that there are many wage setters, namely firms all of which unilaterally set wages immutably for the length of the current period.   Each firm has to decide and declare its wage rates without knowledge of the wage rates being similarly set by the other firms, and the money supply is simultaneously set by the Bank.   We maintain the Natural Rate hypothesis and the Quantity Theory.

It seems to be widely assumed that the existing decentralization of wage setting throughout the economy does nothing to dissolve the difficulty of achieving permanent disinflation without the pain of an intervening slump (no matter whether wage setting is actually synchronous or not). One argument to this conclusion sometimes heard—it is not the only argument—is the following: If each wage setter expects all other wage setters to increase their wages as usual for the upcoming period whether or not they believe the central bank is going to carry out its threat to tighten the money supply in the interest of disinflation, and if each wage setter believes with certainty that the central bank will with immediacy drop its intention to rein in the money supply the moment that wages are seen (without lag) to have increased again as usual, then each wage setter will be motivated to increase its own wages in the same proportion—thus to maintain its real and relative position. In short, the general expectation of general wage growth as usual is self-warranting if each wage setter sees the central bank's threat as lacking all credibility.

Of course, it is not very realistic to suppose that the central bank will observe the rise of wages without any lag and that it will be able to increase the money supply in time to prevent any damage to aggregate demand within the current period; and those assumptions are just as crucial to the argument as the assumption I am going to focus on. Perhaps the weakest reed in the argument, however, is the assumption that the central bank will withdraw its threat *with certainty* once it sees that wages have increased as usual (or by less than the desired amount at any rate). Would not the central bank have hired Thomas Schelling to instruct it on the "threat that leaves something to chance"?

Let us then suppose instead that each wage-setter assigns some positive probability to the decision by the central bank not to increase the money supply, to carry out its threat, in response to (or in spite of) the average wage increase which the bank observes before it acts. Letting f denote the rate of wage inflation and $p_i(f)$ the ith wage setter's probability, we have $p_i(0) = 1$ for in the event that $f = 0$ the central bank has obtained what it wants and will not increase the money supply to jeopardize the permanence of its victory. But for the less successful outcomes $f>0$, we have $0<p_i(f)<1$ for every i. It is not required that the wage setters possess the identical p_i function, but it will be supposed that each wage setter believes quite correctly that all the other wage-setters also have positive probabilities.

It is then possible to show, upon attributing to wage-setters a rather high order of rationality, that the central bank can have its way—can induce f to be zero (or any other target inflation rate) without even a temporary slump. For if each wage setter at first provisionally assumed that other wage setters would increase wages as usual, so that f would equal the accustomed f of the previous period, then each wage–setter, upon recognizing the chance that the central bank would then carry out its threat to withhold an increase of the money supply, would want to increase its own wage rates by less than that customary amount--in order to take advantage of the implied chance of a weakening of the labor market. But then each wage–setter will reasonably assume that other wage-setters are making similar calculations and thus deciding to raise their wage rates by somewhat less than the accustomed amount. It is plausible to suppose that this downward revision in the expectation of other firms' wage rates induces each wage–setter to decide provisionally to reduce its own provisionally planned wage increase a bit more. But then, again, each wage setter will reasonably assume that other wage-setters are thinking similarly and thus also lower again their planned wage increases. That consideration leads to yet another iteration until finally the conclusion is ineluctable that the other firms are not going to increase their wages in view of the central bank's threat. Although the central bank's money-supply policy is understood to be probabilistic, no weight is attached to outcomes that would tempt the central bank not to carry out its threat, so the rationally expected growth of the money supply is zero. Likewise, the rationally expected rate of wage inflation is also zero.

This is the world of Lucas and Sargent. In it the central bank holds complete sway over the price level (in an appropriate expected value sense), without risk to the level of employment, as long as the central bank makes clear what it is going to do--and maybe what it forecasts will result. The only difficulty is one that Sargent noted. Once asset holders reduce to zero their expectation of the rate of price inflation over the future, the real value of cash balances associated with the new (full employment) equilibrium will be increased in proportion to the interest-sensitivity of the demand for money--a sensitivity excluded by the Quantity Theory. It follows that if the central bank's plan is to stop the *money supply* in its tracks, both the price level and the average wage must *fall* if full employment is to be maintained. The central bank will presumably want to estimate the size of the necessary decline of wages in order to inculcate the desirable expectations of wage behavior by wage setters; some difficulties may arise if this estimate is not widely agreed upon throughout the economy. If instead the central bank's plan is to stop the *wage* and price level from rising further beyond their previous levels, the bank must paradoxically *increase* the *money supply*—though not, one hopes, by the amount that would have been necessary to ratify the usual rate of wage growth. It seems to me that in that case the central bank may have to devise a somewhat more complicated threat strategy: the threat of a lesser increase of the money supply if wages rise. We should not make too much of these fine points, however. They do not loom large if our interest is only in a small adjustment of inflation—from 9 percent per annum, say, to 5 or 6 percent per annum.

The view that disinflation is problematic, even when wage setting is synchronous, is sometimes based on an argument quite different from the above, purely expectational, sort of considerations. It is held that money wages in the current period cannot be held to the level in the previous period if prices last period were up over those the period before that—except at the cost of labor strife and unemployment. And without a cessation of wage growth, there cannot of course be any cessation of price inflation.   This contention about money wage behavior is a prominent element of some versions of what is generally known as implicit labor contract doctrine.

If that contention is correct, there is nothing that monetary policy can do to restore price stability, or to achieve more generally a lower rate of inflation, as long as it is desired sooner or later to return to full employment. The fiscal authorities could lighten payroll and excise taxation, although by itself such an act would tend to slow capital formation and productivity growth thus intensifying the inflation problem in the farther future. They could offset the stimulus to consumption by imposing higher taxes on wage incomes, but if the contention about wage behavior is correct maybe it is the after-tax real-wage income of employees that firms are sworn to protect, in which case inflation will grow worse in the short run. Or the fiscal authorities could lighten the implicit taxation of saving which is present in the taxation of interest income at virtually the same rates as wage income. Such an act would perhaps increase the rate of capital formation, but it might also increase the growth of the public debt by enough to cause a net injury to the stream of future generations. Finally, the government could invoke price controls or Lerner-Colander controls on prices, in

either of which cases money wage rates would catch up to prices
and some firms might consequently pare down their employment
rolls; or the government could institute wage controls or Lerner-
Colander controls on wages, in either of which cases wages
would then be free to catch up to prices as soon as the controls
were removed. The latter problem would arise too if there were
temporary controls on both wages and prices.

My own reading of American experience, however, is that the
tie between current wages and the previous price level is not a
widespread phenomenon.   Granted, there are many union contracts with explicit COLA (cost of living adjustment) clauses;
the eventual expiration of these contracts, however, offers
renewed latitude for a slackening of wage rates in the succeed-
ing contracts.   The contention that unions and employers pre-
designate a path of real wages for existing employees over the
rest of their working lives, revising it upwards on occasion but
never downwards by one iota, does not seem to me to be a very
accurate description of money wage behavior in the United
States over recent years. It does not stand up very well, at least
in my eyes, to the almost experimental evidence offered by the
supply shocks in oil and food of 1973-74, especially if one takes
account of the end of the last stage of wage controls in the
spring of 1974.

If the indexation of current money wage rates to the previous
period's price level were present yet confined to just one sector
of the labor market, monetary policy might still contrive to end
price inflation without an interim rise of general unemploy-
ment--at least if wage setting is synchronous as we have been
assuming. Nominal rents to land and quasi-rents to workers not
having indexed wages would presumably fall until firms could
produce the equilibrium GNP at last period's price level despite
the one-time rise of the wages that are indexed; any rise of
unemployment would be largely localized within specialized
trades where wages are indexed. The prospect of bankruptcy
would presumably induce the renegotiation of some indexed
arrangements.   The seriousness of the difficulties that would
arise from announced and anticipated disinflation in this   synchronous and periodic type of economy depend presumably upon
the interval of time between wage-setting dates. The seriousness also depends upon the rate of productivity growth. If the
period is a year or less in length and productivity advances 2 or 3
per cent per period, the unindexed rents and quasi-rents might
not have to fall to accommodate the last automatic rise of the
indexed wages. Yet all this is rather hard to think about without

laughing, or sighing, because we do not after all inhabit the synchronized world heretofore posited.

NONSYNCHRONOUS WAGE-SETTING

The general tenor of my conclusions above, as I read them, is that disinflation would not pose grave difficulties if wage-setting were synchronized. Monetary policy could do the job alone, although it would not hurt to throw in some monetary education, some indicative wage guideposts, some real-wage insurance against the risk to wage-setters of their doing the right thing, and some Lerner-Colander disincentives to do the wrong thing. The trouble is that wage-setting in our economy is not synchronized. In a recent paper entitled "Disinflation without Recession" [3], I tried to show how very intricate is the task of unwinding inflation when in each period there is an array of overlapping fixed-wage contracts or commitments, only one (or one sub-set) of which is open for fresh determination currently. It should be mentioned that these wage commitments contain no indexing of any kind, no contingency provisions; and each new wage is as free to fall as to rise without trauma to interested parties. In a full-employment scenario, each fresh wage commitment aims only to set a money wage that will produce the equilibrium average relative wage over the life of the commitment.

The conclusion of that analysis is that it is possible to wind down the rate of inflation without departing from full employment if rational expectations, alias perfect foresight, prevails among wage setters and if, of course, the central bank adheres to the right growth-path of the money supply. But it is not possible to end inflation instantaneously. In the simplest case of wage commitments on April 1 and running for a year's time, followed by wage commitments on September 1 also for a year's time, and so on, the contracts expiring at the outset of the antiinflation era must be replaced by new commitments which make those new wages catch up to the ones set most recently; subsequently, all money wages can be perpetuated in a state of constancy and equality. That initial onetime catch-up of wages produces a onetime and last-time rise of the price level. The triannual and quadriannual cases are a great deal more complicated.

That model of inflation leads me to a simple but interesting point. It will do no permanent good to institute a system of wage controls that leaves wages of every "vintage" at their original relative levels by the end of the controls—as would a perfectly effective program that froze all wages over its whole duration. It is a little like an equitable slowdown in an auto race; it has only a temporary effect on the velocity of the vehicles. If wage relatives are exactly restored to their original pattern at the end of the control period, as would be the case if all commitments ran for a year's time and the controls lasted for an integer number of years (1, 2, 3, . . .), then the average level of money wages and prices will have been put back behind schedule: a given integral of wage inflation will have been stretched out over a longer period of time than would have elapsed without controls. But this "lost time" presents no reason for wage-setters to form different expectations about wage inflation over the future than were held previously when the same pattern of wage relatives prevailed. The only reason wage-setters might have for re-forming their expectations of wage inflation lies in the possibility that a disinflationary monetary policy is going to be adopted—but that could have been adopted before, without a prelude of wage controls.

The point, then, is that two or three years of perfect wage and price stability, while winning the plaudits of columnists and smiles all around, will be neither necessary nor sufficient for achieving a lower rate of wage inflation thereafter. However, that conclusion is drawn from a formal model in which expectations are rational. If a calming episode of wage and price stability can lull wage-setters into forming irrational expectations of more of the same even after the removal of controls, the monetary authorities might see in this expectational change the new opportunity for a quicker or surer victory over inflation than any existing before. A further qualification to my point is that no controls program is perfect—which fact may very well be its greatest virtue. If at the end of the controls period, by secret design or by accident, all the out-of-date wage rates existing before the controls were to have been permitted and induced to rise just up to the level of the latest wage rate set before the advent of the controls, the road would then be paved for an inflation-less future. In short, a controls program that sought abruptly to move the rate of wage inflation from 10 percent per annum, say, to 7 percent per annum or to 4 percent or to zero had better wink and connive at leakages in order to ready the pattern of relative wages for a future path of reduced inflation.

Another kind of controls program, an alternative to the severe program of total wage and price stabilization just discussed, would aim explicitly at a sequence of wage adjustments (as old wage commitments successively expired) that finally eradicated the inflation-caused (and inflation-causing) wage differentials existing at the start of the controls program.   As shown in my earlier paper cited above, under perfect foresight there exists one and only one path of wages that ultimately erases inflation while all the time permitting full employment (actual unemployment always equal to the Natural Rate).   Without rational expectations, engineering such a path would require some kind of controls program and perhaps divine assistance as well.   Incidentally, this path entails that the last wages to have been set before the start of controls would have to be replaced (on expiration of those commitments) by lower wages because the "new wages" established in the intervening periods would not have been motivated to come all the way up to the level of those last wages.   But if one is willing to entertain programs involving temporary overemployment, then one can equally well deduce the existence under perfect foresight of a sequence of wage rates that leads asymptotically to a state in which all wage rates have just come up to equal the last wage rate set before the new disinflationary program.   This is an attractive case because it is easy to picture, although not necessarily more attractive than the other case, all things considered.   In either case there is a sequence of allowable algebraic increases of new wages over the old wages they are replacing in the currently expiring commitment, and in the latter case these increases reach zero once all the wage rates have had a turn in which to catch up to the highest wage (the last one to have been set before the disinflationary program).

A PARTING QUESTION

So much for formal analysis, informally presented. What of the practicability of disinflation without a temporary or even permanent slump? The question seems to me to come down to two issues.

The first issue is whether those last wage rates to have been set before controls, wage rates which were expected to be ahead of the others for a while and later behind the others until expiration of the commitment, will "permit themselves" to be "caught up" by the general price level and/or the general wage level. My earlier paper affirms that they will do so, the wage theory of that paper being purely "forward looking": only the expectation of the relative (or else real) value of the wage over the life of the commitment matters, and that expectation is the same after disinflation as it was before. But insofar as the true theory of wage increases is partially or wholly indexationist, not just expectationist, there will be trouble. If contracts prevent workers from suffering an observable decline of their relative (or real) wages, even when it is guessed by everyone that the old relative wage was merely temporarily inflated until other wage-setters had their chances to catch up and even go ahead temporarily, then permanent disinflation would require a permanent rise of unemployment—unless and until some lucky supply shock came along. But, as I ventured earlier, it is my belief that such written and unwritten index clauses are confined to a rather small sector of the American labor market and that many of these conventions and understandings might collapse under a little stress. So on this score I ally myself with those who would be labeled optimists by the other camp.

The other issue, as I indicated in the previous section of this chapter, is whether any controls program might be managed with the ingenuity required to wipe out the wage differentials which were generating, and in turn were regenerated by, the inflation-ary process before the interruption of controls. It is not evident, not to this observer at any rate, that any thought has ever been given by administrators of wage control programs to the appro-priate sequence of wage-inflation targets in view of the time-structure of wage commitments. They think like lawyers and economists when what is wanted is, well, a Herbert Hoover. Moreover, a controls program tends to grant exceptions after a needs test, rather than the catch-up test that is alone appro-priate, no matter how repellent the garish level of wages already achieved by the petitioner. So on this score, both in respect to economic wit and political nerve, I could hardly be less hopeful.

NOTES

1. A game is any event whose outcome depends upon the separate actions of interdependent participants. Each player in the game has several courses of action, or strategies, which might be pursued, and these are summarized in the pay-off matrix. The game envisioned here is of the constant-sum type, where the sum of the winnings of players remains the same regardless of its distribution among participants. For a detailed

description of games and game theory, see C. E. Ferguson and J. P. Gould, *Microeconomic Theory*, 4th ed. (Homewood, Ill.: Richard D. Irwin, Inc., 1975), pp. 340-47.

2. A formal description of a Nash solution can be found in Blaine Roberts and David L. Schulze, *Modern Mathematics and Economic Analysis* (New York: W. W. Norton and Company, 1973), pp. 470-71.

3. Edmund S. Phelps, "Disinflation without Recession."

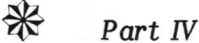 *Part IV*

THE MARKET SOLUTION TO INFLATION

Chapter 11

RATIONALITY, EXPECTATIONS AND
FUNCTIONAL FINANCE

David C. Colander*

Imagine yourself in a Buck Rogers interplanetary adventure, looking at a highway in a City of Tomorrow. The highway is wide and straight, and its edges are turned up so that it is almost impossible for a car to run off the road. What appears to be a runaway car is speeding along the road and veering off to one side. As it approaches the rising edge of the highway, its front wheels are turned so that it gets back onto the road and goes off at an angle, making for the other side, where the wheels are turned again. This happens many times, the car zigzagging but keeping on the highway until it is out of sight. You are wondering how long it will take for it to crash when another car appears which behaves in the same fashion. When it comes near you it stops with a jerk. A door is opened, and an occupant asks whether you would like a lift. You look into the car, and before you can control yourself, you cry out, "Why there's no steering wheel. . ." [1].

A CHALLENGE TO KEYNESIANISM

When Abba Lerner first wrote this parable in 1951, he ended it with the question, "Well, want a ride?" His rational expectations were that everyone would answer, emphatically, "No!" In the 1950s and 1960s, his expectations were fulfilled,

*Visiting Scholar, Nuffield College, Oxford University.

albeit belatedly, as economists accepted Keynesian economics, and almost everyone realized the need for government stabilization. The 1960s style monetarist theory modified, but did not fundamentally alter, Lerner's parable; within the Keynesian-monetarist reconciliation, there remained a role for active government stabilization policy, limited mainly by our lack of knowledge.

Today, however, more and more economists are changing their views, and answering "Yes!" to Lerner's question: A car without a steering wheel may not be ideal, but it may be better than one with a steering wheel when the driver is either blind or myopic. And with these views gaining more credibility and acceptance, Lerner's three rules of functional finance are being questioned and criticized:

(1) Rather than a rule for the government to maintain a reasonable level of spending, the call is for a balanced budget.
(2) Rather than maintaining a rate of interest which induces an optimal amount of investment, the government is now being advised to avoid affecting the rate of interest.
(3) Rather than printing money which is needed to carry out the first two rules, the government is now advised to set a rule for money supply growth which would take precedent over them.

These new policy recommendations are definitely not Keynesian, or even modifications of Keynesian policies; in fact, the new "rules" are distinctly classical, which means that we have come full circle in our thinking. The long run has arrived.

The reason for the changing views is inflation's persistence in the past five years. Keynesian theory has been unable to cope with the problem, and government authorities have been forced to reexamine their policies. The new challenge to Keynesian policies has its origins in the monetarists' position, but has far stronger implications. It is not only argued that Keynesian theory cannot handle inflation, but also that Keynesian policies are themselves the cause of inflation; only by discarding Keynesian policies will we be able to control inflation. This influential challenge is made in the name of "rational expectations," and is directed at the heart of Lerner's principles of functional finance [2].

It seems, therefore, appropriate to reconsider Lerner's principles in light of the rational expectations critique, and to evaluate how those principles stand up. I will begin with a brief discussion of rational expectations, explaining what they are and what kinds of expectations may be considered rational. This will provide the framework for the section in which the rational expectations critique of functional finance is considered. My discussion suggests that rational expectations are neither necessary nor sufficient to reject Lerner's "rules" of functional finance, and that while the issues raised by rational expectations have merit, they do not necessarily lead to the policy recommendations often associated with them. The only clear-cut recommendation that follows from the rational expectations hypothesis (hereafter REH) is that inflation must be considered in designing policy.

Finally, in the concluding section, I suggest how Keynesian theory and functional finance "rules" might be supplemented to meet the rational expectations challenge. I argue that stabilization must be seen as a two-part goal, and that all stabilization tools must be directed toward achieving both full employment and price level stability simultaneously. In effect, a new steering wheel must be designed.

My approach will be heuristic and generally untechnical, ignoring the myriad of complex issues which have formed much of the debate. To delve into these issues would lead me away from my purpose which is to explore the intuitive meaning of the rational expectations arguments. Only by considering whether ideas make intuitive sense when reduced to their simplest form can we assess the usefulness and the validity of the high-powered arguments. Whether I succeed in correctly simplifying the issues will be debatable, but the attempt is, I believe, appropriate, to a chapter in a volume dedicated to Abba Lerner, an economist who has consistently followed this intuitive approach.

WHAT ARE RATIONAL EXPECTATIONS?

The specific hypothesis which has played the key role in forming the new classical challenge was first suggested by John Muth in 1961 [3]. Extending some ideas which originated in the Stockholm expectational school, Muth suggested an improvement to the ad hoc method by which expectations were analyzed in discussing price movements. Before Muth's pathbreaking article, it was contended that individuals used some average of past and present prices as predictors of future prices. It was not clear how weights were chosen, nor was it clear how valid this entire method was. This led Muth to raise two fundamental questions: (1) What kind of information is, in fact, used, and how is it processed to estimate future conditions? (2) How can we predict how expectations will change with a change in the amount of available information, or with a change in the structure of the system?

His answers to these questions were delightfully simple: Assume that since expectations are the informed predictions of future events, they are essentially the same as those that would be derived by the relevant economic theory. This became the basis for the rational expectations hypothesis, REH.

The mathematics which brought Muth to this hypothesis are not simple, but one central idea emerges which is necessary to understand the implications of rational expectations in all possible circumstances. The idea is that at any point in time, no one can expect to make a speculative profit, and in this limited sense the economy is always in equilibrium. If one assumes that there are no costs of adjustment or learning, then the REH becomes identical to assuming the long run has arrived. This is the way in which REH has been used by critics of functional finance, such as Robert Lucas, Thomas Sargent and Neil Wallace, and Finn Kydland and Edward Prescott [4].

It need not be used in this strong sense, however [5]. It can be used with any specification of adjustment and learning costs; given these costs, adjustment to long-run equilibrium need not be instantaneous. Instead of being in long-run equilibrium, individuals will be on an equilibrium adjustment path. Thus the assumption does not rule out disequilibrium; it merely transforms it into an equilibrium analysis.

The simple logic equating REH with the notion that speculative profits cannot be expected is as follows. If expected profits existed, there would be potential gains from trade which individuals would immediately capture; thus if individuals are rational, we can reasonably assume that all potential profits are in fact realized. The argument is not unusual; this same argument is used to justify why individuals are always on their indifference curve. It is neither a stronger nor a weaker argument.

Because it will become important in discussing the implications of the REH, I should emphasize a significant point. REH rules out speculative profit but it does not rule out rent. If any specific agent has a comparative advantage in an activity, he can make a rent in equilibrium. However, if there is a market

for his services, the market valuation of his ability will capita
lize the value of that expected rent so that the rate of return on
the capitalized value would be the normal rate of profit.

In my view, Muth's general concept of rational expectations
is extremely useful for theoretical considerations. In fact, it is
not so much an assumption as it is an equilibrium condition
necessary to understand the nature of a model in dynamic
equilibrium. Thus, for any specific model, some type of rational
expectations assumption is a logical necessity [6].

Whether those expectations will be rational, specifically in
the sense which Muth suggested, is unclear. He assumes both a
well-defined model and costless learning. In econometric work,
such assumptions may be relevant, but in reality they involve
major problems. Consider now the more general notion of the
REH. What possibilities arise? First consider what happens
when the process being modeled is not one where all agents
agree on the underlying model. What if there are two, three or
four models of the same process, each predicting a different
result? One would then need a composite rationality.

Alternatively, what if there are costs of decisionmaking?
Herbert Simon convincingly argued for the need to consider
these costs and noted the limitations on the human mind which
they imposed [7]. He coined the phrase "bounded rationality" to
describe an analysis which considered such costs. Clearly, by
including such costs in the REH, some type of bounded rational
expectations would emerge.

While the preceding possibilities can be incorporated into the
modified REH, a third complication may be even more damaging
for any simple application of REH to specific policy questions.
The difficulty is: What are rational expectations when the
underlying structure is game theoretic? No deterministic result
exists for most game theoretic models, and the uncertainty that
exists with them eliminates the use of certainty equivalents [8].
An almost infinite number of rational expectations exist.
Keynes, in his discussion of investment, had such a world in
mind. He writes [9]:

> The social object of skilled investment should be to
> defeat the dark forces of time and ignorance which
> develop our future. The actual private object of the most
> skilled investment today is "to beat the gun" as the
> Americans so well express it, to outwit the crowd, and to
> pass the bad, or depreciating, half crown to the other

fellow. . . .We have reached the third degree where we devote our intelligence to anticipating what average opinion expects average opinion to be and there are some, I believe, who practice the fourth, fifth, and higher degrees. . . .

There is no clear evidence from experience that the investment policy which is socially advantageous coincides with that which is most profitable. It needs more intelligence to defeat the forces of time and our ignorance of the future than to beat the gun. Moreover life is not long enough.

Notice that every individual in Keynes's world has rational expectations, but unfortunately because the underlying model is game theoretic, the individual rational expectations are not the socially optimal expectations. Individuals and society are caught in a "prisoner's dilemma" where the possibility that the aggregate of individual decisions might throw the economy into a downspin is not considered by each individual. Only if all individuals could collude to limit such activities could such speculation be stopped.

My purpose in discussing such possibilities is to underscore the distinction between the theoretical and policy uses of REH. For modeling, REH is an important advance which is fundamental to our understanding of the nature of dynamic equilibrium. It offers potential for major advances in designing models of the economy. For policy considerations, the general REH is an inclusive hypothesis that can be reconciled with almost any type of expectations, depending on the specifications of the model. Since we do not know the underlying objective model, in discussing practical policy applications of the REH, it must be used with extreme care. In fact, given the present state of economic modeling, belief in the REH would lead me to rely on revealed expectations as an analogue for expectations in the true economic model, rather than to rely on the economic model to analogue the real world expectations.

The potential problem of confusing the process of modeling with an understanding of the economy was beautifully expressed by F. A. Hayek [10]:

Any approach, such as that of much of mathematical economics with its simultaneous equations which in effect starts from the assumption that people's knowledge corresponds with the objective *facts* of the situation, system-atically leaves out what is our main task to explain. I am far from denying that in our system equilibrium analysis has a useful function to preform. But when it comes to the point where it misleads some of our leading thinkers into believing that the situation which it describes has direct relevance to the solution of practical problems, it is then that we remember that it does not deal with the social process at all and that it is no more than a useful preliminary to the study of the main problem.

POLICY IMPLICATIONS OF THE STRONG REH

Significant interest in the REH only developed with its application to macroeconomic policy, and with the suggestion that it greatly modified or eliminated government's role in the stabilization process. Two quite distinct hypotheses have been advanced. William Fellner [11] produced a dramatic reconstruction of macroeconomics organized around a game theoretic rational expectations argument. He argued that wages and prices no longer respond to restrictions in demand because individuals have been conditioned to believe—through thirty years of commitment to full employment—that the government will not maintain its resolve in restricting demand to control inflation. In Fellner's view, the government's full employment guarantee has undermined its ability to control the price level. Consequently, the government is faced today with an almost intractable problem: How to convince individuals that it is committed to price stability. This component of the REH argument is, in my opinion, extremely powerful, and demonstrates the insufficiency of functional finance to cope with inflation.

However, a second group of REH supporters has made much broader claims [12]. In their view, the REH not only makes price stability maintenance impossible, but it also makes functional finance ineffective as a short-run stabilization tool. These stronger claims fall into three categories:

(1) REH negates monetary policy's role in the short run.
(2) REH implies that a fixed monetary rule is preferable to discretionary policy.
(3) REH implies that fiscal policy will have no effect and therefore the government should balance the budget.

While the claims are often not put so directly, these underlying themes are discernible in the literature.

The initial focus of the debate concerned Category 1, and considered the question of whether monetary policy can have any short run effect in an economy characterized by rational expectations and a natural rate of unemployment as depicted by Edmund Phelps and Milton Friedman [13]. Such an economy would have a short-run Phillips curve tradeoff, but the long-run or steady state Phillips curve would be vertical. In a major contribution to the debate, Sargent and Wallace demonstrated that an adaptive expectations hypothesis led to a short-run role for monetary policy, while a rational expectations hypothesis led to no short-run role. In developing this model, similar to many others in the literature, they used an aggregate supply specification suggested by Lucas [14] which required any effect on real output to be achieved through an unexpected movement in the price level. This assumption was crucial to their conclusions because, from this assumption, it followed that in order for the monetary authority to affect real output, it must induce an unexpected movement in the price level. Rational expectations eliminated that possibility by assumption and thus removed the potential role for monetary policy.

In evaluating the relevance of their conclusion to functional finance, it is useful to reinterpret the question they posed in the following manner: Can the government cause an economy to deviate from the natural rate, which by assumption is given exogenously? I think all would agree that the answer to that question is no. However, that question is fundamentally different from the one implicitly posed by Lerner's parable in which the "natural rate" or the "equilibrium rate of unemployment" in any particular short run fluctuated [15]. Cast into a modern framework, Lerner's question could be rephrased in the following manner: Is it possible for the government to reduce the loss function associated with the variance in the short run natural rate [16]?

Notice that the difference in the two stories is in their interpretation of the short run. For Sargent and Wallace, the short run is a transition phase to a long-run steady-state equilibrium; the short run in which monetary policy can be effective, and which I argue Keynesian economics meant (or should have meant) is in a specific subperiod of a steady-state equilibrium in which random disturbances occur. In the first case the road is straight and the policymakers are trying to steer off the road—deviate from the natural rate—whereas in the second, the road is curved and the policymakers are attempting to stay on the road—optimally adjusting to the temporary random shocks.

In both cases, the policy prescriptions follow from the specification of supply conditions and not from the assumption of REH. In the Sargent and Wallace world, even if monetary policies could have a short-run effect, it would do little good because expectations would finally adapt. In my suggested example, supply was constantly shifting and the relevant question was how best to adjust to the temporary shocks that hit the system—through government action or through private action. If the strong REH claim is to hold, REH must imply that it is not optimal for the government to adjust; the private sector would eliminate all possible gains. This, I suggest, does not follow because of the central difference between possibilities for rents and possibilities for profits within the REH. Government cannot make a profit, but since there is no market for government services, there is no way of knowing whether the government can make a potential rent in equilibrium. Whether or not it can depends on the government's cost of stabilization relative to the private sector's cost of stabilization. If the adjustment can best be achieved through government action, then government action is optimal even in a strong REH model.

The following example from the *General Theory* provides a reason why the government might be able to achieve stabilization in a less costly manner through flexible monetary policy than the private sector could through relative price and wage adjustment [17]:

> ...while a flexible wage policy and a flexible money policy come, analytically, to the same thing, inasmuch as they are alternative means of changing the quantity of money in terms of wage-units, in other respects there is, of course, a world of difference between them. Let me briefly recall to the reader's mind (an) outstanding consideration.
>
> Except in a socialized community where wage policy is settled by decree, there is no means of securing uniform wage reduction for every class of labour. The result can only be brought about by a series of gradual, irregular changes, justifiable on no criterion of social justice or economic expediency.... A change in the quantity of

money, on the other hand, is already within the power of most governments by open-market policy or analogous measures. Having regard to human nature and our institutions, it can only be a foolish person who would prefer a flexible wage policy to a flexible money policy, unless he can point to advantages from the former which are not obtainable from the latter.

Thus, within the Keynesian paradigm, an activist monetary policy of the government may be totally consistent with rational expectations, because it is rationally expected that the government is the correct agent to undertake the stabilizing role, and it is merely accomplishing a result which the free market would have achieved in a more costly fashion.

Keynes's discussion of both money wages and prices has a very modern flavor to it, and is suggestive of the implicit contract literature that has developed to explain wage and price rigidity [18]. Interpreted in modern terminology, Keynes's suggestion is that the nature of the optimal contingency contract is such that when uniform changes in real wages and real prices are needed, it is less costly to achieve that desired result through government action than by initially writing it into the contingency contract or by renegotiating their contract. Changing the money supply is not meant to fool anyone.

Individuals will rationally expect that numerous contingencies might occur and will include them in their contract; however, negotiating involved contingent contracts for events that will most likely never occur is a costly prospect. Thus individuals negotiate the contract in money terms with the implicit understanding that the monetary authorities will react optimally to contingencies, pushing the price level up or down as the need arises. Thus an activist monetary policy is a necessary part of the contract, and is merely a public good supplied for private individuals by the government [19].

As an example, consider a sudden exogenous foreign supply shock which has the real effect of lowering domestic income by two percent on the average. Since contracts did not specify this contingency, the optimal monetary policy is to accommodate this higher price, reducing everyone's income by inflation, and allowing individual adjustments to this general change to take place by private recontracting.

If the above argument is accepted, the answer to whether there is a short-run role for monetary stabilization within a strong REH depends on two conditions: (1) Does the short-run equilibrium rate of unemployment and short-run price level shift from period to period? (2) If it does, do the monetary authorities have a comparative advantage in achieving the desired result.

A similar argument can be made concerning the possibility of short run fiscal policy. The question is again one of comparative costs. If government can adjust its revenues and expenditures with a lower cost of adjustment than can the private sector, then optimally they should stabilize in this manner; if they cannot, then they should not.

The third policy tenet of the strong REH group—that rules are preferable to discretion—is again similar to the monetarist position. Support for that tenet is, however, derived from quite different principles. The monetarists base their arguments on limited availability of information about the magnitude and timing of monetary effects, emphasizing the lags in recognizing the need for policy changes and the uncertainty in predicting short-run effects. While the strong REH group would accept these arguments, they have made a stronger claim: that superiority of rules over discretion is a deductive truth, not an empirical argument [20].

Their argument is based on a difference between consistency and optimality. The consistent policy maximizes a social welfare function in each period over the future horizon taking the past as given. The optimal policy maximizes a social welfare function over the entire period. Because the consistent policy implicitly does not allow agreements over time, it can easily be demonstrated that a consistent policy is dominated by an optimal policy. To see why, consider the following example given by Kydland and Prescott [21]:

> . . . suppose the socially desirable outcome is not to have houses built in a particular flood plain but, given that they are there, to take certain costly flood-control measures. If the government's policy were not to build the dams and levees needed for flood protection and agents knew this was the case, even if houses were built there, rational agents would not live in the flood plains. But the rational agent knows that, if he and others build houses there, the government will take the necessary flood control measures. Consequently, in the absense of a law prohibiting the construction of houses in the flood plain, houses are built there, and the army corp of engineers subsequently builds the dams and levees.

In this example, building the dam is the consistent policy; not building the dam is the optimal policy. The problem with this argument is, in my view, not with the proof, but with the interpretation. Kydland and Prescott equate rules with optimal policies and discretionary action with consistent policy, concluding that rules are preferable to discretion because optimality is preferable to consistency. While theirs is one possible definition of rules, where there is uncertainty about the future, it is not an especially helpful definition. A rule in the Kydland–Prescott definition involves full specification of what will be done in every possible contingency; they are what I would call full contingency rules. Given this definition, any proof of the superiority of rules over discretion is trivial. The very definition of rules includes all possible discretionary action. It is totally possible within the Kydland–Prescott definition of rules to say that the rule which the government should follow is to act optimally, subject to a well specified social welfare function. This "rule" is not what most individuals consider when they speak of rules. Most individuals' definitions of rules are of limited contingency, and there is no *a priori* case for the superiority of limited contingency rules over discretion.

My objection to Kydland and Prescott is that they jump from their mathematics which demonstrates the superiority of a full contingency rule to a discussion of policy in which they suggest a very simple monetary rule [22]. That a simple monetary growth rule may not be correct can be seen in the following example: Say the rule states that the government will increase the money supply by 3 percent regardless of what happens. Then in the second period, half the world sinks into the sea because of some shift in the underlying geostructure of the earth. Most people would believe that the money supply should be reduced to prevent inflation in such a situation, but if you follow the 3 percent rule, you cannot take this into account.

Rejection of their argument does not imply that discretion is preferable to rules, only that *a priori* one cannot prove the superiority of either in a meaningful sense. Specific rules and specific discretionary actions must be compared by calculating the expected loss function under both possibilities. The steady-state rule will usually be followed, but the possibility of discretionary action remains, if any situation is a sufficiently unanticipated contingency.

I suspect that in many cases rules are preferable to discretion; in fact, it is one of the reasons why one should not use a perfectly classical model of the economy which assumes optimal discretionary pricing in each period. The same arguments for rules hold for private agents as they do for government. Thus if rules over discretion are superior, pricing policy is—as monetary policy—likely to be determined by a few simple rules invariant to many changes in actual circumstances. But if rules are superior, there is no reason to assume that the economy leads to full employment in any specific time period, in which case there is a potential role for government stabilization.

Summary of Policy Implications of REH

The above discussion of the strong Rational Expectations Hypothesis (REH) can be briefly summarized. Assume that the REH implies that the relevant consideration for policy evaluation is a comparison of steady state effects after structural effects of the policy are considered. If one adds to the REH an assumption that steady-state policy actions can have no effect, then there is no role for steady state policy. Assuming an invariant steady-state natural rate is such an assumption. However, if one adds to the REH an assumption that steady-state policy actions can have a positive effect, then there is a potential role for policy. Assuming a stochastic steady-state natural rate is such an assumption.

Whether there is an actual role for government depends on whether one assumes that the government has a comparative advantage in adjusting to short-run fluctuations. If it does have a comparative advantage, then it can have a positive effect even though the REH ruled out potential profit [23]. The reason for a potential role is that comparative advantage implies rent, not profit.

Functional finance implicitly assumes that government has a comparative advantage in achieving steady-state stabilization, and, in justifying policy actions, Keynes gave plausible reasons why government did have a comparative advantage. Until the strong REH critics demonstrate that the government does not have a comparative advantage, functional finance meets the REH challenge.

REDESIGNING THE WHEEL

Despite the above arguments, Lerner's rules of functional finance do not escape the REH critique; the parable of the steering wheel misses an important point. The steering wheel gives the economy horizontal (employment) control but does not provide vertical (price stability) control. Under functional finance, full employment and a stable price level seem to be incompatible, and as the REH suggests, a likely reason is structural changes induced by functional finance [24]. In today's world, expectations of government accommodation of specific price and wage setting policies have become built into expectations so that the threat of long-term unemployment consequences of any particular decision is lessened. Therefore the fear of unemployment no longer has a significant dampening effect on prices or wages.

The policy question is: What to do? The rational expectationalists propose that the government should abandon all functional finance rules; above I argued that this conclusion does not follow. Instead of retreating to classical economics, forgetting the experience of the last thirty years, we should recognize both the insights and the flaws of the old rules and modify, but not discard, them. This entails supplementing the three rules of functional finance with a fourth rule:

(4) The government must establish policies which stabilize the price level and coordinate both the money supply rule and the aggregate total spending rule with this stable price level.

With this additional rule the structural effects of functional finance on price stability will be incorporated into the policy, and the new policies will be stabilizing for both employment and the price level. To many this fourth rule raises the specter of price control, much as functional finance first raised fears of impending socialism. My fears are of a different kind. I fear that unless economists find a way to implement Rule 4, the market economy is endangered. Thus the issue is not controls versus the market. The issue is how to design controls so that they are compatible with the market.

There are two potential economic methods by which this price stability control can be implemented. One method is to incorporate price stability control directly into the existing stabilization tools. To suggest how this might be accomplished, consider the unemployment insurance program. Initially the program was designed to achieve both humanitarian and functional finance goals. However, its design made the price and wage level more rigid and also increased the average level of unemployment in the long-run, shifting the short-run Phillips

curve upward. The reason is as follows: Unemployment insurance acts as a subsidy for individuals who are fully unemployed.
In designing long run contracts, the firm and workers will take
that subsidy into account, choosing a contract with a higher
probability of layoff and less wage flexibility than it would
otherwise have [25]. Thus a group of workers who met a
downturn in demand by reducing wages by 5 percent, or by
reducing everyone's hours of work by 5 percent, would receive no
subsidy, whereas workers who had a contract which included
potential layoffs would receive a higher expected income inclusive of the insurance program.

Suppose that instead of our present system, a similar program
of wage rate insurance were instituted, under which workers who
accepted a lower wage rate in response to a decrease in
aggregate demand would be subsidized. Such a wage rate
insurance plan would accomplish the identical stabilization effect as would unemployment insurance, but it would decrease
wage rates paid by the firm, encouraging the employment of
additional workers along with holding wage rates low when there
is decreased demand. This specific plan may be impractical, but
there are other methods of accomplishing the desired result.
The concept is what is important. Functional finance policies
must be designed with their effects on price stabilization in mind
[26].

However, even if the tools are not redesigned, there is an
alternative method of implementing Rule 4. It could be done
directly under the Market Antiinflation Plan which Abba Lerner
discusses in the following chapter [27]. Under MAP, the price
level is determined by law, and the money supply aggregate
demand, and expectations of inflation are adjusted to that price
level. Individuals do not have to worry about how to rationally
predict the price level; the government has set it by a direct
rule.

Theoretically, implementing Rule 4 is possible. The real
problems are technical and practical difficulties, and I can think
of no better statement about those problems than the one Abba
Lerner wrote in 1951 when he was commenting on the difficulties of implementing the first three rules of functional finance
[28]:

> ...these problems...will make life difficult for the ad-
> ministrators of the economy....But there is no reason
> for supposing that life will be any more difficult than in

any other financial system which does not give the society the benefits of Functional Finance. . . .Functional Finance will not inaugurate a problemless world. Life will not be effortless. There will still be struggles and conflicts and difficulties and defeats. . . .But it is an important step forward.

NOTES

1.   Abba P. Lerner, *Economics of Employment* (New York: McGraw-Hill, 1951), p. 3.

2.   As will become apparent in this chapter, in my view "rational expectations" is a broad hypothesis about how expectations are formed and is not tied to any specific group or specific method of forming expectations. Generally, however, it has been used to describe a specific group of critics of functional finance such as Robert Lucas, Thomas Sargent, and Edward Prescott.

3.   John Muth, "Rational Expectations and the Theory of Price Movements," *Econometrica* 29 (July 1961): 315-35.

4. See, respectively, Robert E. Lucas, Jr., "Expectations and the Neutrality of Money," *Journal of Economic Theory* 4 (April 1972): 103-24; Thomas Sargent and Neil Wallace, "Rational Expectations, the Optimal Monetary Instrument and the Optimal Money Supply Rule," *Journal of Political Economy* 83 (April 1975): 241-54; and Finn Kydland and Edward Prescott, "Rules Rather than Discretion: The Inconsistency of Optimal Plans," *Journal of Political Economy* 85 (June 1977): 473-91.

5.   The literature on rational expectations has expanded enormously in the last few years, and numerous weaker variants of the REH have been suggested. For a discussion of alternative formulations of rationality, see James G. March, "Bounded Rationality, Ambiguity, and the Engineering of Choice," *Bell Journal of Economics* 9 (Autumn 1978): 587-608.

6.   I therefore agree with many of the REH advocates' criticisms of macroeconomic policy models which do not take into account possible structural changes in the model induced by the policy. However, since policymakers have only a slight idea of what the underlying structure of the model is, and arc generally using a black box method with an acknowledged high degree of error, it is not clear how important such shifts will be. Notice also that the argument holds for any change in policy;

thus a shift from an active policy to a passive policy is as likely to change the underlying structure as is any other policy change. The argument only supports the status quo policy.

7. Herbert Simon, *Models of Man* (New York: John Wiley and Sons, 1959).

8. In game theory a game refers to any situation in which interdependent individuals compete by exercising various courses of action. For a detailed discussion of game theory, see C.E. Ferguson and J.P. Gould, *Microeconomic Theory*, 4th ed. (Homewood, Ill.: Richard D. Irwin, Inc., 1975), pp. 340-47.

Certainty equivalence, loosely interpreted, is a theorem which states that random values can be replaced by their mean. Certainty equivalence, however, holds only under restrictive conditions. See Henri Theil, "Linear Decision Rules for Macrodynamic Policy Problems," in *Quantitative Planning of Economic Policy*, ed. Bert G. Hickman (Washington, D.C.: The Brookings Institution, 1965), pp. 23-25.

9. John Maynard Keynes, *The General Theory of Employment, Interest, and Money* (New York: Harcourt, Brace and World, Inc., 1936), pp. 155-56.

10. Frederick A. Hayek, "The Use of Knowledge in Society," *American Economic Review* (1945), p. 530.

11. William Fellner, *Towards a Reconstruction of Macroeconomics* (Washington, D.C.: American Enterprise Institute, 1976).

12. The specific writers to which I refer are Robert Lucas, Thomas Sargent and Neil Wallace, and Finn Kydland and Edward Prescott. See note 4 for complete citations.

13. Edmund S. Phelps, "Phillips Curves, Expectations of Inflation and Optimal Unemployment Over Time," *Economica* 34 (August 1967): 254-81; and Milton Friedman, "The Role of Monetary Policy," *American Economic Review* 58 (March 1968): 1-17.

14. Robert E. Lucas, Jr., "Some International Evidence on Output-Inflation Tradeoffs," *American Economic Review* 63 (June 1973): 326-34.

15. What I am suggesting is that in the steady-state solution to the dynamic programming model, the natural unemployment rate varies in each period; thus the natural rate hypothesis has a random component in it. The solutions for equilibrium unemployment rate are interpreted as the steady-state solutions in a single period of a dynamic process. Graphically, the natural rate will fluctuate from period to period and will have a short-run Phillips curve associated with each period.

The Phillips curve tradeoff literature of the 1960s did not specify this type of underlying model and thus, in my view, deviated from Keynes's and Lerner's concept. Thus the natural rate hypothesis correctly criticized the short-run Phillips curve literature. This formulation is, however, quite different from the one I am proposing.

16. Specified in a stochastic dynamic equilibrium model, there is no necessary welfare cost of unemployment. Overemployment may be as costly as underemployment. This is a concept quite different from the one the early Keynesian writers used. They were writing for a specific period when almost all believed the "natural rate" was lower than it optimally should have been. Thus increases in employment were associated with definite welfare gains.

17. Keynes, *The General Theory*, pp. 267-68.

18. Examples of the implicit contract literature include Martin Neil Baily, "Wages and Employment under Uncertain Demand," *Review of Economic Studies* 41 (January 1974): 21-36 and Costas Azariadis, "Implicit Contracts and Underemployment Equilibria," *Journal of Political Economy* 83 (December 1975): 1183-1202.

19. Robert J. Gordon suggested such a rule in a discussion of supply shocks. See his "Alternative Responses of Policy to External Supply Shocks, *"Brookings Papers on Economic Activity* 1 (1975): 183-204.

20. The specific argument being criticized here is made by Finn Kydland and Edward Prescott, "Rules Rather than Discretion."

21. Ibid., p. 477.

22. Ibid., p. 487.

23. Most discussions of the REH have suggested that it is the information assumptions of the strong REH that lead to its conclusions. My belief is that it is only the differential information costs between individuals and government that will be important to determining a role for government in stabilization, and that these information costs are part of a broader group of relative cost differentials which can lead to a role for government.

24. I am not arguing that early writers did not recognize the problem. For example, Abba P. Lerner, in his *Economics of Employment* (p. 384), wrote:

> Yet another set of problems is provided by the necessity of obtaining agreement to such plans as the scheme

for prevention of inflation through the operation of wage bargaining in times of full employment when the "reserve army of unemployed" is no longer available as a stabilizer of the general level of wages.

25. I have made this argument rigorously in my "The Implicit Contract Theory Meets the Wage Bill Argument: Round II," mimeographed, 1979 [available from the author by request].

26. The proposals for tax-based incomes policies and real wage insurance are indications that policy is moving in this direction.

27. See also Abba Lerner and David C. Colander, "MAP: A Cure for Inflation," in *Solutions to Inflation*, ed. David C. Colander (New York: Harcourt Brace Jovanovich, Inc., 1979), pp. 210-20, and *MAP: The Market Antiinflation Plan* (New York: Harcourt, Brace, and Jovanovich, Inc., forthcoming).

28. Lerner, *Economics of Employment*, pp. 384-85.

Chapter 12

THE MARKET ANTIINFLATION PLAN:
A CURE FOR STAGFLATION

*Abba P. Lerner**

INTRODUCTION

I shall discuss inflation, and the possibility of curing it. I shall try to keep this chapter as straightforward as possible by spelling out as cleanly as I can the nature of the problem and where we have to go if we want to solve it.

To begin with, we have to know what is meant by inflation. By inflation I mean rising prices in general and, at the same time, the rising incomes out of which the rising prices are paid. (The rising incomes are, of course, essentially the same rising prices as seen by those receiving them.) In the second place, I think of inflation as a continuing process. This means that it cannot be explained in terms of individual events, accidents, shocks, and so on, all of which are not continuing influences. In the third place, we must discover the cause of the inflation before we can devise a cure.

INFLATIONS I AND II

Before the development of economic science, inflation was regarded as an act of God, something about which we had no way of doing anything. Then came the idea that it was caused by wicked people such as speculators. This theory appeared as far back as ancient China, but we still hear it today. Then the

---

*Professor of Economics, and Professor of Policy Sciences, Florida State University.

realization that inflation had something to do with the money supply led, unfortunately, to the exaggeration that made the supply of money the *only* factor.

In my book *Flation* [1] I refer to three different kinds of inflation: Inflation I, Inflation II, and Inflation III. Inflation I is effectively described by the phrase "too much money chasing too few goods." But inflation is a continuing process, and so we need to know what it is that keeps the chase going on. In the first place, it is not enough to say that the inflation is due to "too much money" in the sense of the stock of money in existence. It is only the active *spending* of money that can have any inflationary effect. But we may take it that by "too much money" is meant "too much spending of money" or "excess demand." However, saying "too much spending" is still not sufficient. Too much spending would merely bid up prices until the spending were no longer too much—no longer more than enough to buy at the higher prices, all the goods that are available—and that would be the end. Thereafter prices would be stable. We would have no ongoing inflation.

The same thing is true of cost-push inflation. To say that inflation is due to wages being pushed up, and so costs being pushed up, is not a satisfactory explanation because wage-push also is not in itself a process. It leaves open the question, "What makes it keep on pushing?" just as in the case of the excess demand, or the "demand pull," explanation of inflation one could ask "what makes it keep on pulling?" You must have a continuing process.

To explain an ongoing inflation we must be able to point to a cause which is itself a continuing force. A clue to where one can find such a continuing process is provided by the motto, "If at first you don't succeed, try, try again." A continuing process is what results when someone tries to do something that cannot be done. He fails, tries again, is bound to fail again, and keeps on trying. We have a continuing process.

Such a continuing process can come about as the result of a government's needing money for current expenses but able to obtain it only by creating new money with which it buys the goods it needs. This leaves fewer goods for the citizens. But when the citizens receive the new money paid by the government for the goods it buys, they try, with this money, to buy those goods for themselves in competition with the government. This action bids up prices, and the government has to print more money each time to buy the same goods at higher prices. As this process continues, citizens keep receiving more and more money with which they perpetuate their competition with the government. The citizens and the government together are trying to buy more than is available to be bought. Of course, they can never succeed in doing this, but as long as they persist in trying, the inflationary process continues. This kind of inflation, Inflation I, due to too much total spending, has a very simple cure: Remove the excess spending. (This solution could mean removing that kind of government.)

Inflation II is also due to a process in which people repeatedly try to do something in which they cannot succeed. This time they are not trying to buy more than there is to buy. They may, in fact, be buying less than the economy can provide. But the various parties engaged in production are all trying to be rewarded by shares of the product which add up to more than 100 percent of the product. It is, of course, not possible for them to enjoy more than 100 percent of the product among them, but each party demands more *money* as its share. Labor succeeds in reaping more money as wages, and business then obtains more money by raising the prices of the products by more than their increased cost from the increased wages. But both labor and business still find that the increased money cannot give them more than 100 percent of the product—only higher prices. Consequently, they raise wages and prices again and again, and once more a continuing inflation results. An Inflation II comes to an end when both parties decide that they are getting nowhere and that they must stop demanding shares which come to more than the total product. But when this finally happens, we nevertheless do not observe price stability. We only observe a different kind of inflation—Inflation III.

The same thing happens to Inflation I if its cause disappears and there is no more excess demand. We do not witness price stability; we witness Inflation III.

INFLATION III

Once an inflation has been proceeding for some time, a vicious circle is created in which everybody is concerned with protecting himself from the expected continuation of the inflation. There is now neither an attempt by buyers to buy more than 100 percent of the total available nor a pressure by the parties to production to acquire shares that add up to more than 100 percent of the product. Their concern is only to protect themselves from obtaining *less* in real goods and services than what they have been receiving. Now they are not trying to do something that is impossible, but to protect themselves from the expected higher prices, they still demand and extract higher pay, and the employers have to raise the prices of products to cover the higher costs. They, too, expect prices to rise and to protect themselves they raise their prices even more. In this way the expected price increase is brought into being by the expectation of price increases. At the higher prices the expectation of price rise, having been confirmed by an actual price rise, continues at least as strong as before and the whole process repeats. Although there is now no attempt to achieve the impossible, as in Inflations I and II, nevertheless there is a continuing process of rising prices and wages—an Expectational Inflation—Inflation III.

An Inflation III may have been started by an attempt to buy more than is available (Inflation I). It may have been started by an attempt to gain larger shares than the parties were enjoying before (Inflation II). There are many other ways in which it may have been started. Several of the chapters in this volume describe what happens if there is a decrease in what is available as a result of an increase in the price of oil (where "oil" stands for other troubles, too), if the terms of trade worsen, or if more resources are used for social purposes, leaving less for whatever people are in the habit of buying. Any of these factors may activate an Inflation I or an Inflation II, but when people give up trying to acquire the impossible it turns into Inflation III. Wages are still continually being raised by labor, and everybody sympathizes and understands its demand for higher pay. This understanding is made easy for the employers who can be sympathetic, kindly, and considerate because they can recover the higher pay when they raise prices to their customers. And they have to raise their prices because otherwise they would go broke. But, as the Monetarists remind us again and again, this cannot go on for long without an increase in Money. Enter the government.

The government, like other participants, finds itself caught in the vicious circle of expectational inflation. With rising wages and prices, it is essential that there be a continuing increase in the total amount of spending. If this increase does not happen, then every time prices rise, people will be able to buy less. Less will then be produced, fewer workers will be employed, and the economy will fall into a depression. As the inflation continues, less and less can be purchased, and the depression and the unemployment will grow progressively worse. The pressure on the government to do something constructive becomes absolutely irresistible. The government always gives in to the pressure and provides the increasing money supply necessary to make possible the increasing total spending that it takes to buy, at the increasing prices, the goods and services essential to keep the economy alive. The government may struggle against the pressures, but it finally must concede. The struggle becomes only a pretended struggle.

The vicious circle thus evolves into a tripartite inflationary process with wages, prices, and spending chasing each other. The spending is accompanied by an increase in the quantity of money because it is not possible for spending to keep on increasing if the money stock does not increase as well [2].

SOME VIEWS OF INFLATION CONTROL

There is no difficulty deciding what needs to be done to control Inflation I. If an inflation is due to a continuing process of too much spending, the cure is to reduce the excessive spending. Of course, if we cannot remove the forces that provide a continuous process of continuing excess demand, then we cannot stop the demand inflation. An Inflation II cannot be cured as long as the shares to which the productive partners believe they are justly entitled sum to more than 100 percent of the product. Until these feelings are abandoned, no cure can seem just enough to be acceptable. No such major obstacles plague the case of Inflation III. The fact that there is more unemployment than seems technically necessary shows clearly that there is not enough spending to give us prosperity. We cannot blame the inflation on "too much spending" or on "too much money chasing too few goods." Nor is there a demand for impossible shares in the total real product. The trouble is only in monetary expectations of rising prices. If these expectations could vanish, there would no longer be the pressures on workers to demand higher pay. This pressure for higher prices would then disappear and so would the pressure on the government to provide the increased spending required by increasing prices.

This view has led to attempts to try to cure inflation by telling people to stop expecting inflation. Of course, this tack does not work because people do not believe any such speeches when they can see inflation going on all the time, perhaps even escalating. These attempts to persuade people that inflation will stop has earned the unpolite name of "jawboning." It just does not work. The tripartite inflationary process must be ended some other way.

A temptingly easy other way seemed to be to curb just one of the three elements in the tripartite inflationary race. The other two would then no longer be able to keep up the race, and so the actual inflation would cease. Expectations would also stop when people saw that the actual inflation had, in fact, come to an end. But this strategy does not work, either. I have already indicated what happens if the government tries to cure inflation by just ceasing the increase in spending: This practice works only through creating more depression, unemployment, and starvation than the society can stand, and therefore it is always abandoned before it can succeed in eliminating, or even moderating, the inflation.

Preventing prices or wages from rising seems to be an alternative, but that does not work, either. Attempts to slow down or eliminate price increases become much too complicated to handle. There are too many prices, and it is much too easy to disguise a price increase by changing the quality, shape, or some other aspect of the commodity. Technically, it is much easier to stop the race by working on the third of the characters in the race—wages—because wages are in fact already being regulated by those who are negotiating the collective bargaining agreements and because average costs and prices would stabilize even if wages kept on rising at a rate equaling, on average, the rate of national productivity growth. This strategy, however, has a serious flaw because organized labor sees any such attempts as biased against labor and in favor of profits, and it is impossible, in a democratic society, to carry out any such scheme in opposition to the whole labor movement and all its sympathizers. No one of the three elements in the tripartite inflationary process can be singled out for attack in order to put an end to the expectational inflation process.

I should make it clear that I am not talking about wage controls and price controls and the administrative nightmare to which these lead. I am referring here to much more promising plans which have been developed to establish monetary incentives in the form of government taxes (sometimes combined with subsidies) which would discourage wage increases without calling upon impossible administrative tasks. These would work not through any government regulation of wage or price increases, but through the establishment of a charge, price, or tax which is increased when wages are increased. Such Tax-based Incomes

Policies (TIPs) avoid the greatest difficulty, the administrative nightmare. However, they leave severe political and legislative problems connected with the determination of the incidence and the size of the tax (and any accompanying subsidy) and with the necessary adjustments in these as conditions change. Furthermore, they suffer from the fatal objection that they do not seem fair enough to labor to be acceptable in a democratic society.

THE ANATOMY OF MAP

Needed for curing inflation is a method which will attack all three elements in the inflationary process simultaneously. MAP, the Market Antiinflation Plan, is designed to work simultaneously on wage rates and on prices—that is, on wages and on profits—making it possible for the government simultaneously to cooperate in a "Sound Monetary Policy" of increasing the money supply in the amount just needed for the economic health of the economy. With MAP the government is no longer forced to increase the money supply to ratify an inflation, and thus all three elements in the tripartite inflation process can come to rest simultaneously.

The main principles underlying MAP are as follows:

(1) The objective is to stabilize the *average* price while leaving all *actual* prices and wages free to adjust to changing conditions through the existing free market and free bargaining procedures.

(2) If average price is not to rise, total national (money) Net Sales must not rise more than the total national (real) net output.

(3) As relative prices change, some firms will find their Net Sales per unit of input (of productive resources) growing more than the national average. It is then essential that other firms should be offsetting this by their Net Sales per unit of input growing correspondingly less than the national average.

(4) To reduce the increases in Net Sales (and induce decreases in Net Sales) so as to bring the total national increase in Net Sales into equality with the total national increase in net output, a counterinflationary disincentive must be applied at the point where the wage and price decisions are made

(5) The same disincentive must be applied to all firms and must be based on Net Sales (which consist of profits plus wages combined) so as to avoid any bias against business or against labor or between different products.

(6) The disincentive must be just strong enough to bring all this about. It must be set not by the government but by the market. This feature can insulate it from politics and adjust it to the appropriate strength and to changing conditions.

MAP satisfies all these requirements by the following device: It creates a new commodity, "Anti-Inflation Accounting Credit," which I will here call "MAP-credit." It requires each firm to buy or rent MAP-credit equal to the excess growth of its Net Sales over the national average or to sell MAP-credit equal to the deficit in its growth of Net Sales below the national average (always in relation to its net input). It lets a free market set the equilibrium price of MAP-credit. The market price of MAP-credit does what a free price always does. It moves to the level at which supply and demand are equal. Since the demand for MAP-credit is the sum of the excess net sales and the supply is the sum of the deficit net sales, the two just cancel out and total net sales are kept proportional to total output. Inflation is stopped. The free market price of the MAP-credit is the counterinflationary incentive needed. It is of just the right strength, and it is continually adjusted by the market as conditions change. Firms are induced by the price of MAP-credit to reduce their Net Sales in order to save money by buying less MAP credit or in order to earn money by selling more of it. For this they must reduce their *prices*. Reducing their Net Sales by reducing real output by reducing inputs would *lose* them MAP-credit.

The actual rules for MAP are the following:

1. The Federal Reserve now carries responsibility for maintaining a sound money supply, which means one which is *compatible* with prosperity and with price stability. This responsibility is extended by Congress to include responsibility for the *maintenance* of price stability through MAP.

2. A Federal Reserve MAP-credit Office credits each firm with basic MAP-credit equal to 102 percent of its previous year's Net Sales (2 percent being the estimated national increase in productivity). Net Sales is gross sales minus purchases from other firms, which makes it equal to profit plus wages paid to individuals.

3. When a firm hires a new employee, it receives additional free MAP-credit equal to his Wage (including fringe benefits) in his previous employment. (It has to be his Wage in his

previous employment to avoid the device of employers firing people and then rehiring them at a higher pay to gain extra free MAP-credits.) Conversely, on the separation of an employee from a firm, its MAP-credit is reduced by the amount of the Wage. New capital investment similarly entitles a firm to additional free MAP-credit equal to the interest on the new investment at the prime rate of interest. This represents a payment for the services of the new capital. And, conversely, when invested capital is retired, this reduces the firm's MAP-credit correspondingly.

4. Net Sales in excess of a firm's MAP-credit require the firm to buy or rent that additional amount of MAP-credit. A deficit in a firm's Net Sales below its MAP-credit calls for the sale or renting out of its unused MAP-credit.

5. The MAP-credit Office starts up a free market in MAP-credit, buying, selling, borrowing, and lending it freely to all comers at the market price or rental.

6. In the case of government enterprises or nonprofit institutions, the same rule holds except that instead of Net Sales (which is inapplicable) the rules apply to "Individual Incomes Generated" (which is what Net Sales come to if profit is taken out.)

Let me go through a drastically simplified example of how MAP would work. If MAP is imposed when prices have been rising at 6 percent (annually), with productivity increasing at 2 percent and the inputs of labor and capital services increasing at 2 percent, then total Net Sales will have been increasing at 10 percent. Suddenly the increase in Net Sales is reduced to 4 percent, this being the total increase in MAP-credit to which the Net Sales have to conform (2 percent for "productivity" plus an additional 2 percent for the annual increase in inputs of labor and capital services). This amount is just enough to buy the increased output at last year's prices. There will be a demand for additional MAP-credit to legitimize an expected increase in Net Sales from an expected continuation in the increase in prices. The price of MAP-credit will be correspondingly high. But as it becomes apparent that the actual increase in Net Sales is only 4 percent, the expectation of price increases will diminish and with it the demand for extra MAP-credit and its price.

As MAP deflates the inflation, it also deflates itself. When the inflation and the expectation of inflation cease, the price of

MAP-credit falls to zero (or to whatever counterinflationary pressure is still needed to offset any remaining inflationary pressures other than inflationary expectations).

As with all antiinflation plans, there is a temptation for firms and unions to beat the gun and to establish higher basic MAP-credit claims by raising Net Sales before the plan starts. Once MAP is installed, however, average price stabilization would still be reached as soon as the rules are understood and obeyed. If, as seems fairly certain, there is a lively prior discussion, the price stabilization would take very little time, no time at all, or even less than no time!

MAP could never be adopted without a general expectation having been established that MAP would at least reduce the inflation. Such an anticipation of smaller future price increases would create a readiness of sellers to accept lower price increases now rather than to wait, and a willingness of buyers to wait rather than to buy now. This could stop the inflation even before MAP came into effect.

As outlined above, MAP is directed at quickly and completely eliminating the expectational inflation. This raises serious problems of the possible necessity of abrogating contracts based on expectations of continuing, or even accelerating, inflation. A case can therefore be made for a slow MAP which would reduce the inflation gradually at the cost of delaying the cure.

A gradual disinflation is easily arranged by granting each firm additional, transitional, diminishing, free MAP-credit; say, 5 percent the first year, 4 percent the next, and so on ending with 1 percent the fifth year. This would permit total Net Sales to increase not by 4 but by 9 percent the first year (2 percent for productivity, 2 percent for increased inputs and 5 percent for price increases), 8 percent the next year (with a 4 percent price increase) and so on. In this way it would take six years to reach the 4 percent Net Sales increase (2 percent for productivity, 2 percent for increased inputs and 0 percent for price increases).

MAP may seem too strange and too good to be true, but it is only a new application of a device of daily experience, so familiar that it has become invisible—like G. K. Chesterton's invisible postman. Stabilizing the *average* quantity of some item while each *actual* quantity remains unregulated is no new invention. The market, an ancient and honorable device, does just this under our noses all the time. The market sets the price of oranges so as to make the average number of oranges demanded per consumer just equal to the average number available, even while leaving each consumer free to choose the actual number he wants to buy. What makes MAP seem strange is only that the item to which the device is applied is a new one. In MAP the market sets the price of MAP-credit at the level where supply equals demand, and this is the level which makes the average increase in the Net Sales per unit of input just equal to the average increase in net output per unit of input, even while leaving each firm free to choose its actual Net Sales by buying (or selling) the corresponding quantity of MAP-credit.

This description of the operation of a very simple form of MAP is, of course, little more than an outline, and David Colander and I amplify the details elsewhere [3]. So far, however, nearly all of the objections to MAP have turned out to be either misunderstandings or problems for which we have found satisfactory solutions. Other problems may come to light for which there are no satisfactory solutions, but since we have so far met no fatal objections, we are led to think that MAP may indicate the way to cure our inflation-stagflation.

MAP: A PAINLESS SUBSTITUTE

I want to make one more point about MAP. Why is it necessary to have this new device? Why don't things work the way they worked, or were supposed to work, at the time of Adam Smith? Well, something has changed, causing a flaw in our automatic economic system that MAP is designed to remove. The monetarist idea holds that if there is inflation due to too much spending, then removing the excessive spending is the proper treatment. This view is just as much Keynesian as it is monetarist. But if we have an expectational inflation, with serious unemployment, then it is only the monetarists who claim that the same cure would solve this problem, too. Reducing the volume of spending would cause workers to be unemployed. In Adam Smith's or Karl Marx's time, as soon as workers were unemployed, they would starve and they would offer to work for less money. What has happened since then is that we have eliminated the starvation, and one result is that this method no longer works. We can no longer force the unemployed to become "scabs" and to offer to work for less money. It would take a depression deep enough and long enough to wipe away the government, and perhaps civilization, before they do that. We have reached a situation in the more well-to-do countries where we cannot use the instrument of starvation, and therefore something else is required to take its place—something that will adjust wages and prices directly instead of working indirectly through starvation.

Classical microeconomic theory teaches that if there is an excess supply of a commodity over the demand for it, the price will fall and restore equality of supply and demand in a new equilibrium by reducing the supply and increasing the demand. This procedure works in the case of individual commodities because of the availability of alternatives, both on the supply side and on the demand side. Buyers substitute the cheapened commodity for alternative purchases and producers shift from producing the cheapened commodity to producing something else instead. But in the case of labor as a whole, the substitution does not work. There is no substitute. For the clarification in macroeconomics of a different way in which the classical result of a full employment equilibrium could theoretically be reached, we owe a great deal to Professor Pigou and to Professor Patinkin's work in neoclassical economics. They did a great deal to make it more clear (although I have always felt it clear enough in Keynes) that full employment could be achieved through falling prices increasing the value of the money stock—not by substitution but by a "cash balance effect."

Unfortunately, the cash balance effect depends on the lowered prices, the lowering of the prices depends on lowered costs, the lowering of costs depends on lowered wages, and the lowering of wages depends on thelowering of the classical "subsistence level" or on Marx's "reserve army of unemployed." To speak more plainly, it depends on starvation. The neoclassical clarification, in completing the picture, only makes it more clear that it is starvation that is the instrument depended on to turn the deflation of employment into a deflation of money wage demands and so of the cost and price inflation. This process does not work because we can no longer use starvation as an instrument for adjusting wages and prices for economic stability. MAP is the painless substitute that fills this gap.

NOTES

1. Abba P. Lerner, *Flation* (Baltimore, Md.: Penguin Books, Inc., 1973).

2. I cannot resist repeating my conversations with the president of the Bank of Israel in the corridors of the Treasury in Jerusalem. He would say, "Professor Lerner, once more the government is pressing me to create more money, but I shall

resist it till the last ditch." To which my answer was, "I see you're getting ready for the last ditch." Of course, he always had to submit to the government's pressure, just as the government had to submit to the social (and political) pressure.

3. Abba P. Lerner and David C. Colander, *MAP, A Market Anti-Inflation Plan* (New York: Harcourt Brace Jovanovich, Inc., 1979).

Chapter 13

A TIP FOR MAP

Sidney Weintraub *

INTRODUCTION

The American Stagflation Sickness continued unabated in 1979, actually gathering a more manifest fever. One legacy of the Carter cosmetics after the Nixon-Ford fiasco, the double-trouble of too much inflation and too much unemployment seems certain to endure. The 11-year ordeal (to date) has entailed a colossal output and income drain, inflicting shattering damage and untold anguish on individual lives through devastating, indiscriminate wealth transfers. Rational decision-making has been impaired. Our world leadership has eroded [1].

There is some sentiment to blame OPEC for our plight, and the Carter administration has grabbed at this scapegoat as a rationalization for the seamy 1979 outturn. The energy price debauch, however, only confirms a deeper malaise requiring more adamant policies to arrest the gushing energy price tide. On a firmer grasp of the issues in official quarters, entailing less concern with imagery, and with the application of vigorous pertinent policies to enforce price level stability, energy prices would have to be relatively higher: there would be no contention over this by economists, regardless of their theoretical and policy stripe.

---

*Professor of Economics, University of Pennsylvania.

TIP

The simultaneous outbreak of inflation and unemployment over about the last decade is literally a new phenomenon for the United States and other affluent western market economies. Farcical buffoonery that only occurred in comic operas, or 'banana republics,' where everything went wrong in concert, finally hit the most affluent, technically advanced, politically stable, mature economy. In older business cycles, in recession and depression, unemployment edged up and prices dipped. In recovery toward fuller employment, the sequence reversed: unemployment down, prices up. The relations were so consistent and normal that either a price, or unemployment, series was invoked to measure the trade cycle oscillation. In the new concatenation both prices and unemployment move in unison. Recession in jobs and output and growing unemployment have lost their claim to arrest the price level binge: inflation persists. United States prices have escalated by over 100 percent since 1968 despite chronic joblessness.

The invocation of monetary policy to thwart the unruly price trend has only compounded the iniquities: conscription to the army of unemployed has been augmented, without any discernible interruption of the price pace. Keynesian fiscal policy has been equally bumbling, too often myopic, in countering the inflation distress. Proponents of monetary policy have dredged up recipes advising stronger doses of the bitter monetary pill to widen the unemployment sea, despite cumulating signs that the enforced madness would contribute little to break the inflation impasse while inviting a gigantic job and output collapse. What was certain was a cruel and costly relapse; subsequent recovery without inflation was dubious.

It was the stagflation circumstance that led Dr. Henry Wallich, then of Yale University and now Governor of the Federal Reserve, and myself to devise what has become known as the Wallich-Weintraub Tax-Based Incomes Policy (TIP) [2]. Variations on the theme, such as that of Dr. Arthur Okun, formerly Chairman of the Council of Economic Advisers and now at Brookings, were sponsored subsequently. A diversity of proposals, as an extended family of TIP, now dot the landscape with the Lerner-Colander MAP being the tantalizing newcomer. Wider realization has ensued that something might be done to abort inflation without plunging the economy into a dismal recession-depression wasteland by mischievous twists on the monetary screw. Mostly in sorrow, it is nonetheless possible to characterized the Federal Reserve Board as "the 7 maids futilely sweeping back the 7 seas."

The lost faith in the monetary myth, and its posturing, motivate the TIP to MAP array. At a time when other luminaries in the economics profession were reluctant to adopt a public stand, despite the oppressive stagflation tangle, the approximately uniform expression of interest in the Wallich-Weintraub TIP by Abba Lerner, James Tobin, Arthur Okun, and Lawrence Seidman enormously facilitated an advance of dialogue beyond the narrow confines of the monetarist and fiscalist-Keynesian vacuities where each school advocated half-a-stability loaf; the former visualized inflation as the ubiquitous foe, while the latter was obsessed with perpetual unemployment. Policy attacks by their venerable medicines succeeded only in perpetuating the double-trouble. With TIP, a range of policy antidotes were opened, as thought was released from a veritable Stone Age of intellectual inertia conditioned by habitual responses.

The TIP Theory

The theory buttressing the TIP proposal might be sketched briefly. From:

(1) $PQ = kwN$, then $P = kwN/Q$ or $P = kw/A$

where PQ = Gross Business Product (GBP)
         P = GBP price level
         Q = Gross physical output
         w = average money wage *and* salary
         N = employment
         A = (Q/N) = average product of labor
         k = average markup of prices over unit labor costs (w/A); this is also equal to the reciprocal of the wage share for k = (PQ/wN) or $(1/k) = (wN)/(PQ)$

Historically, of the 'great ratios' of economics, such as the capital-output ratio, capital-labor ratio, income-velocity of money $(V = PQ/M)$, and the savings ratio, k is most nearly constant, being just short of $k = 2$ (or 1.9 approximately) in GBP. Taking $k = \bar{k}$ for expository brevity, and as a good factual approximation, then the price level moves in tandem with the flex in unit labor costs (w/A). Assuming causation from right to left—and causation is *always* a mental way of interpreting phenomena, and incapable of being 'proved' but which must stand the test of logic and experience—whenever the movement of money wages jumps out of alignment with advances in the average productivity of labor, then prices must rise. Historically, average productivity has tended to inch forward by about 2 to 3 percent per annum in the United States. Whenever money wages stay on an annual course of increments in this range, prices are stable.

Over the 1970 decade, the annual percentage increase in A tended to dip closer to 1 percent, with money wages lurching ahead by nearly 10 percent. Small wonder that in this frenetic assault on the laws of arithmetic the price level lunged higher each year to close the gap in the malalignment of w and A. In 1974 the productivity figure turned *negative*; the same wayward result seems to be in prospect for 1979. Without severe average money wage and salary restraint, a price level bulge over the decade has been inescapable especially with the limited maneuverability in depressing k [3].

TIP Policy

Out of this theoretical model it has seemed paramount that to control P it is necessary to coerce the (w/A) ratio into alignment. Note that the theory omits ascribing any direct weight to money in inflation: a money term is nowhere to be seen in the formula. But it would be a misreading of the theoretical perception to suppose that money is impotent in the economy; instead, its main impact, and a major one at that, is in determining the level of output. Only indirectly, and via a very roundabout channel, can money have a price level incident: if tight money creates enough unemployment, the money policy can slow down the annual increments in money wages. This, to be sure, is good Phillips-curve doctrine: unemployment is the route through which money policy can affect the price level. But if undue money wage hikes flout widespread unemployment, the effort to invoke money tightness to fight inflation will yield stagflation, with too much unemployment, and without inflation surcease.

There are those who would rip unions. Apart from the politics of union-busting, and the ideological battle turmoil that would be generated, 'union-busting' simply evades the underlying issue of the annual magnitudes of pay increase, and not for union labor alone but for *all* labor, including managerial, executive, professional, clerical, etc. Manifestly, it would be utterly unfair to hold only union labor culpable, or to strive to subjugate union members while permitting all other personal incomes to rise disproportionately to average productivity gains.

TIP is thus far less ideological, emotional, strife-prone, or partisan in this respect [4]. Under the Wallich-Weintraub proposal, what is conceived is an extra corporate income tax on about the largest 2,000 firms in the economy whenever the *average* pay hike in the firm exceeds the normal economy-wide pace of productivity improvement. Assuming the norm to be set at 5 percent, firms which increase pay, on average, by more than 5 percent would be penalized by an extra corporate income tax levy. Those which grant an average pay increase of 7 percent, say, would have their effective tax rate raised, say, by 3 percent; those who transgress by shooting up by 9 percent, say, would face a progressively larger tax bite.

The objective, it must be emphasized, is *not* to collect taxes, or to raise the corporate tax take. If TIP recouped heavily in tax revenue it would be a monstrous failure, ripe for dismantlement, just as a traffic fine for speeding is an admission of the non-observance of speed limits. To the extent that there were *some* TIP collections, the normal corporate tax rate could be reduced. As TIP succeeded in giving us a better price level record, and monetary and fiscal policy were made conducive to full employ-ment, the corporate income tax could be *reduced*; the reduction could be mandated on the date of adoption of TIP. The TIP objective is not to collect taxes, or to erode corporate venture capital; it is instead to provide a rational motive for firms to resist exorbitant pay boosts which ignite the inflationary spiral of higher pay, higher prices, higher pay, etc.

Applying TIP to the largest 1,000 firms (in terms of value produced) would cover about 55 percent of the GBP. Placing the largest 2,000 firms under its umbrella would erect a pay re-straint tent for about 85 percent of the GBP. Administratively, to calculate TIP tax liability, about 7 extra lines on an income tax form would be required, consisting of information already reported by firms to the Internal Revenue Service on the wage bill in computing profits, and the withholding tax data listing employees. On the assumption that an auditor could examine one set of 7 lines per day, about 10 extra employees in the IRS might be needed. Even magnifying the number of auditors several-fold, when one considers annual GBP (or GNP) losses estimated at $100 billions or so each year through the dismal underemployed economy of the 1970s, the administrative outlay is piddling compared to the prospective rewards. In the trade-off, the operational cost is nil and the chance for huge gains is enormous.

TIP Adjuncts

The economic world is not so neat and tidy as to permit an unalloyed TIP to serve alone. For example, government employees would have to be brought under restraint; this could be accomplished by permitting average 5 percent annual increments in pay, corrected every 2 or 3 years for any lag of the government sector behind the private sector.   Trucking and construction trades, likewise, would escape TIP, for smaller firms dominate in this sector. Various possible methods exist to reduce conformity to the average pay scales.   Likewise, physicians and hospitals might prompt special provisions consistent with the main objective. In farming and at the gas pump, where prices are mainly demand-oriented (for agriculture especially), insofar as average money incomes are brought under discipline, market demand will reflect the income restraints and product prices would not pierce the stable orbit [5] .

Money wages and salaries are the primary ingredients in business costs and, simultaneously, they constitute far and away the major component of consumer demand: perhaps 85 percent of the goods and services bought at the supermarkets, auto dealers, garages, appliance shops, etc. emanate from wage and salary recipients.   It is a half-truth to gauge TIP as concerned with wage-push or cost-push inflation: wages are simultaneously costs *and* the stuff of consumer market *demand*.

Ours is foremost a money wage (and salary) economy, with prices evolving from the money income payments. Firms hire labor in the expectation of demand; they pay out money wage--salary incomes, thereby setting up the cost side of the market equation.   The self-same incomes determine consumer demand outlays directly, and indirectly, they are the well-spring in the ultimate demand for capital goods.   To provide the money lubrication, banks enter the process but *at the secondary phase*: depending on average incomes and the volume of labor hire, firms borrow money.   It thus is not the money supply that "causes" inflation but the fact that money incomes are speeding at a stiffer pace than average productivity; it thus is the higher costs and higher prices which leads firms--and the economy--to *require* more money. Money *follows* the price-making process.

TIP Supplements

A variety of supplements to the basic TIP policy can be devised, for example, to allow more generous pay hikes for enhanced productivity, or to assist firms that abide by the TIP policy in labor negotiations in the face of union adamancy, or to sponsor the FTC or Anti-Trust Division to monitor sectors in which k-margins are widening despite rapid productivity improvements, etc. The refinements and extensions to comprise a complete program to attack the inflation problem are developed in other places [6].

Obviously, TIP makes no attempt to control individual prices or individual wages. *Average* pay hikes are alone the target. Contemplated firm-size would limit oversight to instances of 20,000 or more employees. Union labor, for example, might secure more than, say 5 percent, if managerial and executive personnel are held to smaller increments. Thus TIP could contribute to placing the onus of collective bargaining where it properly belongs, to wit, in a concern with *relative* incomes in a stable price level structure.

The TIP Safety Valve Feature

Like good legislation generally, TIP does not prohibit firms from puncturing the norm: firms can pay more—but at a price, in cognizance of penalty taxes. Firms may have good reason, in individual cases, to violate the general rules and, under TIP, they could be free to do so. Incentive to transgress would depend on the militancy of labor, or special obstacles to firms in hiring labor, with each factor measured against the burden of the penalty rate structure.

For a stable price level the basic norm would have to be the economy-wide productivity increment. To illustrate, if productivity within the firm were the basis for pay increments, the result would be that in an industry which showed abnormal increases in productivity, say 10 percent per annum, in a few years its pay scale would double. In another sector, where productivity was nil, pay would stay fixed. Almost equivalent work skills could yield widely disparate pay, and reveal discriminatory pay distortion.

MAP

Before passing from TIP to MAP, Professor Lerner earlier made a brief sojourn as the parent of WIPP, the acronym for a Wage Increase Permit Plan. Most of my remarks will concern the artful MAP, as drawn by Professor Lerner and David Colander, his able and agile collaborating cartographer.

I am as yet unpersuaded by any apparent advantages of MAP over TIP. I see it as an ingenious tracing, but vague in imagining terrain that I think dimly futuristic; it deviates too much from known staked, and practical travel routes. For computers and poll-takers a century hence, and with social attitudes hitherto unknown, it may evolve from an orgy of requited inflation, and become a relevant expedient, but that is not yet the case.

I list below what I deem to be questionable features. Most of the points will be elaborated subsequently; others are either fairly self-explanatory or they will evoke space on another occasion.

Some Blurs on the MAP

The MAP appears blurred to me in several areas. (1) It tells us nothing at all about how the MAP is to be enforced, or how it is to be administered and yet, as it poses obstacles to conduct, it cannot be 'led by an invisible hand.' (2) The MAP does not inject a single remark on penalties for evasion or non-compliance. I find this strange for *this is the cardinal feature of TIP*; the outline of a theory, it may be argued, is subsidiary to a blueprint for application; yet it is in its policy perspective that the spirit of a theory is best captured. (3) MAP, it should be conceded, marks a more substantial institutional departure than TIP; there is not a word on the response of its authors for an interim policy if MAP is rejected; Is there no contingency plan if the MAP is vetoed as impractical? (I have frequently expressed myself in favor of the old fashioned controls while TIP is being debated). (4) What does MAP offer by way of enforcement for compliance if labor strikes, or business boycotts operations under MAP? Or is the prospect so outlandish as not to warrant any comment? (5) MAP professes to be more even-handed' or less 'anti-labor' than TIP. I dispute the charge that TIP is anti-labor, for reasons frequently given: it is anti-inflation, pro-full employment. On the other hand, when MAP intimates that labor can, on average, secure more than the annual productivity increments, or very much more over an extended time frame, the cartographers can be criticized for foisting an emotional delusion on an audience not ncessarily informed of the concatenation of facts; this sets back the educational aspect: money wages and salaries cannot for long surpass average productivity trends. The greatest opportunity for a more egalitarian income division lies in intralabor shifts. (6) MAP needlessly, and for reasons that elude me, places restraints on *output* expansion by firms. (This aspect may have since been withdrawn or corrected.) (7) Despite the air of urgency imparted to the proposal, it seems to me that the severity of the inflation impairment is treated casually, and the ordeal minimized, by the prescription to usher in a 'gradual' abatement of the price scourge. (8) MAP, as I read it, appears clouded by a vision of solely an industrial economy based on large firms, of big globs in the economic universe having homogeneous labor hire, and production behavior patterns. Can we really overlook government employees, professionals, farmers, trucking, and the construction industry? TIP may be laconic at times, but it is not silent in available expositions. (9) The authors go needlessly to a great exercise in ingenuity to encompass 'value-added'—which would have to be a gross concept to avoid fudging through accounting—when the sweeping coverage might be achieved more simply on recognition of wage share or markup constancy. The neglect of k, in my view, vitiates the claim of 'evenhandedness,' which holds the prospect of important departures of wage hikes from productivity gains. Then (10), the omission of an enforcement or compliance mechanism is noted in (1-2) above. Are criminal penalties intended? Presumably not. Fines for evasion? Will these approximate TIP taxes, or will they come to a slap on the wrist? The consideration is vital to MAP for inasmuch as the coupon 'rights' can have a significant market value at times, the plan would have to carry rather universal coverage extending to about 13 million firms in lieu of the 2,000 or so TIP'sters. In respect of coverage, the defect of universality is shared by the Okun TIP which contemplated tax rebates to participating firms. (11) The theoretical underpinning of MAP appears to be an ideological fascination with the price mechanism to elicit the 'optimal' price that producers will pay for the 'right to inflate' their particular prices, and thus to perturb the price level.

A far-fetched analogy may be injected to make a point. There may be a market price that could be extracted for the 'right to commit mayhem.' Some of us may be old-fashioned enough, and divested of wholesale devotion to the pecuniary system, as to eschew the sale of indulgences which conflict with communal purposes: there are areas where we may prefer to eject from our political constitution, and deny the status of 'natural right,' activities that could be accommodated by the market mechanism. Slavery is a case in point, along with a list of lesser crimes against humans.   It is thus possible to be underwhelmed by the 'right to inflate' calculable damage through the market system.   The expression of a 'right to inflate' elevates, to the uppermost heights of decision-making, a procurement department concerned not with efficient production but with contemplated (speculative?) dealings in inflation privileges.

Hence suppressed enthusiasm is a not unreasonable reaction to the establishment of new ventures in inflation-rights, and all that it would entail, as yet dimly perceived and exposed. If the function of the economic system is to produce goods efficiently, a process for erecting a substantial superstructure to ascertain the 'optimal' price of 'inflation rights' constitutes a digressive detour, wasteful of energies and resources until, at a minimum, we are shown otherwise by expository details in which 'financial strength' is shown to be a plausible subordinate element.

Most of these objections invite further elaboration. Before examining MAP, or as a prelude to some survey, a useful beginning is with WIPP, the original parent of MAP and a lineal descendent of TIP. To be sure, the genealogical line stems more as a reaction to the Okun TIP, which Lerner rejected when he detected some major litigational shortcomings which were sometimes, by several participants, mistakenly attributed to the Wallich-Weintraub TIP.

FROM WIPP TO MAP

WIPP was built around a scheme whereby firms would be handed tickets, ration coupons in effect, or a second kind of money, and then would trade them (as Walrasian *bons*?) for cash insofar as they wanted to have enough legal coupons to raise average money wages (and salaries) by more than, say, 3 percent. Firms that did not intend to raise wages by the *legally* permissible 3 percent would be the sellers of the *bons* [7] .

One can admire the subtlety of it all. The point was to let market pricing of the *bons* express the degree to which firms would pay for the legal right to inflate, or stipulate the price at which they would agree to refrain from inflationary behavior. The idea was that repressing the wage bulge would tend to keep unit labor costs more stable and check price level inflationary flare-ups.

Nonfeasibility comes, I believe, because WIPP assumes fairly automatic and assured compliance, sans administration.   Monitoring and policing, and sanctions for offenders, go unmentioned.

(This is the very focus of TIP). Without any enforcement mechanism, however, there would be no reason to play the WIPP game: coupons could be costly to procure. Labor, too, without a monitoring structure for compliance, would insist that firms forget the whole thing insofar as their pay claims were at stake. Perhaps these objections help to explain why Lerner's own evaluation of WIPP turned negative as he now supports the new proposal, MAP. For myself, I defer to the ingenuity of WIPP, even as I reject the design.

MAP now constitutes the current Lerner theoretical version written in collaboration with David Colander. (Heretofore, for Colander, it has been MIP, for Market Based Incomes Policy [8]). Unfortunately, MAP, as with WIPP, at too many places puts the onus on the reader to spell out the details to give the notion operational significance and, in my case, this leads to an adverse judgment on its prospects for the here and now. Even someone who has followed closely the evolution of the income policy literature is apt to be more than a mite bewildered by the incomplete MAP: it is as sparing in legislative outline as WIPP, and far less instructional as a legislative mandate than TIP. In this respect, although the urgency of coping with inflation is reiterated, MAP is devoid of operational specifics [9].

Envisaged, as before, are grants of coupons, the ration *bons* as a second form of money, this time to legitimatize firms which intend to expand their *net* sales—value added—to 102 percent of the previous year value sum. Net sales for the previous year are a compound of prices and quantities. They are implicitly assumed to be known at the very start of the year as a definite aggregate, rather than being initially merely a fuzzy sum: apparently New Year's Day is to be an intense work session for accountants. Firms which contemplated an expansory thrust surpassing the 102 percent norm would have to buy *bons*, or legitimate "rights," from other firms at whatever prices the traffic would bear—to coin a vague phrase from obsolete texts.

This, at least, is what I derive from the paper. According to statistics available, the plan would have to cover some 13 million firms: each would surely want tickets, and they would be aggrieved if valuable privileges, in sum unknown but which they could sell in the market, were denied to them [10]. TIP, in the Wallich-Weintraub version, would in contrast be limited at most to 2,000 firms.

No remarks appear, at least in the early Lerner-Colander work, on the matter of evasion, of firms selling over 102 percent of their previous year's norm, and without a matching number of ration coupons (or expansory "rights"). How could firms be checked for compliance? What penalties would be levied on violators? Criminal verdicts would erect a new-fangled white-collar crime, and courts would be hard pressed to measure economic damage. Levying fines, as civil offenses? In a way, this penalty of undefined magnitude could parallel or greatly surpass, after far more roundabout routes, the tax imposts conjectured under TIP which would nevertheless rank MAP by virtue of clarity and administrative feasibility. Without discussion of compliance and enforcement, we have bathwater without a baby.

So far as I can see there seem to be no administrative benefits in MAP to compensate severe comparative shortcomings in enforcement. TIP would rely on the IRS service, and entail audits of about seven extra lines on the corporate tax form, while restricted in its applicability to no more than about 2,000 firms.

As I read the MAP, Lerner must subscribe to nearly this assessment, for he writes: "This is not to say that we think we have a finished blueprint." This declaration comes as a forlorn letdown inasmuch as the urgency of the mission of stopping inflation pervades the paper.

Apart from not distinguishing adequately the litigational and administrative burden that divides the Wallich-Weintraub penalty TIP from the Arthur Okun reward TIP—the "stick" versus the "carrot"—the Lerner-Colander MAP projects a deceptive benign image, professing that TIP is aimed at reining labor in holding money wages at bay while winking at prices and profits. This is condemned as less than even-handed in assigning "blame" to labor.

This invites some pause. If MAP is to be less sedulous in monitoring money wages, it simply will not do as an inflation control vehicle. It can only create a false illusion to suggest that where, truistically, prices are an outcome of money incomes outpacing production, it is possible to play soft with labor despite its garnering 75 percent of the money income total, the portion which happens to constitute employee compensation. There is no way of keeping the price level at bay without restraint on the lion's income share. Too, it is a mystery to me that the authors have nowhere confronted the facts on the year-to-year near constancy in the wage share, and the longer period slow downward drift in the non-wage share, as supporting the presumption that profits will behave once the big portion of unit costs is brought in check [11]. MAP conveys a false expectation in being touted as superior to TIP in not suppressing *money*—not real—wages when, operationally, it *must* reach precisely equivalent money wage–salary impacts for price level stability.

Omitted is any discussion at all of what happens if labor strikes and insists on higher pay increases beyond any 2 or 3 percent norm. Under TIP a profit onus prevails on firms to resist; if the firm submits, it is faced with the incidence of the higher corporate income tax. Under MAP, if the movement for excessive pay increase is general, so that firms bid feverishly for coupons to raise net sales value—consisting of prices times output—and if labor is adamant and coupon prices jump high, the upshot will be a rise in unit costs and thus in prices, and an ensuing erosion in output. In short, *MAP would usher in stagflation*, the very situation it seeks to avert.

If the pay move is more localized, confined to a few large industries, all sorts of questions arise in respect to market dealings in *bons*. Do firms try to procure them in advance of labor negotiations? After negotiations? Can the tickets be resold? How does a firm receiving sporadic orders, say a bulge toward year-end that is unexpected, operate in a *bons* market? Why confine firms that want to expand by more than 2 percent in output to this narrow limit? Surely this would hamper the very resource allocation features that MAP professes to foster.

Are speculative dealings in *bons* to be encouraged? By specialist speculators? Would speculation favor firms with superior financial strength? What resources would have to be devoted to new *bons* by specialist procurement or purchasing departments in firms? How large an effective administration agency might be required to enforce the MAP?

On this, every reader must become his own script writer. The authors owe us more detailed information and discussion. If we conjure *voluntary* wage and price acquiescence at non-inflationary norms the stagflation problem can be instantly dispelled—in imagination.

GRADUALISM

The Lerner–Colander theme, and the works of some other authors, takes another baffling twist for which this reader is unprepared, in pleading for a "gradual" unwinding of the price surge. The argument is that if a mere precipitate approach is taken, those who banked on the inflation binge would be sorely disenchanted in a turnabout. This conclusion mitigates the sense of urgency pervading the Lerner–Colander and other antiinflation proposals, to wit, that inflation is so insidious a matter that it must be checked. The inflation sting loses its venom in the pinch for gradual de-escalation. Certainly, perpetuating the price climb will continue to ravage those who have been ravished already, while giving aid and comfort to long-term beneficiaries--home owners, and bankers, for example--of the spiraling process. Gradualism comforts those who have benefitted already, with less thought for the afflicted.

Hard facts are most elusive on the subject of gains or losses under inflation, even on the most meticulous empirical studies; it is still possible, however, to state an ideological preference that the way to stop inflation is to stop it, and forthwith. "Gradualism" has been the ideological preference of the Carter administration, where, in the name of fighting inflation, the attack has been mounted merely to cap it, while Federal Reserve Chairman Miller talks vaguely of a five, six, seven-year effort--on top of eleven years past.

Readers may be misled by a dubious passage toward the close of the available Lerner–Colander work on "the possibility that there is an inherent pressure on wages and prices even at less than full employment, and even in the absence of any expectations of inflation." Some of us already have concluded that the one significant lesson of the 1970s was that even with important surges in the unemployment rate, inflation was capable of bounding ahead. This fact has been exemplified in our own country, as well as in Canada, the United Kingdom, and Australia, to name only the English speaking world of my reasonably close experience. Theoretically, the phenomenon was long ago discerned by Keynes in reference to "semicritical" points of inflation.

On the importance of "expectations of inflation," there are the revealing lines by Mr. Wooky, in a World War II play of that name, on being told that the morale of the troops was low. He expostulated: "There's a job to do. Morale, that's a dirty French word." Expectations, too, have an ambiguity. They have a base which, I think, consists in wage-cost movements. A load of graduate courses in economics is really superfluous to apprehend that when construction workers' pay jumps four-fold, while productivity stands still, new home prices will soar. Control incomes, and price expectations will come back to ground level.

The Baumol Assessment

The tentative assessment of Professor Baumol, judiciously expressed and neatly expounded, seems to me to misfire.   He writes that "theoretically" the "advantages in terms of potential effectiveness all lie with the [inflation permits]." And: "the free market . . . should assign them to those products where they are most urgently needed."

Before the MAP can be effective, it should at least be shown that the idea can be implemented.   The discussion, so far, has been chary on this elemental detail.   Too, to talk of a 'free market' is a mite premature considering that no attention at all has been given: (1) financial strength in bidding for the *bons*, (2) any destabilizing speculation, and (3) the diversion of resources to departments of *bon* procurement.   Conceivably, when policing, costly distraction, and penalties for noncompliance and evasion, are investigated—which are the nuts and bolts of feasible policy-- the presumed 'advantages' will shake out as a mirage. As a MAP cannot automatically survive without monitoring and punishing violators, a theoretical assessment which omits these aspects is suspect for being incomplete and thereby inappropriate.

In passing it is also possible to be less sympathetic to an evaluation that depends on the 'long-run' 'free markets,' Phillips curves, and 'equilibrium.'   TIP can operate—as the corporate income tax does—in a less tidy, less competitive, and more dynamic world of short runs.   Too, it is the Phillips curve stagflation woes that TIP is designed to eliminate, to the end that the vicious Hobson's choice may be empirically precluded by damping unemployment to an 'irreducible minimum' based on new operational forces in a TIP'd institutional environment.

CONCLUSION

What strikes me as a fundamental difference with the early pages of the formulation of the Lerner-Colander MAP is their confidence that by maintaining a close grasp on net value added or total money income—money expenditures are especially emphasized at the beginning—the price level will be stabilized. This sounds very much like the monetarist's desire to stabilize income—why not stabilize money income through money emissions and a stable MV aggregate?   As remarked, this could mean stagflation, with P going up and Q going down.   In an economy in which *unit* labor costs bulk so large and mark-ups stay so firm—the missing MAP road sign—a sidewise price level trend requires better control of the average money pay so long as strong productivity gains are precluded.

This aspect leads me to think that MAP is misconceived in its focus on value added where the latter must become mainly a euphemism for average wage cost.

The analytical controversy may disolve as a semantic digression. Yet I fear an inability to even locate the MAP until symbols for compliance and enforcement are featured prominently. MAP cannot chart direction until these aspects are drawn. When they are entered I suspect the MAP will be a more complicated TIP.

NOTES

1. The economic costs of inflation, and an elaboration of consequences, appears in my *Capitalism's Inflation and Unemployment Crisis* (Reading, Mass.: Addison-Wesley, 1978), Chapters 1 and 2.

2. For the original collaboration, see "A Tax-Based Incomes Policy," *Journal of Economic Issues* (June 1971) reprinted in my *Keynes, Keynesians, and Monetarist* (University of Penn., 1978).

3. Extended discussion appears in *Capitalism's Crisis*, Chapter 3.

4. cf., Lawrence Seidman, "TIP: Feasibility and Equity," *Journal of Post-Keynesian Economics* (Summer 1979).

5. cf., A more thorough discussion of supporting measures appears in my "A TIP Package," *Challenge* (Sept. 1978).

6. See TIP-CAP, devised to encourage productivity boosts. *Capitalism's Crisis*, Chapter 6.

7. See David Colander, "Incomes Policies: MIP, WIPP, and TIP," *Journal of Post-Keynesian Economics* (Spring 1979).

8. The lack of specifics is especially disappointing in that Lerner originally saw the administrative and litigational problems of TIP as a drawback. Most of these criticisms, I think, applied to the Okun "carrot" TIP.

9. Lerner/Colander.

10. For 1974 there were about 2 million active corporations and about 11 million proprietorships. See Richard E. Slitor, *Tax Based Incomes Policy: Technical and Administrative Aspects, A Report Prepared for the Board of Governors of the Federal*

Reserve System, pp. 15, 37. Reprinted in "Anti-Inflation Proposals," *Hearings*, Senate Banking Committee, 95th Congress, May 22-23, 1978.

11.   TIP draws its intellectual sustenance from the empirical relationship of unit costs and prices, in view of the near-constancy of the average mark-up in Gross Business Product data. See, *Capitalism's Crisis*, Chapter 3.

 *Part V*

POLICY INGREDIENTS

Chapter 14

POLITICAL AND ECONOMIC PARTNERSHIP IN REGULATORY REFORM

*Elizabeth E. Bailey**

INTRODUCTION

The deregulation of airlines shows dramatically how a partnership between political strategy and economic analysis can result in successful regulatory reform. I will describe the political and economic interactions that proved helpful in each of two distinct phases of the reform process: the pre-reform stage and the period of reform.

I will not focus on regulatory reform as an anti-inflation measure, even in a volume whose primary focus is inflation. My reason is simply this: where regulatory reform is justified on the merits, it should be encouraged whether the U.S. economy is in a period of rapid or slow inflation. The increases in economic efficiency that occur with reform of traditional economic regulation are warranted for their own sake, and least costly solutions to problems in social regulation are also warranted for their own sake.

Regulatory reform can, of course, potentially offer substantial savings to the U.S. public. Estimates made by Robert Crandall [1] of the Brookings Institution show that the potential annual savings from deregulation of airlines is between $3.4 and $5.0 billion, and that from deregulating trucking is between $1.8 and $5.2 billion. In aviation, during 1977, the first year in which widespread deep discount fares were permitted, price (as mea-

---

*Member, Civil Aeronautics Board.

sured by operating revenue per revenue passenger mile) declined in constant dollars by 2.8 percent; by the end of 1978, the second year of greatly increased opportunities for downward fare flexibility, price declined in constant dollars by 10.8 percent. For an industry with revenues of $18.5 billion, this represented a savings of $2 billion in 1978. Unless fuel costs increase substantially or the scarcity of capacity in aviation worsens, we expect that price will continue to decline in real terms for the next year or two as unrestricted low fares spread and as other efficiencies are achieved. But when deregulation has been completed, a new equilibrium price level will be reached, after which prices will again rise if input prices rise faster than productivity. Deregulation will not prevent the price level from rising over time, although by encouraging innovation and productivity, it may help hold the rate of increase at a level somewhat lower than otherwise. Thus, deregulation is at best a measure that can be an adjunct to a more broadly based counter-inflationary program [2].

My purpose in this paper will be to describe, quite apart from the inflation issue, how reform has been accomplished in aviation.

PRE-REFORM STAGE

It is difficult to say who took the first steps in aviation reform-- the businessmen in California who adopted low-fare pricing practices or the academicians who analyzed these practices and compared them to the way in which the Civil Aeronautics Board (CAB) was regulating the industry. In either case, the comparison revealed various forms of economic damage caused by Federal regulatory policy and led to a number of further studies both by academicians and by other agencies in the executive branch.

The academic investigators, however, were not able to provide the political impetus to begin a reform movement. This impetus was supplied by Senator Edward Kennedy in 1975 through oversight hearings that dramatized the issues in an economically careful as well as a politically visible way [3]. The hearings reshaped the research evidence to address political fears of harm from change and to convince others in government of the benefits from reform. An effort was made to expose as myths the positions taken by those resisting reform that did not correspond to the true character of the industry. The value of specific evidence in counteracting such general rhetoric was enormous. The value of the political visibility was also enormous. Such visibility attracted a support base for reform and permitted the movement for reform to gather momentum.

It is instructive to describe some of the ways in which available research was combined with newly generated data to address head-on some of the industry's allegations of potential harm from reform.

One myth current in the industry was that lower prices would lead to economic ruin, and that price competition, if permitted, would be destructive and would bankrupt small carriers. Studies of Michael Levine [4] and William Jordan [5] showed that a group of non-CAB certificated airlines operating solely within state boundaries in California had adopted prices approximately half as high as CAB regulated levels for markets of similar distance. The airlines offering these rates were highly profitable. Moreover, the relatively small intrastate airlines had been able to resist strong competitive responses by large CAB-certificated carriers. Similar experiences were accumulating in Texas. In spite of this evidence, the certificated airlines maintained that the California and Texas experiences were attributable to unique operating conditions, such as good California weather. The Kennedy staff did additional analysis to establish just how much merit these arguments had, and showed, for example, that poor visibility in Los Angeles occurred for 228 hours in 1974 as contrasted with 233 hours in Boston; thus, weather delay differences were insubstantial. Similarly, interlining costs, which were not incurred in intrastate operations, were shown to add about $3 to a ticket price, which would make a San Francisco to Los Angeles ticket cost $21.75 in 1974 instead of $18.75, still well below the $41.67 charged at this time between Boston and Washington. The major explanatory variables were found to be load factor and seating capacity, with American Airlines configuring its Boeing 727-200 jet aircraft for 121 seats flown 55 percent full, as contrasted with a PSA configuration of 158 seats flown 60 percent full. This fact alone was shown to account for more than half the fare difference.

A second issue dealt with in the pre-reform stage was the arguments offered by Lucille Keyes [6] and Richard Caves [7] that the CAB was creating regulatory barriers to entry in what appeared to be a structurally competitive industry. The hearings cited evidence that between 1950 and 1974 there had been 70 applications for new entry into the domestic scheduled airline industry and that none was granted. The only new entry permitted was that of carriers providing specialized or geographically limited or otherwise circumscribed services in peripheral markets: they included subsidized small community, charter, all cargo, small aircraft commuter, Alaskan and helicopter service. Despite an almost 300-fold increase in revenue passenger miles since 1938, the original grandfather carriers continued to provide over 90 percent of the revenue passenger miles in the 48-state domestic market in 1972 [8].

A third issue addressed in the oversight hearings concerned the extent that profits from dense routes were being used to subsidize service to small communities. George Eads' research [9] supplied evidence that such communities were served for the most part by local service and commuter carriers not by the trunk carriers. The Douglas and Miller study [10] supplied evidence that current prices could indeed produce large profits in the long-haul markets but that the existing carriers had competed this profit away by means of scheduling competition—planes in long-haul markets were flying about 40 percent full in markets that had four competing carriers, 50 percent full in markets that had two competing carriers, and 60 percent full in monopoly markets.

Fears concerning small community service continued to be on the minds of Congressmen, however, and were fed by industry representatives who stated that under deregulation their airlines would pull out of a substantial number of "losing" city-pairs. The Kennedy staff responded by conducting a detailed analysis of 327 "losing" city-pairs cited by United Air Lines, where "losing" refers to failure to cover fully distributed costs. A similar analysis was later carried out by the Department of Transportation for a list of 160 "losing" domestic segments provided by Eastern Air Lines [11]. In both cases, it was found that all but two dozen or so of the losing segments were served on a discretionary, not on a mandatory, basis and that in the majority of these more service was being provided than was required by the CAB. Of the remaining city-pair markets, pull-out by a trunk carrier would, as it had in the past, in most cases lead to unsubsidized replacement service by other carriers. Only in a few instances would direct subsidy be needed. Because of this evidence, subsequent policy in this area endorsed not the cross subsidy idea, but instead the formulation of special subsidy-eligible provisions to guarantee essential air service to small communities.

Shortly after the Kennedy hearings, a task force was set up at the CAB to study the need for regulatory reform. This task force, under the leadership of Roy Pulsifer, issued a report supporting reform and offering the first blueprint for sunset of the Board's rate and route authority [12]. Other executive branch agencies also issued supportive documents. Senator Cannon, Chairman of the Aviation Subcommittee of the Senate Commerce Committee, held further hearings. President Ford named John Robson as a reform Chairman at the CAB. Cannon and Kennedy together devised reform legislation, using information gathered from the hearings, from the CAB reform report, and from DOT and other agency studies.

Still, almost no change in policy was instituted by the CAB itself, in part, because of Robson's philosophy that legislative change was a precondition for successful reform. The moment of actual reform in aviation policy came when President Carter used his power of appointment to name economist Alfred E. Kahn as Chairman at the CAB. It has recently been written that whereas "under Chairman John Robson, the Board began flirting with competitive principles, under Chairman Alfred Kahn that flirtation grew into a passionate and notorious love affair." I agree with this. With Kahn's arrival, and with my own arrival shortly thereafter, the time had come to institute reform. Our philosophy was to do all and everything we could to bring reform about, whether or not the anticipated new legislation was available to help.

REFORM STAGE

Kahn immediately began to recruit new leadership for the agency. Darius Gaskins was brought in as a "can-do" economist, and greatly influenced the initial steps toward reform from within. Phil Bakes, who had been on Kennedy's staff during the hearings and had later been Chief Counsel at the Senate Commerce Committee, was brought in to be a "can-do" General Counsel. A third key appointment was Michael Levine to head the reform of both price and entry (rates and routes) regulation. Levine's strong policy views and his strategic orientation had a profound influence, shaping long-run reform policy both domestically and internationally.

Reform itself was also begun. It rapidly became clear that the profound changes we wanted to accomplish would all require time—time to design and propose the new policies and time for legal process; that is, time for all the affected parties to have their say.

So our initial strategy as policymakers was to work toward our longer term goal of broad reform while looking for and instituting any narrow reforms that could readily be carried out. We took any beneficial action we could within the existing regulatory framework, while simultaneously beginning to lay the groundwork for major changes in regulatory structure. We knew that our long-term strategy for reform entailed the encouragement of enough competition to make the industry workably competitive; our idea was that with sufficient new entry, it would be hard to undo our reforms. Meanwhile, we settled for whatever measures of reform could be carried out immediately. We looked particularly for policies that would result in immediate gains to consumers. Consumer and political awareness of and support for the gains provided momentum for further steps.

Fare policy was the obvious place to begin. In the short run, we were locked into the price-making rules of the Domestic Passenger Fare Investigation (DPFI) in which equal fares were required to be charged for transport over equal distances regardless of cost differences. However, discount fare policy could readily be made to serve the purpose of reform; indeed, the Robson Board had begun to use it this way. Kahn could, and did, vastly expand the acceptability of discount fare proposals and encouraged new proposals of this sort. One major discount fare idea was Texas International's Peanuts fare, in which certan off-peak flights were sold at unrestricted low fares. A second was American's SuperSaver fare, in which deep discounts were offered in the New York to San Francisco and New York to Los Angeles markets, subject to capacity constraints and limited to round trips of restricted duration (7-45 days). The SuperSaver fare was initially highly discriminatory geographically—since the low fares were offered in only two markets—but it was approved on an experimental basis in order to enable carriers to discover without great risk to themselves exactly how consumers would respond to the lower fares. If their discovery was that low fares were profitable, as the Board surmised, then the carriers themselves would have the incentive to let the fares spread.

This fare strategy proved successful, and the new fares did indeed begin to spread. The SuperSaver initially spread to all east coast cities as the carriers sought to counteract the tendency of passengers to re-route themselves to obtain the cost savings. By March 1978, the fares had spread to virtually all of the cities served by trunk carriers. Off-peak fare concepts, such as the Peanuts fare, also spread with the introduction of "tag-end," "simple-saver," "fill-up" and other fares.

A third type of fare reduction was inaugurated after the CAB indicated to the trunks that it would no longer adhere to its formerly rigid ideas on the proper ratio of first-class to coach fares. It took about two weeks for the trunks to settle on a first-class fare level approximately 130 percent of that of coach (as contrasted with the previous 160 percent figure), and within a few months this was reduced further to the current 120 percent level.

Another incentive we gave for lower prices was to expedite those route cases which involved new entrants, and those route cases which involved one or more carriers who were willing to offer low-fare proposals. The *Transcontinental Low Fare Route Proceeding* [13] is perhaps the best known example of this.

The success of this fare policy in lowering prices has already been cited. But it was not consumers alone who gained. So did the carriers. The combination of lower fares and the general economic upsurge resulted in sales, as measured in revenue ton miles, that were up 12 percent in 1978 over 1977. Load factors also went up five percentage points (from 56 to 61 percent for the trunks, from 54 to 59 percent for the local service carriers), indicating that the new fare policies were enabling the airlines to fill a greater fraction of their empty seats. Net income for trunk and local service carriers rose from $665 million in 1977 to $1207 million in 1978, a staggering increase of 82 percent [14].

One of the miracles, or puzzles, of regulatory reform in aviation is that reform was so resisted when every party was to gain so enormously. One of the great assets that Alfred Kahn brought to the reform effort was immediate recognition of and willingness to publicize the good results. Kahn was stunningly effective in publicizing the gains from our pricing policies--both for consumers and for carriers--and stunningly effective also in using the good will so generated to fuel our longer term reform goals. Kahn lent an almost magical aura to reform, never failing to communicate enthusiasm for reform. Just as Kennedy's visibility aided reform in its inception, so Kahn's visibility aided immeasurably in the acceptance of reform as it unfolded.

Let me turn now to some of our longer-term reform policies. By the summer of 1978, a little more than a year after Kahn's arrival, a zone of fare flexibility was put in place [15]. This zone was formed with the presumption that any fare in the zone would be lawful unless there was clear and convincing evidence to the contrary. The zone was set up with large downward fare flexibility, so that a reduction of prices would be relatively easy. However, we recognized that it would be several years at least before we could introduce entrants into most monopoly air routes; therefore, we limited upward fare flexibility to prevent an abuse of monopoly power during the period when there would still be substantial barriers to entry. The ceiling on upward flexibility was set at 10 percent, as contrasted to the 50 percent downward fare flexibility, and it was limited to markets with four or more authorized carriers.

In the area of entry, we began to make changes in the legal standards used in route cases. Traditionally, carriers' routes had been restricted so that in many cases a carrier serving two cities could not fly between them without making stops. Route realignments, in which some of these and other restrictions were removed, were well under way at the time Kahn and I arrived at the Board. The realignments used show-cause procedures rather than a hearing process to remove restrictions in thousands of markets, each of which was individually small, but the sum total of which contributed substantially to increased operating efficiency and flexibility for the carrier.

Traditional route cases were handled by oral evidentiary hearings after which at most one carrier would be granted new or competitive authority. We began to explore the use of show-cause procedures in route cases, by setting new standards of what constituted material evidence. For example, we put carriers on notice that unless they were prepared to show that revenue loss from new competition on a particular route would threaten their solvency as a carrier so as to impair their ability to provide essential air transportation which would not be replaced, calculations of revenue loss would no longer be considered to create an issue of material fact requiring a hearing. Another step in our program of easing entry barriers was tentatively to adopt a policy of granting routes to all fit carriers rather than granting it to only one carrier. Two of the most significant applications of this policy occurred in the *Chicago-Midway Low-Fare Route Proceeding* [16] and the *Oakland Service Case* [17], both of which involved the opening up of underutilized airports.

FROM REFORM TO DEREGULATION

Our policies were only partly in effect when Congress began reshaping its aviation reform legislation in 1978. It soon became clear that there was an enormous synergy between reform from within and reform from without. By moving as quickly as we could, on as many fronts as we could, and by taking all the small steps we could while waiting for the legal process to permit the larger steps, Kahn had made it possible for a legislative and agency partnership to operate effectively. The CAB was showing that reform could be managed in a way that brought economic benefits to all, and our demonstration of this had very positive political benefits. Senator Cannon was able to gain enormous Senate support for reform. Congressman Levitas went so far as to get the House to vote for complete deregulation and suddenly the stage was set for a move all the way from reform to deregulation. While the CAB supported the idea of deregulation, and sunset, it was the conference committee which proposed the compromise, a compromise which looked like the sunset provisions of the Pulsifer report.

The Airline Deregulation Act of October 1978 provided a schedule for the successive elimination of various powers of the Board—ability to regulate routes disappears at the end of 1981, ability to regulate rates disappears at the end of 1982, and so on. The policy of setting fixed dates for the elimination of protective controls permits effective planning by both carriers and the CAB. The setting of differing dates for the removal of different powers means that there is no target about which opponents of reform can rally. Thus, both of these sunset features are excellent aids in administering the transition. The process of transition has also been aided by our earlier policies. We, at the time the Act passed, had completed the launching of the multiple and permissive entry program, and we are now routinely using show-cause orders to carry it out case-by-case. The transition to full freedom of pricing will be slower, in part because of the effect of eliminating mandatory joint fares on our program of essential air service to small communities. However, the zone of fare flexibility which we instituted closely and strongly parallels that of the statute and provides a mechanism for price change as new entry begins to become a reality.

CLOSING COMMENTS

The economic area that is of great concern to us now is the reduction in service to some U.S. communities. A staff study was requested which examines this issue in detail. It provides a far more felicitous picture than we had feared. Although the new Act's provisions for easier exit have meant that some communities have experienced reductions in air service, in most cases the reductions have been accompanied by increases in service at other nearby communities. Indeed, the losing communities are often those near other airports or major highways while gainers are communities farther away. For example, departures at Providence, R.I. (near Boston's Logan Airport) went down 10.6 percent while more remote Hartford, Conn. experienced an 18.2 percent increase in departures. Moreover, overall service at airports of all sizes increased an average of 8.4 percent from February 1978 to February 1979. Non-hub airports had increases of only 5.2 percent, but the most valuable forms of service at the nation's non-hub, small hub and medium hub airports, those providing connecting opportunities to the larger hubs, experienced gains in the 9 to 13 percent range.

The lesson from all this is that research without political astuteness cannot achieve substantial change; but political insight without analysis can produce change that is ill advised or can effectively block urgent reform. Only their partnership carried out with dedication on mutual understanding can offer to the public all of the benefits which the analyses carried out by our colleagues over so many years have revealed but have so far often failed to put into operation.

NOTES

1. Robert W. Crandall, "Federal Government Initiatives to Reduce the Price Level, *Brookings Papers on Economic Activity*, 2 (1978): 419.

2. See, for example, Robert E. Hall, "Controlling Inflation," The Hoover Institution and Department of Economics, Stanford University, November 1978.

3. See Civil Aeronautics Board Practices and Procedures, Report of the Subcommittee on Administrative Practice and Procedure of the Committee on the Judiciary of the United States Senate (Washington, D.C.: U.S. Government Printing Office, 1975).

4.   Michael E. Levine, "Is Regulation Necessary: California Air Transportation and National Regulatory Policy," *Yale Law Journal* 74 (1964-1965): 1416-1447.

5.   William A. Jordan, *Airline Regulation in America: Effects and Imperfections* (Baltimore: The Johns Hopkins Press, 1970).

6.   Lucille Sheppard Keyes, *Federal Control of Entry Into Air Transportation* (Cambridge, Mass: Harvard University Press, 1951).

7.   Richard E. Caves, *Air Transport and Its Regulators: An Industry Study* (Cambridge, Mass.:   Harvard University Press, 1962).

8.   Civil Aeronautics Board Practics and Procedures, pp. 78-80.

9.   George C. Eads, *The Local Service Airline Experiment* (Washington, D.C.: the Brookings Institution, 1972).

10.   George W. Douglas and James C. Miller, III.   *Economic Regulation of Air Transport: Theory and Policy* (Washington, D.C.: the Brookings Institution, 1979), p. 91.

11.   Regulatory Policy Staff, U.S. Department of Transportation, "Analysis of Eastern Air Lines' Unprofitable Domestic Route Segments," in *Regulation of Passenger Fares and Competition Among the Airlines*, eds. Paul W. MacAvoy and John W. Snow (Washington, D.C.: American Enterprise Institute, 1977), pp. 141-154.

12.   *Regulatory Reform*, Report of the CAB Special Staff, July, 1975.

13.   Order 79-1-79.

14.   Fourth Quarter 1978, Quarterly Financial Review, Trunk Carriers, Local Service Carriers, 4-78 (March 1979).

15.   CAB Regulation PS-80, 22 August 1978.

16.   Orders 78-7-40 and 78-8-203.

17.   Order 78-4-121.

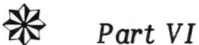 *Part VI*

TRIBUTE TO A PIONEER

Chapter 15

ABBA LERNER ON EMPLOYMENT AND INFLATION: A POST-KEYNESIAN PERSPECTIVE

Irvin Sobel *

INTRODUCTION

Any work which attempts to delineate the present state of the arts in regard to inflation and hopefully offer suggestions for what currently is our major concern would be seriously incomplete without according major attention to Abba P. Lerner's over thirty years of writing on this subject.

Professor Lerner's concern, if not preoccupation, with inflation was apparent even before the end of World War II, during a period in which the majority of economists, in surveying the postwar scene, were more inclined to predict deflation expressed in terms of a high volume of unemployment, rather than inflation. In his classic work *The Economics of Control*, published in 1944 but actually completed as his Ph.D. dissertation in 1942, Abba Lerner introduced his then revolutionary idea of functional finance in the following way:

> A conscious policy for avoiding the evils of inflation and the evils of deflation we shall call functional finance. The government is responsible to maintain adequate levels of consumption and investment but not inflation.

---

*Professor of Economics, Florida State University.

PHASE ONE: COLLECTIVE BARGAINING AND INFLATION

Events, and sometimes unwanted ones, have an unfortunate habit of overtaking and putting to the test ideas and theories.   The rapid inflation of the immediate post-World War II era provided such a test.   While that inflation which had been suppressed by price controls might have been expected to have taken place after their removal, the resultant price reaction was much more rapid and protracted than most economists had anticipated. Thus, from 1946 onward, concern with the rising price level became the subject of a major proportion of Abba Lerner's writings either in more generalized writings on employment theory and Keynesian economics or in particular works addressed to specific aspects of the inflationary problem.

Such a preoccupation with inflation, and especially the con- tribution to inflation of changes in wage rates induced through "free" collective bargaining, begins to show in Professor Lerner's works by the end of 1945.   The unions, especially those in the mass production industries, had been demanding large wage increases (later settling for 18.5 percent), contending that such increases would augment consumption and prevent the predicted postwar recession.   The more extreme proponents of this view, citing decreasing costs, even contended that prices of final products would not have to rise at all.   The opposition, led by the late Professor Sumner H. Schlichter of Harvard, argued on marginal productivity grounds that a change in wage-price ratios, favorable to wage earners, would cause unemployment.

In a symposium "The Problem of Full Employment," printed in the May 1946 Proceedings of the American Economic Associa- tion, Abba Lerner pointed out that wage policy cannot be employed as a means of implementing employment policy.   In general he contended, a rise in wages by itself by raising costs and aggregate demand in equal proportion would have no general effect on employment but would bring with it a rise in the price level.   No change in wage-price ratios would result from a wage increase since employers would still maintain their current mark-ups or profit rates.   Governmental authorities could pre- vent this rise in prices only by bringing about a decline in employment. Without stating the difference explicitly Lerner at this very early stage implicitly recognized the differences be- tween price rises induced by too high a level of spending at full employment and those resulting from wage increases in excess of average productivity gains. Functional finance techniques, that is, reducing spending, would stabilize the price level for the first type of inflation. The same functional finance policies applied in the "wage inflation" case would bring about a decline in employment.

The result of this early recognition was his contention that full employment, free collective bargaining, and price stability were an incompatible trio and that only two of the three were feasible at any given time.

The effect of rising wages through collective bargaining upon the economy, and upon the ability of functional finance to satisfy the dual objective of full employment and stable prices, constituted the theme of Dr. Lerner's May 1947 AEA Proceedings article "Money as a Creature of the State." The article unequivocally starts out by declaring,

> The second most important problem that modern civilization has to solve if it is to survive threats to its existence is the prevention of severe inflation and depression. While the government through some form of functional finance is in a position to keep the rate of spending at the level required to fulfill these responsibilities, so far it has been less able to maintain the value of its money.

He concludes that the techniques for maintaining the value of money have not yet been worked out because government is unable to work out rules for the regulation of money wage rates. This is despite the fact that the government is able to regulate if not determine the level of total spending. The key unregulated matters are the determination of wage rates and rates of mark-up over cost. The power of trade unions over wages (now that the depression influence over wages no longer prevails) has become too great to allow the policy of determining wages by collective bargaining. The only way price stability can be maintained is through wage guidelines in which the rate of average wage increases is limited to the rate of increase in productivity. Thus by 1947 Lerner was arguing that some form of an incomes policy to achieve price stability was a prerequisite to the maintenance of full employment.

He was explicitly concerned that wage markup induced inflation would reduce the willingness of policymakers to fully implement functional finance policies. Thus, he not only had raised the question of whether functional finance (used as a shorthand for compensatory monetary and fiscal policy) could be successfully employed against price rises attributed to wage rates and associated mark-ups, but also whether in the event of such inflation policymakers would be willing to fully implement functional finance policies.

Other changes in Lerner's position were beginning to be apparent. Whereas he initially had felt that only at full employment would the ability of trade unions to raise wages above the rate of average productivity increase assert itself, he now began to see the possibility that wage inflation could exist even below the full employment level. In a 1947 symposium titled "Ten Economists on Inflation" [1], he stated, "Nonetheless the workers' bargaining power may still be too great for price stability even when economic activity is below the optimum level." This statement represents the first explicit indication either by him or any other well known economic theorist, of the possible existence of that theoretical anomaly we now label stagflation.

In a 1949 article, "The Inflationary Process: Some Theoretical Aspects" [2], Lerner differentiated between the effects of rising prices which could be foreseen and those which were unforeseen. While decisionmakers could adjust expectations to the foreseen type and thus minimize its harm, unforeseen price rises result in disappointment of some expectations and thus could cause adverse cyclical movements.

The germs of his first specifically stated wage stabilization plan appear in this article. While he would limit average money wage increases to the level of productivity increases he recognized the adverse allocative effect of the generalization of a single rate of increase. He thus proposed that in those industries defined as attractive, that is, in which the number of job seekers is more than double the number of jobs available, wage increases of one half the average rate be granted; and, in those less attractive industries, in which the number of vacancies more than doubles the number of job seekers, wage increases double the national productivity average rate be granted. He emphasized the point which he has consistently made; namely, that any incomes policy must either replicate market processes and results, or fail in the process. He has consistently made this point during the 1951-53 wage-price stabilization era, the Kennedy-Johnson guidelines period, the various stabilization phases of Nixon, and that belief is central to his current MAP (Market Mechanism Anti-Inflation Plan).

In the same work Dr. Lerner reveals his own preferences regarding his willingness to trade off employment gains for reduction in the rate of inflation. He stated that the then prevailing level of unemployment (around 8-9 percent) was substantially more harmful to economic welfare than the relatively severe inflation between 1946-49. The position taken is that inflation is dangerous and must be controlled not primarily because it engenders high welfare losses but because it generates pressures upon policymakers which would induce them to allow or even pursue deflationary monetary and fiscal policies at less than full employment. In short, the full implementation of functional finance becomes an impossibility if wage increases in excess of productivity gains keep prices rising in a situation of less than "high full" employment.

This was essentially the position taken by Lerner in his August 1951 work, "Controversy Over Monetary Policy." [3] He contended that we, including trade unions and management, are all determined in the abstract to fight inflation but each one of us is also determined "not to be made the goat." Thus no one with sufficient power to influence wages and prices will restrain himself for fear of being "caught short" by the actions of others.

By this time, at least one year before John Kenneth Galbraith published his *American Capitalism: A Theory of Countervailing Power*, Professor Lerner was well aware that the willingess of management to resist inflated union wage demands was limited, if nonexistent. In fact, in administered price industries, since the normal mark-up could be added to wage increases, an increase in wage costs meant an increase in money profits resulting in much lesser resistance if not acquiescence by management to inflationary wage demands. Given this inability or unwillingness by the two parties to countervail each other's power Lerner viewed government, the other countervailing power, as needed to constrain people from ultimately hurting themselves. As he explains in the "Controversy" article, it is the fact that, "given its druthers," our society prefers the 10 percent of added output consonant with high full employment which leads to the ability of unions and management to increase prices. Despite the concern about inflation, Lerner again cautioned against the attempt to impose that degree of restrictive monetary and fiscal policy required to achieve price stability. Price stability, he contended, would be reached at an approximately 4-6 percent higher level of unemployment than full employment, and would result in a sacrifice of at least 10 percent of national output.

PHASE TWO: HIGH AND LOW FULL EMPLOYMENT

Professor Lerner's evolving position in regard to inflation was summarized and put into a more theoretical Keynesian framework in his second major work of book length, *Economics of Employment*, published in 1951. Because that work contains his fullest exposition, not only of Keynesian economics and his developing position on inflation, but also a more explicit treatment regarding the existence of rising prices and unemployment than his previous works, it merits full scrutiny.

The work was commissioned as an elementary textual account and exposition of Keynesian economics. It proved to be much more than that. Important original contributions of the book include its treatment of the multiplier, its discussion of low and high level full employment, its analysis of the conflict of private and social interests with attendant danger to stabilization objectives, and its handling of Say's law.

In this work the concept of high full and low full employment is highly original and central to the further progression of Lerner's view regarding inflation. The high full employment level was defined, at the time, as about 3 percent or 2 million workers without jobs. Unemployment at high full employment is solely frictional, and all increases in total spending lead solely to price level increases. At high full employment the only way of increasing employment and real output without inflation is through improved functioning of the labor market. The low full employment level defined, at the time, as approximately 9 percent unemployment or 6 million workers without jobs, is that level of employment which is compatible with price stability; namely, as a situation in which average wage increases just equal productivity increases. The low full employment level is further defined as that state at which unemployment or unutilized capacity is not regarded as sufficiently high as to induce the major market protagonists to reduce either wages or prices in order to stimulate output and employment.

One can see in his distinction between high and low full employment the essence of the Phillips curve, substantially before it was enunciated and discussed by the profession. Since our post World War II level of unemployment very rarely has been higher than the 9 percent level, what was then defined by Abba Lerner as the low full employment level represents a very early explicit recognition of the existence of what is now almost universally termed stagflation. He stated,

This is what is meant by saying there is a range between 2 million and 6 million unemployed in which we have both depression and inflation. The lower extreme of the range at which wages and prices both begin to rise we shall call 'low full employment.'

In this distinction between high and low full employment Professor Lerner had, in his own later words, "spotted the fatal flaw in the Keynesian schema." His identification with Keynesian theory and his own predilection against any policy which might have an adverse effect upon employment prevented him at that time from grasping the full significance of what seemed to be a theoretical, if not semantic, paradox. In referring to this unwillingness to accept the theoretical flaw inherent in the paradox he stated in the 1966 Ely Lecture before the American Economic Association,

In my first encounter with the indecent entrance of the inflation dragon on the stage before his cue was called, i.e., before full employment was reached, some remnant of the brainwashing made me give the name full employment (albeit low full employment) to the point where the dragon first appeared. . .to legitimize the dragon's prematurity.

The Phillips curve was a reformation of this idea, suggesting that we could do business with the dragon by feeding him a certain number of jobs. [4]

Lerner's objection to the Phillips curve approach rests less on its empirical content than in his unwillingness to accept its implications. The Phillips curve, he contends, implies that we can, by the appropriate monetary and fiscal mix, choose where we want to be. He stated the issue thusly:

It is questionable whether we can obtain a general reduction in prices at the cost of lower levels of employment. We can get higher or lower levels of employment by providing higher or lower levels of spending but between the politically and morally impermissible catastrophic depression that crushes Inflation II (Sellers Inflation) and the excessive demand of Inflation I (Buyers Inflation) the effects on prices and inflation are questionable. [5]

This unwillingness to accept the full theoretical implication, if not contradictions, inherent in the 1951 "low full employment" designation he explained later, in the following statement.

The only excuse I can give for calling this any kind of full employment is that I had not at the time recognized that this was a basic departure from the Keynesian view in which both of these full employments were regarded as identical. It had assumed that the right amount of spending is all that is needed for flation—neither inflation nor deflation. In this language this would mean that low full employment which is required for price stability and which at that time I described as corresponding to 6 million unemployment is identical with only frictional unemployment corresponding to 2 million unemployed in the United States. It is this failure to see the existence or even the possibility of this gap which constituted the inadequacy of the Keynesian theory of inflation and of the functional finance policies for dealing with these problems. [6]

In the course of his work on *Employment* and in subsequent discussions of the problem, Abba Lerner not only reinforced his previously expressed concern that long before high full employment was attained, prices would rise sufficiently to cause policy makers to reverse expansionary functional finance policies, but also utilized that concern to argue for his version of wage guidelines. He stated:

A wage policy is needed to prevent excessive bargaining power of labor from causing inflation as soon as the low level of full employment is reached and thereby preventing the attaining of the high level of full employment. [7]

PHASE THREE: BUYERS AND SELLERS INFLATION

These early views point to the next, that is, late 1950s and early 1960s, phase of Lerner's thinking; namely, of an economy trapped between the high and low full employment level alternating between "administered inflation and administered recession."

Between 1951 and 1960 Dr. Lerner's interest in the problems of inflation and his desire to prevent restrictive monetary and fiscal policy, resulting from the conventional monetarist view that the only cause of inflation was excess monetary demand, did not wane, although superficially the lack of any books or even articles in major journals written by him explicitly about inflation would so indicate. He merely shifted the focal point of his interest to the public policy arena, and to the more popular nonprofessional media, both in Israel, where he was located for three years (1953-56) and subsequently in the United States.

Abba Lerner served as adviser to the Israeli prime minister for two years and for another year as adviser to the Treasury and to the Bank of Israel. This was during a period when Israel was plagued by persistent inflation. These inflationary problems resulted from a high rate of immigration, a high intake of foreign aid and German reparations, most of which became monetized, and a rapid rate of absorption of capital. During this same period Israel also had a fair amount of unemployment.

A considerable body of public opinion reinforced by a number of prominent economists contended that the inflation was the result of high levels of both immigration and capital formation and that any attempt at restrictive policy would be antithetical to both economic growth and immigration. At the same time, it was emphasized, or at least argued, by a number of more traditionally oriented economists that price level stabilization was necessary for any ultimate solution to the balance of payments problem and was a prerequisite to "economic independence." While considerable stabilization had taken place prior to 1955 and the rate of inflation had fallen to about 10 percent, the inflation rate was still relatively much higher than desired.

In his works "Stabilization and Economic Independence" in the Israeli *Quarterly Journal of Economics* (1955) and "Inflation: Will It Wreck The Israeli Economy?" a 1955 memo to Levi Eshkol (Secretary of Treasury), Abba Lerner dealt with these problems and cautioned against restrictive policies which could negate growth, immigrant absorption, capital formation, and employment. However, Lerner soon began to link the inflationary pressures in Israel to wage inflation and in this context he soon was arrayed against the Histadrut, both a huge labor movement and a major owner of industry, which also was the bulwark of the labor political parties.

The Histadrut wage policy had featured a cost of living escalator for all workers plus relatively large wage increases which they justified by rapidly rising man-hour productivity in specific industries. Abba Lerner, in several articles in the

Histadrut newspaper *Davar*, in his *Midstream* article "The Histadrut and the Israeli Economy" (October 1957), and in articles in Israel's *Journal of News and Comment*, hammered on the theme that Histadrut's wage policy, especially the Cost of Living Escalator, not only perpetuated the inflation, but added to costs which made Israel's (and the Histadrut's own industries) output less competitive in world markets. Nominal wages, he argued, should be reduced instead of being allowed to rise. This position aroused considerable controversy within the party and conflict among the responsible cabinet ministers, mainly former Histadrut leaders and the current Histadrut leadership.

Upon his return to the United States, Abba Lerner's attention centered on the American political-economic scene and the late 1950s resurgence of inflation and recession. In a February 1958 article on "Halting the Current Recession—A Proposal for Dealing with Sellers Inflation," he differentiated--as had Professor Sidney Weintraub--Sellers Inflation from Buyers Inflation and reiterated his proposal to restrict wage increases to productivity increases, while allowing market replicated differentials around the average productivity rate. [8, 9] The titles of his written statements mainly before the Joint Economic Committee then headed by the late Senator Paul Douglas, himself an economist of stature, are indicative of the evolution of his thought. [10]

In sum, Abba Lerner's position was that "Sellers Inflation" resulting from the ability of the wage and price—or as alternatively titled markup--administrators to raise wages and prices before full employment is attained, causes policymakers to employ restrictive policies. Although these policymakers had finally and belatedly accepted basic Keynesian employment theory, they continued to believe that all inflation was buyers, or demand pull inflation, and thus attempted to eliminate or at least reduce what they perceived as traditional inflation by restrictive monetary and fiscal policies, including premature budget balancing before full employment was attained.

These fiscal and monetary restrictions, erroneously aimed at restricting aggregate demand, caused what was originally a sellers (or cost push) inflation to become a government administered recession. When the level of unemployment increases sufficiently, as it did in late 1958, more expansionary monetary and fiscal policy ensues, increasing employment until, as happened in late 1959 and early 1960, despite the failure to attain high full employment enough "sellers inflation" has taken place to cause a repeat of the same restrictionist pressures, and another administered recession. This Gordian knot, Lerner contended, can only be cut by preventing a sellers inflation by means of the type of incomes policy which he had been advocating.

The fullest exposition of Dr. Lerner's position during this phase of his career is in his March 31, 1958, paper submitted to the Conference on Economic Stability and Growth. In this paper he contrasts Buyers Inflation (Inflation I) with Sellers Inflation (Inflation II) and attempts to analyze the implications of misconceptions arising from our thinking that inflation and excess demand of buyers are integrally linked. It is paradoxical, he argues, that we use one word (inflation) to describe two different things, rising prices and excess demand, which are not always identical. Excess demand is not the sole cause of rising prices, and prices can rise, as they have most recently, without buyers trying to buy more goods at current prices than are available when productive resources are fully employed. Prices may rise because sellers, that is, wage and price administrators, have the power to raise their prices even though they would like to sell more goods and services. Each type of inflation is the result of the attempt to do what is economically impossible. In the case of Buyers Inflation buyers try to buy more than 100 percent of the goods available at current prices, while Sellers Inflation results from the attempt by the different sellers (labor and management) each to increase their share of the total product, in short causing the sum of their wage and profit claims to exceed 100 percent. The result is that wage increases bring increased selling prices, since producers also attempt to add on their desired share, and then when the increased wages do not buy what was anticipated another round of money wage increases to restore labor's desired share and another increase in selling prices are generated.

The failure to recognize Inflation II as an equally significant cause of inflation, he argued, is not only attributable to the fact that economic theory recognized only excess demand from buyers as the unitary cause of inflation but also because Sellers Inflation frequently is masked by rising aggregate demand, especially if the authorities attempt to maintain full employment by pursuing policies which increase aggregate spending. Thus when rising prices force the authorities to remove what they believe is excess demand they remove demand which was not in excess, causing unemployment but not in sufficient amounts to remove pressure from sellers.

The contention by some economists that the behavior of prices in the competitive sector belies the possible existence of sellers inflation, according to Lerner, overlooks the process by which inflation spreads from the administered price sector to the competitive one.   As Lerner saw it, although unemployment exists in the administered sector, prices are still rising, and thus the change in relative prices causes demand to spill over to the competitive sector.   Under these conditions, if government increases demand to prevent more unemployment in the admini- stered price sector, demand spillovers intensify; and thus, what originally was sellers inflation has become a self-fulfilling pro- phecy in the competitive sector, which is likely to be an even more price volatile one.

In sum, sellers inflation starts in the administered sector, spreads to the competitive sector, and the end consequence is inflationary depression.   To prevent this, the wage and price administrators should be regulated just as public utilities are. This is the case for wage guidelines designed to remove pressure upon the two sets of mark-up administration which induce them to try to obtain more than 100 percent of the total product.

Drs. Lerner and Weintraub were not the only prominent economic theorists at this time to enunciate these cost push views. Dr. Gardner Ackley, later to become Chairman of the President's Council of Economic Advisors during the Johnson administration, and Dr. Charles L. Schultze, the current incum- bent of this post, both maintained similar views.   Ackley's statement at the same Joint Economic Committee hearings is equally pointed in this regard. He states:

> My views on this question are clear cut.   They are that post-war inflation is not basically the direct result of excess demand. It has continued in the face of consider- able deficiency of demand. It seems to me that inflation in our post-war economy can be understood primarily as a process of jockeying for relative position between capital and labor. In effect, the two groups extend claims that add up to more than the total product. Not only do administered prices and wages not fall in response to excess supply, they can and do rise if costs rise. Since every price is someone else's cost, all costs and prices can rise with excess supply. [11]

Although inflation continued to occupy Lerner's interests and concern during the rest of the 1960s, that interest was in some respects subordinated to other interests, and when he alluded to the problem it was in the context of Keynesian theory and what he increasingly acknowledged as the incompleteness of Keynes's schema.   Underlying this incompleteness, he argued, was the strong implication in Keynes that excess demand was the sole explanation for inflation.

In general, during the early 1960s the problem of inflation was seemingly muted by the Kennedy wage guidelines. Although contending that the Kennedy guideposts would ultimately fail because of their disregard for what should have been market-imposed wage differentials, Lerner nevertheless felt they worked sufficiently well during the first two- to three-year period to assure at least a sufficient degree of price stability so as not to negate the somewhat expansionary fiscal policies pursued.

As Lerner foretold, these guideposts would ultimately break down because workers in high productivity industries at the top of the wage range were able to secure wage increases which were considerably in excess of the average rate of productivity increase.   This high rate of increase tended to be generalized even in industries characterized by low or even negative rates of productivity gain, thus causing a ratchet effect of higher prices originating from the low productivity sector which then spilled over to the highly productive industries.

With the tax rate cut of 1964, which Lerner initially felt was a major step toward full adoption of functional finance policies, the economy went into what he would have termed full employment, and relative price stability prevailed until 1966-67, when the substantial increase in aggregate demand due to the expansion of the military efforts in Vietnam and the failure to raise tax rates generated a conventional buyers inflation.

In the Ely Lecture before the American Economic Association in December 1966 Abba Lerner summed up and restated his central theme concerning inflation. In linking this analysis to a broad review of the state of Keynesian economics after thirty years in this presentation he acknowledged for the first time the flaw in the Keynesian framework which he had inferred, but never explicitly stated.

Dr. Lerner attributed this flaw to several confusions and obscurities in Keynes, which either were not apparent or else not important at the time Keynes wrote. The key element, he contended, was the recognition of downward rigidity of wages and prices which Keynes obscured by focusing on the inability of workers to reduce their real wages.   Lerner wrote:

> This confusion was compounded by Keynes' denial of the classical notion that complete wage flexibility could cure unemployment by increasing the real value of claims to wealth.   Keynes referred to the actual degree of flexibility achievable in the real world which could easily be swamped by decreased expectations.   Both the Keynesians and the classicists were right; but both failed to see that recognition of downward rigidity involved nothing less than the dethronement of the market as the determinant of prices.

> If supply is greater than demand, then the market is telling price to fall; if it does not fall, it is obeying a more powerful master—a price administrator (or administrators) who could just as well tell prices to go up when the market is telling it to go down (or stand still). [12]

This is what we see in the unKeynesian co-existence of unemployment with inflation. He stated:

> [It is] unKeynesian because Keynes not only did not see this possibility himself but even succeeded in banishing it from the vision of others.   In 1935 or 1936 Robert Bryce and I asked Keynes whether the maintenance of sufficient effective demand for full employment would not result in perpetuating inflation.   Keynes could not understand the question, although we persisted until we exhausted his patience and our own, for the question of administered inflation seems to have been washed from my brain for a decade or so after this incident. [13, 14]

In the same Ely Lecture, Abba Lerner again reiterated his view that the alleged trade-off between employment and inflation in the case of sellers inflation is a questionable one.   He argued that acting against a sellers inflation through attempts to reduce aggregate demand merely reduces employment without necessarily reducing the degree of sellers inflation.   In short, with sellers inflation, we could sacrifice jobs and sales to the inflation dragon without deterring the dragon one iota.   He emphasized that because most of us are both buyers and sellers simultaneously, the effects of inflation cancel out in most cases, and thus the degree of welfare loss, which could be attributed to 1 percent of inflation, was estimated by him at the relatively small rate of one sixteenth of a percent. The corresponding output loss for a 1 percent reduction in employment is 2-3 percent of national output. Nevertheless, Lerner believed inflation must be stopped in order to forestall any pressures to reduce aggregate demand. In this trade-off Lerner would not encourage an attempt to reduce demand unless it was certain that the inflationary pressures were of the buyers, or demand-pull, type.

The solution, Lerner argued, to rectifying the fundamental flaw in the Keynesian analysis is a policy through which wages and prices would be induced to behave properly. Wage guideposts which would be based upon the average level of productivity increase and which adjusted the average rate of change to conditions in specific labor and product markets would make wages and prices behave as if market determined. Although wage and price guideposts are not a substitute for monetary and fiscal regulation of effective demand they are a requisite for any stable full employment policy and the restoration of credibility to Keynesian analysis and policies.

PHASE FOUR: EXPECTATIONAL INFLATION

Dr. Lerner's 1972 work *Flation* his only major work specifically addressed to the problem of inflation, not only restated, albeit in somewhat reformulated form, his previous thinking on the subject, but also contributed new concepts and a modified view of the inflationary process. A half decade of continuous and mounting inflationary pressure coincident with a relatively severe recession in 1970-71, the imposition of wage and price controls in the latter half of 1971, all contributed to these modifications in his approach.

In his opening chapter, "Why is This Inflation Different from All Other Inflation?" Professor Lerner differentiates a Sellers Inflation from a Buyers Inflation in the following fashion:

> In the inflation of 1970-71, all the symptoms associated with excess demand were absent. Prices were rising but the sellers who were getting the higher prices were not making unusually high profits. Instead, they were generally making unusually low profits. Producers were not trying to produce more to sell at the higher prices. They were having great difficulty in selling their current out-

put. Shopkeepers, instead of being able to choose among eager buyers, were trying hard to persuade their customers to come in and buy more. They were not limiting their sales of a scarce item to those who agreed to buy some profitable item. On the contrary, the customer was often given something with the item he bought or was given the right to buy something at an especially low price. Sellers were more polite than usual and more eager to sell than usual. They tried to make stores more attractive and to help customers find what they wanted. Buyers, if they had the money to pay the price, found it very easy to buy and sellers found it very difficult to sell. There was a deficiency of demand. [15]

Lerner in this work restates the Keynesian contradiction which associates inflation and deflation with too much or too little spending, but could be construed as arguing, if inverted, that if there is not too much spending, there will be no inflation, and if there is not too little spending, there will be no depression. He argues,

Keynesian theory and functional finance thus seemed to be saying, in the case of stagflation, two contradictory things; namely, that we can have at the same time too little and too much spending. This has led to the loss of credibility of Keynesian theory and the functional finance policies derived from it. [16]

In *Flation* Abba Lerner introduces a new type of inflation which he terms Inflation III or Expectational Inflation. That type of inflation leads to what he terms defensive behavior, that is, the attempt to raise wages and prices in order to defend one's relative position in the face of an expected price increase as contrasted with Type II inflation, which results from "offensive" attempts to improve relative income shares.

Expectational inflation can be triggered by any number of causes; for example, sustained buyers inflation, such as took place during 1967-69, a rise in input or raw material prices in foreign markets, or even an organizational change in the trade union movement. Once buyers and sellers expect a certain level of inflation and act accordingly the "attainment" of that level of inflation becomes a self-fulfilling prophecy.

This recognition of expectational inflation necessitates revision of previously held notions regarding the levels of economic activity at which prices could be expected to be stable. According to Professor Lerner, the belief in full employment at stable prices rested upon an assumption never previously made explicit; namely, a normal expectation by buyers and sellers both of price and wage stability. But when the normal expectations are of 10 percent inflation and wage-price administrators act accordingly, then aggregate supply and demand will be in balance only at a 10 percent level of price rise. Deficiencies in aggregate demand at the levels of employment (or unemployment) currently experienced in the United States would, according to him, lead only to a slightly lower level of inflation than the 10 percent expected. Thus the rise in prices, resulting from defensive actions by the pair of mark-up administrators, tends to cluster around the rate of inflation which, by virtue of previous experience, they now expect.

This formulation redefined low full employment, which Lerner contends is synonymous with Milton Friedman's "Natural Rate of Unemployment." The low full employment level now is defined in terms of the rate of price level increase which approaches the level of expected inflation.

The implication resulting from Inflation III is that the level of unemployment consonant with absolute price stability would be unacceptably high. Thus, until Inflation III pressures could be removed, the attempt to attain absolute price stability through monetary and fiscal measures would prove socially and politically inadmissible.

Dr. Lerner employs the existence of expectational inflation to reinforce his argument for a strong incomes policy. He states:

> The elimination of Inflation III, expectational inflation, even though it is only defensive, is essential for genuine stability. The elimination of Inflation II is not sufficient. Even if we have a sufficiently low level of employment so that attempts to get more than 100 percent are crushed, and even if we have a sufficiently high level of understanding so that the different parties do not try to get more among themselves than is available inflation will continue in the absence of an incomes policy as long as there is an expectation of rising prices. And the parties

to production will perpetuate inflation in their fear of having their shares eaten away by the inflation they are perpetuating. [17, 18, 19]

A major restatement of Dr. Lerner's position in the light of the controversy regarding the "demise" of Keynesian economics appears in a recent work published in the 1977 autumn issue of *Social Research* titled "From Pre-Keynes to Post-Keynes." In this original and provocative article which shows his continuing ability to make important theoretical contributions which convey policy implications, Dr. Lerner summarizes the periods encompassed within his conceptual time frame in the following way:

Pre-Keynes: With a stable money supply, economic prosperity and price stability require only that wages (and thus prices) behave themselves; that is, adjust to the money supply.

Keynes: With steady wages (and thus stable prices) prosperity requires only that the money supply behave itself and adjust to the wage and price level.

Post-Keynes: Both money supply and wages must behave themselves. For prosperity money supply must adjust to wages (prices). For price stability the average wage can rise only with an increase in productivity.

Lerner contended that pre-Keynesian analysis dealt only with microeconomic adjustments while Keynes's analysis was macroeconomic and dealt primarily with governmental adjustments of the money level of aggregate demand. Post-Keynesian analysis involves synchronization of both micro and macroeconomic policy.

In this work Professor Lerner again emphasizes the effect of inflationary expectations to reiterate the need for a plan designed to stabilize expectations as a prerequisite to stabilizing the price level. The plan should not only restrict the average level of wage increase granted in the economy to the rate of average national increase in productivity, but also must preserve the proper microeconomic pattern of wage differentials consonant with market forces. Such a plan, originally titled as WIP (Wage Increase Plan), but now named MAP (Market Anti-Inflation Plan) is the one he and Professor Colander propose in this work.

CONCLUSION

Dr. Lerner's thinking has been manifested in four distinct phases, each of which represent a steadily evolving and increasingly sophisticated formulation of his thought. The first phase emphasized the influence of collective bargaining upon money wages and prices and the resultant incompatibility of free collective bargaining with economic stabilization goals of full employment at stable prices; the second is characterized by the distinction between high and low full employment; the third is one in which the emphasis shifts to sellers inflation as contrasted with buyers inflation; and the last is the phase in which expectational inflation and defensive action by sellers are the focal points of emphasis.

Through all of these phases he has consistently maintained a position that full employment should not be jeopardized by deflationary functional finance policies directed indiscriminately against all forms of inflation; that in the case of sellers inflation the Phillips curve trade-off between price level and employment changes is an illusory one; that departures of any significance from full employment would be far more harmful to national economic and social welfare than inflation, and that an incomes policy which facilitates market replicated wage and price differentials is the only viable solution to maintaining full employment without inflation.

No matter the stand by a particular economist on the cause of and solutions to the inflationary problem and his/her willingness to sacrifice employment objectives—whether one is a monetarist, fiscalist, or an eclecticist—there is full agreement among all that Abba P. Lerner has made important and original contributions to our understanding of, and possible solution to, the inflationary problem.

NOTES

1. This symposium was published in the *Review of Economics and Statistics*, 30:1 (February 1948) p. 1-29.
2. *Review of Economics and Statistics* (August 1949) p. 193-216.
3. *Review of Economics and Statistics*, 33:3 (August 1951) p. 179-200.
4. Ely Lecture, Allied Social Science Association, December 27, 1966 in *Proceedings of American Economic Association*, (May 1967) p. 3.
5. Abba P. Lerner, *Flation*, New York: Quadrangle Books, 1972, p. 126.
6. *Flation*, op. cit., p. 125.

7. *The Economics of Employment*, copywrite in 1951 by McGraw Hill.   Reprinted in 1978 by Greenwood Press, Westport, Conn., p. 193.

8. "Commentary," February 1958.

9. Sidney Weintraub, whose work also appears in this volume, observed the same phenomena and influenced the terminology involved.

10.   These are: "Inflationary Depression and the Regulation of Administered Prices" (March 31 1958); "Inflationary Depression," Summary Opening Statement for the Joint Economic Committee (May 15 1958); "Statement to the Joint Economic Committee for the Study of Employment, Growth, and Price Levels" (September 1959); and a statement made before the Center for Democratic Institutions titled "Administered Depression" (November 1961); a similarly titled article in the *Review of Latin American Economics* in Spanish; and a paper titled "Collective Bargaining" also before the Center for Democratic Institutions.   This phase of Abba's career was concluded by a policy paper, "Sellers Inflation and Administered Depression: Administered Prices," before the subcommittee on Anti-Trust and Monopoly (1963).

11.   Joint Economic Committee, *Hearings*,   May 15 1968, p. 304.

12.   *American Economic Review*, May 1967, op. cit. p. 4.

13.   *American Economic Review*, May 1967, op. cit., p. 2.

14. In his lecture Lerner reiterated his intellectual debt to Sidney Weintraub who had earlier emphasized that sellers inflation resulted from the combined attempt by the parties to obtain more than 100 percent of the product.

15. Op cit, *Flation*, p. 10-11.

16.   Ibid., p. 45.   "In fact, functional finance seemed to be saying that avoiding inflation could not be achieved by bringing about the right amount of public spending."

17. Ibid.

18. *Flation* summarizes and analyzes various proposals, especially TIP (Tax Incentive Plan), espoused by Sidney Weintraub and Henry Wallich, and discussed by Weintraub elsewhere in this volume, which were designed to limit wage increases through taxing or imposing penalties on individuals and firms in which wage increases above a certain level took place.

19.   Dr. Lerner continued to amplify and restate his position relating inflation and Keynesian theory in papers for the Industrial Conference Board; in "Wage Price Policy: The Theoretical Issues," and two lectures at the University of British Columbia

"The Challenge of Full Employment with Price Stability, and Income Policies" (1973) and "Market Power and and the Wage Price Problem" (1974); and in "Wage Price Controls II: Appraisal of U.S. Wage and Price Control System" which appeared in the *American Statistical Association Journal* (1974). In 1974 and 1975 he wrote several letters about the current recession in the *New York Times* and an article, "Stagflation: Its Cause and Cure," appeared in the October 1977 issue of *Challenge Magazine*.

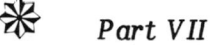 *Part VII*

SYNOPSIS AND SYNTHESIS

※ *Chapter 16*

POST-KEYNESIAN INFLATION: CAUSES, CONSEQUENCES, AND CONTROLS

*James H. Gapinski**
*Charles E. Rockwood**

PROLOGUE

The chapters in this volume indicate a much stronger agreement than might be supposed on where economists stand in the struggle to comprehend and control the post-Keynesian inflation-unemployment dilemma. This consensus emerges despite the fact that the authors were selected not only for their expertise in one or more aspects of the inflation problem, but for the diversity of their viewpoints as well.

Consider but one dichotomy, that most often cited when the inflation-unemployment topic is discussed: monetarists versus fiscalists. The volume contains contributions from both. Yet, the views and conclusions of these two groups, as presented in this work, are surprisingly similar. Neither group appears mystified by stagflation, the simultaneous existence of inflation and unemployment, and both groups assign the same basic reasons for the joint appearance of these two scourges of the modern economy. Both also recognize the importance, and the insufficiency, of monetary policy in dealing with the problem.

The papers in this volume, too, represent an impressive illustration of the depth of professional understanding about the post-Keynesian inflation-unemployment problem. Even to one familiar with the literature, it is remarkable how far the profession has come since the mid-forties. As Irvin Sobel describes, thirty-five years ago economists were likely to view

*Professor of Economics, Florida State University.

deflation as synonymous with depression, and the possibility of inflation occurring in the face of pronounced unemployment was barely acknowledged. Economic thinking then grew to accept that possibility and offered an explanation for it under the heading of cost push. Further refinement in thinking has led to the recent notion of expectational inflation. With this progression of knowledge has come successive insights for inflation control, and in that regard the frontier is now dotted with incomes policies such as WIP, TIP and MAP; namely, the Wage Increase Plan, the Tax-based Incomes Policy and the Market Antiinflation Plan.

During the evolution of the economic perception of inflation, Abba Lerner was a principal trailblazer. Sobel notes that through Lerner the profession uncovered in 1944 propositions of functional finance, in 1947 arguments urging incomes policy via wage guidelines, and also in that year clues to the coexistence of inflation and recession. It witnessed in 1951 the twin concept of high full and low full employment, which served as a precursor of the relationship eventually credited to A.W. Phillips. In 1958 the doctrine of cost push emerged. The latest to bear Lerner's imprint are the concept of expectational inflation and the control programs WIP and MAP.

From the broad perspective painted by Sobel, the cost-push, demand-pull debates of decades past seem annoyingly transparent. True, much remains that is still not understood; the previous chapters make this clear. But the need for more wisdom should not cloud the gains which the profession has made in comprehending the inflation-unemployment problem.

CAUSES OF INFLATION

Several authors in this collection of essays take a careful look at the mechanism of inflation. Tibor Scitovsky, for instance, notes that inflation may occur quite independently of the unemployment level because of incompatible demands over income shares; that is, because of cost-push pressures. Some disturbance to the domestic economy, perhaps from the OPEC cartel, may cause an initial price rise which leads to the realization by entrepreneurs and workers alike that labor is too cheap relative to its marginal worth. In this circumstance workers demand—with or without benefit of union power—a wage increase, and entrepreneurs, knowing that cost increases can be passed forward to consumers, respond favorably to their request. Profits fall, prices rise, and real wages decline. The process repeats. This wage-price spiral emanates, according to Scitovsky, from market forces operating in an economy where producers have the initiative and remain active price makers in both product and labor markets.

E. Ray Canterbery joins Scitovsky in highlighting the struggle over income shares as the basis for a wage-price spiral. He insists, however, that the spiral is more deeply embedded in the economic fabric than has been believed because producers, who generally enjoy the power to raise prices, have succeeded in convincing consumers to expand the number of commodities which they regard as necessities and whose continued purchase during inflationary periods determines the size of wage increases to be demanded. In other words, the magnitude of wage hikes due to producer-induced price increases reflects perceived needs determined in great part by producers themselves. Collective bargaining is more a standard of living issue than it is a money wage dispute.

William Baumol studies the inflation mechanism using two models couched in microeconomic terms. One paradigm, suggested by Fritz Machlup, has as its basis both the high unemployment of unskilled individuals due to minimum wage laws and the political liability which that unemployment represents. That unemployment lures politicians to increase market demand, even though overall unemployment remains low, thereby forcing prices upward. Real wages fall, and to restore the minimum wage to its previous real level it must be raised, generating once again the need for increased aggregate demand. This sequence recurs. The second model considered by Baumol takes the form of a long-run Phillips curve trade-off. In this framework, which emphasizes the importance of expectations in the micro foundation of inflation, the desire by policy makers (alias politicians) to maintain low overall unemployment is sufficient to perpetuate price increases.

While acknowledging the self-generating nature of the wage-price process and the key role of expectations in that process, Leonard Rapping directs his energies to investigating the political underlay of inflation. He points to the erosion of United States power globally and to the consequent inability of the country to control external events. To Rapping, the decline in America's influence and the inability of the government to deal strongly with world events constitute the root cause of inflation. Put differently, inflation is the economic manifestation of a weak government.

The expectational basis of inflation is further discussed by Abba Lerner, who asserts that a wage-price spiral may not reflect the desire by workers and employers to divide *more* than one-hundred percent of aggregate income between them. Rather, it may represent their attempt to protect themselves, given expected higher prices, from obtaining *less* in terms of goods and services than they have been receiving. The government becomes drawn into the inflation race because, without additional spending during inflation, the quantity purchased would fall as would employment. Inflation, therefore, has a tripartite character with prices, wages, and spending all chasing each other. According to Lerner, the demand-pull and cost-push types of price advance can degenerate into this expectational variant.

Monetary and fiscal excesses are accepted by all the authors as potential causes of inflation, and they are underscored by some. Martin Bronfenbrenner, addressing the international dimension of inflation, examines the price response to monetary growth and fiscal deficits prompted by an increase in the import price of a key commodity which is complementary to domestic inputs. Oil serves as the illustration. Bronfenbrenner concludes that the monetary and fiscal indulgence could heighten the domestic price rise occasioned directly by the import price increase.

Similarly, Kenneth Boulding, based on statistical time profiles which he calls maps, attributes the United States inflation between 1947 and 1970 to a rise in the money supply and cites an escalation in the federal deficit as the factor responsible for the inflationary binge after 1970. He wonders, however, if the money supply increases underlying the price increases were not themselves caused by earlier inflationary pressures. Raised, therefore, is a chicken-or-egg issue. Which comes first? Money increases or price increases?

Rapping, while agreeing that demand-pull pressures existed at least in the mid-sixties, regards excessive monetary expansion as at best a proximate cause of inflation. Following Boulding he asks, Why does such money expansion occur? Don Patinkin asks the same question only more technically: Is the quantity of money exogenous or endogenous? Furthermore, notes Patinkin, since alterations in fiscal policy may also lead to inflation, it is the cause of those alterations which must be understood if inflation is to be fully understood.

In his review of the monetary and fiscal underpinnings of inflation, Mancur Olson attacks the prevailing monetarist and

Keynesian orthodoxies for being crucially incomplete. Their parochialism is revealed by a failure both to anticipate stagflation and to explain its existence except through *ad hoc* arguments. This failure, he believes, accounts for the prevalence of the cost-push theory of inflation; it essentially filled the vacuum created by incomplete doctrines. Ignored by the conventional viewpoints is the gradual but nevertheless resolute evolution and accumulation of organizations which attempt to further the interests of their members through combined market action or through political lobbying efforts. This change in economic structure explains to Olson the empirical observation that stagflation is really a progressive phenomenon which has become more pronounced over time. Common-interest organizations are responsible for the downward stickiness of wages and prices, and this rigidity tends to convert a decrease in aggregate demand into a decline in output and a rise in unemployment. According to Olson, common-interest groups lie at the heart of both the short-run and the long-run Phillips curve trade-offs.

CONSEQUENCES OF INFLATION

Effects of inflation are considered by Ray Canterbery, who views purchases by a household as separable into a hierarchy of commodity bundles. Food, clothing, housing, and transportation all compatible with minimum "subsistence" levels comprise four bundles of necessities listed in descending order of utility. Other bundles, yielding even lower utility levels, represent nonnecessities. Given this taxonomy the welfare effects of inflation depend crucially upon the pattern of price rises; specifically, *which* prices are rising? Recent inflation has been especially acute for food, utilities, housing, and fuel--for the necessities--and households respond by shifting expenditures away from nonnecessities in order to maintain their previous level of subsistence items. In the process the household's total utility falls. Moreover, this shift from nonnecessities means that production and employment losses occur in the industries associated with them, and these losses are not matched by corresponding increases in the industries associated with necessities. Thus, on balance, production and employment decline.

Another effect of inflation regards the balance of trade. As Martin Bronfenbrenner shows, inflation tends to create trade deficits. Explained simply, an increase in domestic prices implies that foreign products become cheaper relative to their domestic counterparts, and this change makes foreign goods more desirable to domestic consumers and domestic goods less desirable to foreigners. Thus, imports rise while exports fall. A flexible exchange rate could allow restoration of trade balance equilibrium but only after a delay exceeding one year.

In his discussion of the effects which inflation exerts on behavior patterns, Don Patinkin recalls the Israeli experience in which the price level has risen one-hundred fold in forty years. During the present decade, Israel's annual inflation rate soared to over thirty percent. Yet despite the torrid pace of prices, Israelis have proceeded with their life-styles much as usual. Some adjustments have been made, of course. For instance, people choose to hold assets in real form when possible. Exemplifying this preference is the popularity of condominiums in Israel: most workers own their apartments. These adjustments aside, however, consumer behavior has remained quite stable in the face of appreciable inflation.

An additional reaction to inflation, comments Patinkin, is the emergence of indexation, by which price increases in some sectors of the economy are formally tied to price increases elsewhere in the economy. In Israel, the government began in the early 1950s to issue an indexed bond whose nominal interest rate varied with the level of prices. This action was taken because the government, faced by a doubling of the price level in the period 1949-51, would otherwise have experienced considerable difficulty selling bonds to finance its budget. While indexation still remains in Israel today, there is disillusionment with the policy. To Patinkin, indexation may have had the effect of accelerating inflation, since it has impaired the ability of relative prices to change.

Edmund Phelps expresses agreement with Patinkin on the indexation issue, although Phelps deals with the United States. Phelps remarks that indexation in wage contracts could prevent a change in relative prices (wages) and thus create difficulties for inflation control. Fortunately, suggests Phelps, wage indexation applies to only a small segment of the United States labor market and might easily collapse under stress.

POTENTIAL INFLATION CONTROLS

The authors in this volume agree that the solution to present inflation cannot lie exclusively in traditional monetary and fiscal restraint, but should include other, more direct, forms of market control. Charles Rockwood argues that conventional monetary and fiscal prescriptions for combating inflation can be extremely expensive. Because the short-run Phillips curve is very flat on the contraction side, inflation restraint through traditional policy action would lead to substantial output forfeiture for the short run, and similar prospects exist for the long run. Needed then is some program of direct controls to supplement conventional policy maneuvers. Reviewing econometric evidence on various episodes of wage and price controls, Rockwood concludes that they can be effective but that, since controls have a tendency to break down over time, they must be limited to a short duration, perhaps two to four years. An essential condition for the success of direct controls, according to Rockwood, is restrictive monetary and fiscal policy, which should be invoked before direct controls are applied.

Kenneth Boulding believes that inflation control must involve some interference in financial contracts. Although he grants that inflation could be curbed quickly by Draconian policies such as a twenty percent increase in income taxation or the imposition of a temporary wage-price freeze, he fears that such measures would cause unemployment to soar to intolerable levels. Unemployment would increase, he maintains, because real interest rates would rise above real profit rates, and hence, entrepreneurs would be motivated to purchase securities with their funds rather than to hire workers. To avoid this imbalance between the rates of profit and interest, the government might find it necessary to declare existing financial contracts null and void. Inflation could then be checked without substantial unemployment.

A different type of inflation control is urged by David Colander. He addresses the recent challenge made by the rational expectations, or perfect foresight, hypothesis to the principles of functional finance developed by Abba Lerner many years earlier. According to some proponents of that hypothesis, rational expectations render the maintenance of price stability impossible and make functional finance ineffective as a short-run stabilization tool. The government simply ceases to be important in stabilization activity. Rather than taking such a classical stance, Colander proposes that the scope of functional finance be broadened to include a dictum that the government must establish policies which stabilize prices, and must coordinate its other functional finance rules with the stable price level. As one method of implementing this new desideratum, Colander calls for MAP, the Market Antiinflation Plan, which he and Abba Lerner fashioned jointly. Under MAP the price level is determined by law and expectations, while money and aggregate demand are adjusted to that price level. In this setting individuals need not worry about how to rationally predict the price level because the government sets it by direct decree.

Abba Lerner emphasizes the need for MAP and elaborates some of its details. Because, he claims, expectations form the basis of inflationary behavior—with workers and entrepreneurs raising wages and prices to protect themselves from the effects of anticipated higher prices and with the government increasing expenditures to prevent mass unemployment—the cure lies in eliminating the expectation of inflation. Endorsing William Baumol's position that expectations do not respond promptly to rhetoric, Lerner dismisses "jawboning" as useless for dealing with expectational inflation. He hypothesizes that its elimination can be accomplished only by attacking all three links in the inflation chain simultaneously. MAP does precisely this. It works directly on wages and prices (profits) thus allowing the government to use its more traditional tools to maintain the general health of the economy.

This plan creates a new commodity called an anti-inflation accounting credit, essentially a permission slip to raise price. Credits are bought and sold in the open market, and consequently market forces establish their price. It is this price which acts as the disincentive necessary to restrain inflation. When inflation and its expectational basis cease, the price of MAP credit falls to zero. In Lerner's view, MAP could lead to price stability rather quickly.

An alternative inflation control program is advocated by Sidney Weintraub. Known as TIP, the Tax Incentive Plan, it envisions an additional corporate income tax on those firms in the concentrated sector that raise average money wages and salaries above some target level, say five percent. Only the largest 1,000 or 2,000 firms would fall within the ambit of TIP. Since prices reflect unit labor costs, which would be constrained by the program, price increases, too, would be constrained. Released from the worry about inflation, the government could use its conventional monetary and fiscal instruments to steer the economy closer to full employment.

In reviewing the merits of MAP and TIP, William Baumol appeals to the theory of externalities. Agreeing with Charles Rockwood that the Phillips curve is asymmetric—that it exhibits flatness on the contraction side—Baumol asks why this should be. He notes that the cornerstone of the asymmetry is a separation of individual interests from group interests. Voluntary abstention by an individual or by an individual labor union from demanding wage increases would do little to relieve overall inflationary pressures, and nevertheless would place the individual or the union members at the complete mercy of rising prices. In short, the individual would gain little through separate action, while losing much. Collective action is needed. Inflation can therefore be regarded as an externalities problem, and from this interpretation comes the clue to its treatment.

Baumol recalls that Pigou proposed to control externalities through taxes and subsidies, and Baumol likens TIP to a Pigouvian tax. A second measure to control externalities consists of pollution rights which can be freely traded in the open market. The inflation counterpart of these, of course, are the Lerner-Colander MAP credits. Baumol holds that TIP faces significant drawbacks. Because of expectations TIP may leave relative prices unchanged, and consequently it need not provide any motivation for behavior different from that which would result without TIP. Succinctly, TIP's effort to reduce inflation might be completely frustrated. But worse could occur: TIP, working through inflationary expectations, may have the perverse effect of accelerating inflation. By contrast, Baumol argues, MAP does not share these limitations. Furthermore, it should not distort relative prices and should not misallocate resources. According to Baumol, then, MAP seems superior to TIP.

Rising to the defense of TIP, Sidney Weintraub underscores its practical merit; namely, its ease of implementation and enforcement. It would rely on established functions of the Internal Revenue Service and would require only a few extra lines on the corporate income tax form. Under TIP monitoring, policing, and imposing sanctions are clearly defined features. Weintraub criticizes MAP, claiming it to be an unfinished blueprint devoid of operational specifics regarding compliance and enforcement. Since MAP must cover roughly thirteen million firms, as opposed to TIP's 2,000, these essential elements would be difficult to secure. Furthermore, Weintraub cautions that MAP, unlike TIP, could usher in stagflation, the very anomaly it hopes to avert.

PROSPECTS FOR INFLATION CONTROL

Abba Lerner and David Colander display optimism about the prospects for reining inflation.   So do Sidney Weintraub and Charles Rockwood.   Elizabeth Bailey, in her review of recent experience with airline deregulation, advises that to achieve economic successes such as inflation control, a partnership between scholarly research and political astuteness must be established.   Manifestly, sophisticated research abounds on the subject of inflation, and thus, reminiscent of the exchange between Robert Eisner and W. H. Locke Anderson in the sixties, it might be said that economic "fact" should hope for an early marriage with political "fancy."

Some authors are hardly sanguine about the possibility of controlling inflation.   Kenneth Boulding laments that while a full-employment, anti-inflation policy is feasible, its execution requires more knowledge than now exists.   It also requires a very different political will, and on that point, he is not ebullient. Rapping concurs with Boulding's bleak assessment. Patinkin, too, indicates skepticism that anti-inflation schemes can work and attributes his diffidence to the many past attempts at inflation control which have failed.   Experience has taught him that winning the fight against inflation is difficult.   Edmund Phelps expresses similar sentiments.   While acknowledging that a controls program could restrain inflation, he strongly doubts that policy makers possess the necessary economic wit or political nerve to achieve much success in their quest.

CONCLUDING COMMENT

While it is possible to remain pessimistic about the prospects for inflation control, especially since inadequate remedies for inflation may be one of its causes, the discussion in this volume offers some encouraging signs.   Economists have done their homework on inflation.   They have studied its causes and its consequences, and they have developed a set of strategies to deal with it.   There is consensus that inflation involves a self-perpetuating mechanism, and that expectations play a principal role both in the cause of inflation and in its control.   There is also consensus that indexation, born of the malady, does not qualify as one of its unquestionable tempering agents.   Perhaps most importantly, there is growing agreement that the solution to inflation must entail some form of direct market control.

NAME INDEX

Abramovitz, Moses, 158
Ackley, Gardner, 276-77
Anderson, Paul S., 176
Anderson, W. H. Locke, 298
Archibald, G. C., 60,76
Askin, A. Bradley, 166-67,175-76
Aukrust, Odd, 9,116
Azariadis, Costas,214

Bailey, Elizabeth E., ii,251,298
Baily, Martin Neil, 214
Bakes, Philip, 255
Barnett, Hunter, xvii
Barro,Robert,76
Baumol, William J., ii,55,64,76,245,291, 297
Benjamini, Yael, 65
Bergstrom,A.R., 76
Blackman, Sue Anne Batey, 77
Boulding, Kenneth E., ii,11,292,295,298
Braybrooke, David, 102
Brenner, Reuven, 131
Brinner, Roger, 166,176
Bronfenbrenner, Martin, ii,49,107,292-93
Brown, Robert, xvii
Brown, William A. Jr., 49
Brunner, Karl, 175
Bryce, Robert, 178

Cagan, Phillip, 145-47,149,155-56,158-59
Cannon, John, 255,259
Canterbery, E. Ray, ii,51,79,102-03,291, 293

Carter, James Earl, 115,255
Causseaux, Martha, xvi
Caves, Richard, 253,261
Chesterton, G.K., 226
Chipman, J.S., 102
Churchill, Sir Winston, 157
Colander, David C., ii,174,179,188-89,197, 215,229,238,241-46,282,295-98
Crandall, Robert, 251,260
Crotty, James, 51
Cushing, Brian, 158

Dillard, Dudley, 158
Diocletian [Roman Emperor], 169
Douglas, George W., 254,261
Douglas, Paul H., 274

Eads, George C., 254,261
Eckstein, Otto, 165-66,169,175-76
Eisner, Robert, 298
Eshkol, Levi, 273
Espino, Maria, xvi

Fellner, William, 203,213
Ferguson, C.E., 193,213
Firestone, Harvey, 40
Ford, Gerald, 115,171
Ford, Henry, 40
Franco, Carol, xvii
Friedman, Milton, 103,158,204,214
Frisch, Ragnar, 88,103

Galbraith, John Kenneth, 95,269

Gapinski, James H., ii,iii,289
Garraty, John A., 159
Gaskins, Darius, 255
Girola, James A., 165-66,169,175
Goldthorpe, John H., 33,50
Gordon, Robert J., 166,175-76,214
Gould, J.P., 193,213
Grimes, Nancy, xvi

Haworth, Joan, xvi
Hall, Robert E., 260
Hayek, Frederick A., 213
Hickman, Bert G., 213
Hirsch, Fred, 33,50
Holzman, Franklyn D., 176
Hoover, Herbert, 192
Houthakker, H.S., 88,103
Hume, David, 145
Humphrey, Hubert H., 115

Ironmonger, D.S., 102

Johnson, Harry G., 102,157
Johnson, Lyndon, 117
Jordan, Gennelle, xvi
Jordan, William, 253,261

Kahn, Alfred, 255-59
Kennedy, Edward, 252,255,257-58
Kennedy, John F., 115
Kershaw, Joseph Alexander, 177
Keyes, Lucille, 253,261
Keynes, John M., 29-30, 43-44, 47, 51,
    53,62, 129,137,139,141,144-45,157,
    201-02,205-06, 209,213-15,277-78,282
Kindleberger, Charles, 49
Kinney, Douglas, 158
Kraft, John, 166-67,175-76
Krause, L.B., 9
Kurihara, K.K., 49
Kydland, Finn, 200,207-09,212-14

Laird, William E., xvi
Law, John, 11
Lehman, Ernst, 131
Lerner, Abba P., ii,xv,3,65,79-81,
    101-02,124,125,130-31,133,162,171,
    174,179,188-89, 197-99,205,
    209-12,214-15,217-18,228-29, 232-
    33,237-38,242-46,265-85,290,292,295-
    98
Levine, Michael E., 253,255,261
Levitas, Congressman, 259
Lewis, Naphtalio, 176
Lipsey, R.G., 60,76
Lluch, Constantino, 89,91,103
Lucas, Robert E. Jr., 186,200,204,212-
    13

MacAvoy, Paul W., 261
Macesich, George, xvi
Machlup, Fritz, 58,291
Maier, C.S., 33,53
Maital, Shlomo, 65
Malmud, Bernard, 52
March, James G.,212
Marlin, Matthew, xvi
Marshall, Idelle, xvi
Marx, Karl, 227
Mazek, Warren F., xvi
McGovern, George, 115
Meade, James, 107,124
Mellon, Andrew, 115
Meltzer, A., 175
Meyer, Paul, 158
Miller, James C. III, 254, 261
Miller, William, 244
Minford, Patrick, 158-59
Minsky, Hyman, 52
Mixson, Wayne, xvi
Moerlins, John, xvi
Moss, Milton, 158
Murrell, Peter, 159
Muth, John, 199-202,212

Okun, Arthur, 65,163,175,232-33,239-
    40,242
Olson, Mancur, ii,137-38,293

Pankowski, Mary, xvii
Parkin, Michael, 158
Patinkin, Don, ii,125,228,292,294,298
Perry, George L., 167,176
Phelps, Edmund S., ii,76,179,189,193,204,
    215,294,298
Phillips, A.W.H., 76,290
Pigou, A.C., 65,87,102,228,297
Powell, Alan A., 91,103
Prescott, Edward, 200,207-09,212-14
Pulsifer, Roy, 255,259

Rapping, Leonard A., ii,31,291-92,298
Ricardo, David, 49
Riddell, Craig, 76
Robson, John, 255-56
Rockwood, Charles E., ii,iii,161,176,289,
    295,297-98
Rescher, Nicholas, 102
Redford, Emmette S., 177
Reinhold, Meyer, 176
Roberts, Blaine, 193

Salant, Walter S., 9
Sargent, Thomas, 186,200,204-05,212
Schelling, Thomas, 180,185
Schlichter, Sumner H., 266
Schultze, Charles L., 61,76,276

Schulze, David L., 193
Scitovsky, Tibor, ii,3,290
Seidman, Lawrence, 233
Siebert, Calvin, 167,176
Simon, Herbert, 50,201,213
Sliger, Bernard F., xvi
Slitor, Richard E., 246
Smith, Adam, 227
Snow, John W., 261
Sobel, Irvin, ii,265,289-90

Theil, Henry, 213
Thompson, F.P., 149,159
Throop, Adrian W., 176
Tobin, James, 60,76,233

Wachter, Michael L.,176
Wallace, Neil, 200,204-05,212-14
Wallich, Henry, 162,232,235,240-41,284
Weber, Arnold R., 176
Weintraub, Sidney, ii,65,103,133,171,174,
    231-33,235,240-41,246-47,274,276,284,
    296-98
Whitehead, Donald, 158
Williams, Ross A., 91,103

Zaidi, Mahmood,167,176
Zee, Howell, 158
Zimmerman, Virgil B., 177

SUBJECT INDEX

Administrative Cost
  Wage Price Control and, 170-74
Administered Prices, 269
Aggregate Demand
  Foreign Inflation and, 117
Airline Deregulation Act, 259-60
Ancient Rome
  Wage-Price Controls in, 169-70
Antiinflation Accounting Credit, 224
Argentina, 118-19
Aspirations Gap
  Inflation and, 38-40
Australia, 142,144,168-69,244
Automatic Stabilizers, 144

Balance of Payments
  Equilibrium Model, 108-10
Balanced Budget, 198
Banking School, 49
Banking System
  Stagflation and, 236
Bank Credit
  Inflation and, 41
Bonds
  Stocks and, 30
Boston, 253
Bounded Rationality
  Decision Costs and, 201
Brazil
  Inflation in, 11
Bretton Woods, 31,34,43
British, 119
Britain, 157

Buck Rogers, 197
Budget Shares
  Labor Market Returns and, 93-101
Bureau of Labor Statistics, 173
Buyers Inflation, 271-79
  (see also Demand Inflation)

California, 253
Canada, 116-17,142,144,244
Canadian Dollar Float, 117
Capacity
  Inflation and, 5
Capital Flows
  Currency Depreciation and, 113-14
  Inflation and, 112-14
Capital-Labor Ratio, 100-01,233
Capital-Output Ratio, 233
Carter Administration, 163,231
Cash Balance Effect, 228
Cash Balances
  Inflation and, 129
Central Bank Policy
  Inflation Control and, 180
China, 217
Civil Aeronautics Board
  Barriers to Entry and, 253-54
  Sunset Law for, 255
Class Conflicts
  Inflation and, 143
Class Phenomenon
  Wage Rigidities and, 152-55
Collective Bargaining
  Wage Rigidities and, 153-55

Commercial Banks
  Wage-Price Controls and, 174
Commodity Credit Corporation, 174
Common Market, 114
Consumer Credit
  Inflation and, 51
Corporate Taxes
  Tax Incentive Plan (TIP) and, 235
Cost of Living Adjustment, 273-74
  Inflation Control and, 188-89
Cost of Living Council, 171-72
Cost-Push Inflation, 141-42,219,290
  (see also Inflation)
  Defined, 3
  Discussed, 24-25
  Explained, 5-9
  Monopoly Power and, 141-42
Council of Economic Advisers, 232,276
Countervailing Power, 269
Credit
  Inflation and, 35
Cultural Necessity
  Engle Curve and, 85
Culturally Basic Expenditure, 88-89
Currency Depreciation
  Capital Flows and, 113-14
  Export Demand and, 113-14
Currency School, 49

Decentralized Wage Setting
  Inflation and, 184-86
Deflation
  Early Medieval Period, 11
  Great Depression, 14,16
  India, 11
  Roman Empire, 11
  United States, 11-12,16
Demand
  Utility and, 82-86
Demand for Labor
  Technology and, 97
  Unions and, 96-97
Demand-Pull Inflation
  (see also Inflation)
  Capital Shortage and, 4-5
  Defined, 3
  Discussed, 24-25,290
  Explained, 4-5
  Government Deficits and, 4
  Labor Shortage and, 4
  Record of, 35
Department of Transportation, 254
Deregulation of Airlines, 251-52,254
  Discount Air Fares and, 256-57
  Evidentiary Hearings and, 258
  Load Factors and, 257
  Long Term Strategy for, 256-58
  Monopoly Routes and, 258

Route Realignment and, 258
  Short Term Strategy for, 256-57
Diminishing Marginal Utility
  Probability of, 80-82
Direct Controls
  (see also Wage-Price Controls)
  Usefulness of, 120
Disinflation
  Market Antiinflation Plan (MAP) and, 226
Distributive Efficiency, 79, 101
  Productive Efficiency and, 80
Distributive Shares
  Inflation and, 85-87,291
  Tax Incentive Plan (TIP) and, 237
  Utility of Income and, 80-82
Domestic Inflation
  Trade Balance and, 110-14

Economic Development
  Inflation and, 126
Economic Expansion
  Trade Balance and, 113
Economic Growth, 142
Economic Planning, 35
Eisenhower Administration
  Recession of, 32
  Stabilization Policies of, 45
Employment and Inflation, 32
  Monetarist View of, 36
Employment Policy
  Wage Policy and, 266
Energy Prices, 42,231
Enforcement Problem
  Price-Wage Controls and, 169-70
Engle Curves
  Cultural Necessities and, 85
  Utility and, 85-87
Engle Elasticities, 89
Environmental Protection Agency, 65
Exchange Rates, 41
Exchange Stability
  Marshall-Lerner Condition and, 121-24
Expectational Inflation, 279-82
Expectations, 244
  Inflation and, 36,38,62-63,219-23, 279-82,292
  Inflation 'Rights' and, 67-68
  Stockholm School, 199-200
  Wage-Price Behavior and, 291
Expenditure
  Wealth and, 89
Expenditure Estimates
  Commodity Bundles and, 91-92
Externalities
  Inflation and, 63-65

Factor and Product Markets
  Inflation and, 5-8

Factory Councils, 53
Federal Reserve, 224,233
Federal Trade Commission, 237
Financial Contracts
    Inflation and, 28-29
Fiscal Controls
    Pollution and, 76-77
Fiscal Policy
    Inflation-Unemployment and, 232
    Rational Expectations and, 207-08
Food Prices, 42
Ford Administration, 115,163,171,231
Foreign Inflation
    Aggregate Demand and, 117
Floating Exchange Rates
    Inflation and, 113
France, 148
    Inflation in, 11
    Stabilization Policy of, 45
Free Riders
    Inflation and, 63-65
Frisch Parameter, 89-92
Full Employment
    Stagflation and, 3
Functional Finance, 199-200,209-10,
    265-67,277,280,290
    Rational Expectations and, 203-04,
    210-12

Game Theory, 192-93,213
    Rational Expectations and, 201-03
Germany, 113-14,118-19,142-44,152,157
    Inflation in, 11
Gold Prices, 28-29
Government
    Inflation and, 24-26,220-21
    Money Wages and, 267
Government Budgets
    Inflation and, 129,133
Government Deficits
    Inflation and, 4,35,292
    Rational Expectations and, 203-04
Government Employees
    Tax Incentive Plan (TIP) and, 236
Government Expenditures
    Inflation and, 51
Government Policy
    Inflation Expectations and, 62-63
Gradualism
    Inflation control and, 163-64
Great Britain, 140,148
Gross Business Product, 233,235
Gross Capacity Product, 13-15
Gross National Product, 14-15
    Components, 18
    Per Capita, 14-15
Gross Private Domestic Investment,
    17-18

Growth
    Inflation and, 34-35,47-48
Growth Rates
    Explanation of, 150-52
    Major Countries, 39
    United States, 39-40

Hartford, 260
High-Full Employment, 270-72,290
Human Capital
    Labor Markets and, 95-101
Hungary
    Inflation in, 11
Hyperinflation
    Money Supply and, 145

Implicit Deflator, 14,16
Income
    Purchase Patterns and, 89-92
    Saving and, 90-91
Income Redistribution
    Economic Efficiency and, 79
Incomes Policy, 267,281
    (see also Wage-Price Controls)
Indexation, 188,294
    Inflation and, 130-33
Indexed Loans
    Israel and, 129,294
India
    Deflation and, 11
Indochina, 31
Indulgences, 239
Inflation
    (see also, Demand-Pull, Cost-Push,
    Wage-Push)
    Capital Flows and, 112-14
    Cash Balances and, 129
    Cause of, 275-76
    Class Conflicts and, 143
    Consumer Behavior and, 126-27
    Controversiality of, 137-41
    Cost of Control, 165
    Credit and, 35,51
    Decentralized Wage Setting and,
    184-86
    Definition of, 55-56,128,217,227,275
    Distributional Impact of, 52
    Distributive Shares and, 85-87,291
    Domestic Trade Balance and, 110-14
    Economic Development and, 126
    Expectations and, 62-63,219-23,292
    Externalities and, 63-65
    Financial Contracts and, 28-29
    Floating Exchange Rates and, 113
    Government and, 220-21
    Government Deficits and, 35,292
    Government Expenditures and, 51,129,
    133

Growth and, 34-35,47
Impact of, 244
Income Shares and, 5
Indexation and, 130-33,188
Job Mobility and, 161
Lags and, 57
Minimum Wage and, 58-59
Monetarist View of, 35-36
Monetary Expansion and, 143
Money Supply and, 128,218,234
Necessities and, 92-93
Organization of Petroleum Exporting
   Countries (OPEC) and, 290
Phillips Curve and, 59-60,141
Political Underlay of, 31-35
Price-Wage Rigidity and, 61
Product Quality and, 40-41
Propensity to Import and, 113
Prospects for Control of, 133-34
Protectionism and, 120-21
Rational Expectations and, 140
Recession and, 52,274
Speculation and, 41,217
Static Attribution of, 56-58
Substitution and, 85-87,92-93
Trade Balance and, 293-94
Trade Unions and, 266
Unanticipated, 268
Unemployment and, 24-25,32,45-46,
   59,61,271,290
Union Wage Demands and, 130
U.S. Global Position and, 31-32,291
Wage Behavior and, 219,273
Wage Demands and, 49-50
Wage-Price Controls and, 32,187-91,
   222
Wage-Price Freeze and, 295
Wage Rates and, 266
War and, 34,126
Welfare Effects of, 293
Welfare State and, 130
Inflation as a Tax, 129
Inflation Cause, 218-19
Inflation Control
   Balanced Budget and, 198
   Market Antiinflation Plan and, 223-28,
      296-97
   Monetary and Fiscal Policy and, 295
   Prospects of, 27-29
   Rational Expectations and, 295
   Tax Incentive Plan and, 222-23,
      296-97
Inflation in Customer Countries
   Trade Balance and, 114-18
Inflation Expectations
   Monetary Policy and, 180-82
Inflation Record
   Brazil, 11

Continental U.S. Inflation, 11
   Exchange Rates and, 41
   Food, Energy and, 42
   France and, 11,148
   Germany and, 192-93
   Hungary, 11
   Israel, 125-27,273-74,294
   Korean War, 14,16,31
   Major Countries, 33
   United States, 145-48,279
   Vietnam War, 31
Inflation 'Rights,' 65-70
   Expectations and, 67-68
   Product Shortages and, 69
Inflation-Unemployment,161-62,219,
   232,278,289-90
   Fiscal Policy and, 289
   Historical Record of, 14,16
   Monetarists and, 289
Inflationary Gap, 57
Interest
   Profit and, 22-24
Interest Rates
   Real, 27-28
Internal Revenue Service, 172,235
Intrastate Airlines, 253
Iran
   Inflation in, 36-37
Invisible Industries
   Direct Controls and, 167-68
Israel, 125-34,273-74
   Indexation in, 294
Italy, 118-19

J-Curve, 113-14
Japan, 113-14,142-44,152
Jawboning, 221-22
Job Mobility
   Inflation and, 161
Johnson Administration, 117
Justice Department, 172

Kennedy-Johnson Administration, 174
   Wage Controls during, 167-68
Kennedy Guidelines, 277
Keynesianism
   Rational Expectations and, 202
Keynesian Theory
   Stagflation and, 141-42
   Subsistence Economies and, 144
Korean War, 116
   Inflation during, 31

Labor Market Conditions
   Human Capital and, 95-101
Labor Shortage
   Inflation and, 4

Lags
    Inflation Process and, 57
Learning Costs
    Rational Expectations and, 201
Lehman Committee, 131
Lexicographical Ordering, 102
Lexicographical Utility Function,
    82-86
Logic of Collective Action, 150-52
Los Angeles, 253
Low-Full Employment, 270-72,290

Macroeconomic Theory
    Incompleteness of, 138-39
    Stagflation and, 139-40
Management
    Union Wage Demands and, 269
Marginal Budget Shares
    Income and, 90
Marginal Utility
    Measurability of, 87-92
Marginal Utility of Income
    Saving and, 87
Market Antiinflation Plan (MAP),
    174,211-12,223-28,232-33,237-40,
    268,282,290,296
    Economic Growth and, 239
    Enforcement of, 238
Market Restructuring and, 163-64
Mark-up Inflation, 267
Marshall-Lerner Condition, 115
    Exchange Stability and, 121-24
Measurability of Utility, 87-92
Middle Ages, 98
Military Expenditures
    Unemployment and, 21-22
Minimum Wage
    Inflation Process and, 58-59
    Phillips Curve and, 154
    Unemployment and, 291
Monetarist
    Explanation of Inflation, 35-36,227
    Inflation-Unemployment and, 289
    Natural Rate of Unemployment and,
    145
    Sellers Inflation and, 273-74
Monetary and Fiscal Policy, 269
    Direct Controls and, 168-69
    Inflation Control and, 161-65,292,
    295
    Sellers Inflation and, 274
    Unemployment and, 274-75
    Wage Rigidities and, 154-55
Monetary Expansion
    Inflation and, 143
Monetary Policy
    Effectiveness of, 180
    Expectations and, 62-63

Inflation-Unemployment and, 232
    Rational Expectations and, 203-06
    Stagflation and, 141-42
    Unemployment and, 234
Money Supply, 24-26
    Determinants of, 36
    Inflation and, 128,218
    Prices and, 234
    Rule for Change of, 198
Money Wages
    Business Costs and, 236
Monopoly Power
    Cost-Push Inflation and, 141-42
    Price Rigidities and, 154-55
    Wage Policy and, 154

Nash Equilibrium, 183
Natural Rate of Unemployment, 140,
    164-65,188,213-14,281
    Monetarists and, 145
Necessities
    Inflation and, 92-93
Necessities Inflation
    Impact of, 93
Necessities v Luxuries
    Classical View of, 94-95
    Neoclassical View of, 95-96
Needs v Wants, 102
    Hierarchy of, 82-87
Net Interest, 19-20
New Deal, 14
New Zealand, 142,144
Nixon Administration, 115,231
    Wage-Price Controls of, 171-73
    Wage-Price Freeze, 167-68
Nonsynchronous Wage Setting
    Inflation and, 189-91
National Recovery Act, 14,166

Office of Economic Preparedness, 172
Office of Price Administration, 173-74
Okun's Law, 163
Organization of Petroleum Exporting
    Countries (OPEC), 114-15,130,231
    Inflation and, 290

Pareto-Optimum, 137
Phillips Curve, 23,46-47,70,163-64,
    214,234,245,270-71,291,295
    Inflation and, 59-60,141
    Minimum Wages and, 154
    Rational Expectations and, 204
    Unemployment Compensation and, 211
    Wage Rigidity and, 154-55
Pigouvian Taxes
    Inflation Control and, 65-70,297
Pollution Control, 63-64
    Fees for, 137

Populist Movement, 148
Post-War Inflation
    Cause of, 276
Price Behavior
    Rational Expectations and, 203
Price Competition
    Regulated Industries and, 253
Price Rigidities, 155-57
    Monopoly Power and, 155-56
Price-Wage Controls
    (see Wage-Price Controls)
Price-Wage Equations, 37-38
Price and Wage Rigidity
    Inflation and, 61
Prisoners' Dilemma
    Inflation and, 63-65
Product Demand, 162-63
Productivity
    Inflation Control and, 165
Productivity Change, 234,237
Productivity Improvement
    Tax Incentive Plan (TIP) and, 235
Product Quality
    Inflation and, 40-41
Production Technique
    Employment and, 99-100
Productive Efficiency
    Distributive Efficiency and, 80
Profits, 19-20
Profit and Interest, 22-24
    Employment and, 28-29
Propensity to Import
    Inflation and, 113
Providence, Rhode Island, 260
Purchase Patterns
    Income and, 89-92

Rational Expectations, 189,212-13
    Economic Policy and, 203
    Functional Finance and, 203-04,
    209-11
    Fiscal Policy and, 207-08
    Game Theory and, 201-03
    Government Deficits and, 203-04
    Inflation and, 140,199-209,295
    Keynesian Model and, 202
    Monetary Policy and, 203-06
    Natural Rate of Unemployment and,
    204
    Policy Rules and, 208-09
    Price Behavior and, 203
    Rule for Monetary Policy and, 203-04
Ration 'Bons,' 241-43,245
Ration Division
    Office of Price Administration,
    173-74
Reconstruction Finance Corporation,
    174

Regulatory Reform
    Savings of, 251-52
Repressed Inflation, 170
Roman Empire
    Deflation and, 11
Recession
    Inflation and, 52
Relative Prices
    Trade Balance and, 108-09
Reserve Army of the Unemployed, 228
Rules for Policy
    Rational Expectations and, 208-09

Saving
    Income and, 90-91
    Marginal Utility of Income and,
    87
Say's Law, 270
Scandinavia
    Wage Drift in, 8-9
Scandinavian Countries, 116
Sellers Inflation, 271-79
    (see also Cost-Push Inflation)
    Administered Prices and, 276
    Competitive Prices and, 276
Shortages
    Wage-Price Controls and, 69,170
Slavery, 239-40
Snob Appeal, 98
Soviet Union
    Price-Wage Controls in, 170
Speculation
    Inflation and, 41,217
Speculative Collapse
    Conditions for, 30
Speculative Profit
    Rational Expectations and, 200-01
Spending
    Under Capitalism, 92-93
Stagflation, 231-32,234,246,266,293
    Banking System and, 236
    Keynesian Theory and, 141-42
    Macroeconomic Theory and, 139-40
    Monetary Theory and, 141-42
    Tax Incentive Plan (TIP) and, 243
    Trade Balance and, 115-16
    Trade Unions and, 234-35
Stabilization Policy
    France, 45
    Post-War, 47-48
Steering Wheel of Economics, 197-98,
    209-10
Stockholm School, 199-200
Stocks and Bonds, 30
Structure of Direct Controls,
    Control Breakdown and, 168
Subsistence Economies
    Keynesian Theory and, 144

Substitution
    Inflation and, 92-93
Substitution Effect
    Inflation and, 85-87
Supply of Labor, 162-63
Suppressed Inflation
    World War II and, 14,16
Switzerland, 118-19
Synchronous Wage Setting
    Inflation and, 180-89

Tax Cut
    Stagflation and, 277
Tax Incentive Plan (TIP), 174,222-23,
    232-40,284,290,296-97
Technology
    Demand for Labor and, 97
Texas, 253
Trade Balance
    Domestic Inflation and, 110-14
    Economic Expansion and, 113
    Inflation in Customer Countries and,
    116-18,293-94
    Inflation in Supplier Countries and,
    114-16,293-94
    National Income and, 108-09
    Relative Prices and, 108-09
    Stagflation and, 115-16
Trade Union Behavior
    Inflation and, 180-83,266

Unanticipated Inflation, 268
Unemployment
    Inflation and, 24-25,59,61,271,290
    Minimum Wages and, 291
    Monetary Policy and, 234
    Natural Rate of, 3,164-65
    Origin of Term, 149
    Rate, 17-18
    Record, 270-71
    Wage Inflation and, 268
    Welfare Cost of, 214
Unemployment Compensation
    Phillips Curve and, 211
Unions
    Demand for Labor and, 96-97
    Stagflation and, 234-35
Union Wage Demands
    Inflation and, 130
United Kingdom, 114,142,244
U.S. Conciliation Service, 173
Utility
    Engle Curves and, 85-87
    Wealth and, 89
    Function, 88

Velocity of Money, 233
Vicious Cycle of Inflation, 219-21

Vietnam War, 146
    Inflation during, 31
Visible Industries
    Direct Controls and, 167-68

Wage Demands
    Inflation and, 49-50
Wage Drift, 8-9
Wage Formula
    Non-Inflationary, 24
Wage Guidelines, 267
    (see also Incomes Policy, Wage-Price
    Controls)
Wage Increase Permit Plan (WIPP),
    237,240-41,290
Wage Inflation
    Unemployment and, 268
Wage Policy
    Employment Policy and, 266
Wage-Price Behavior
    Expectations and, 291
Wage-Price Controls, 161-62,222,
    277-78
    Administrative Cost of, 170-74
    Decontrol Problems of, 77-78
    Effective Duration of, 168-69
    Effectiveness of, 165-68,295
    Enforcement of, 169-70
    Inflation Control and, 32,179,187-91
    Monetary and Fiscal Policy and,
    168-69,295
    Nixon Administration and, 171-73
    Productivity and, 267
    Relative Prices and, 69
    Roman Period, 169-70
    Shortages and, 69,170
    Soviet Union and, 170
    World War I and, 49, 169
    World War II and, 49,169,172-74
Wage-Price Freeze
    Effect of, 28
Wage-Price Rigidities
    Inflation and, 277-78
Wage Rates
    Concentrated Industries and, 97-99
    Inflation and, 266
Wage Response Function, 71
Wage Rigidities, 152-55
    Monetary and Fiscal Policy and,
    154-55
    Phillips Curve and, 154-55
Wage Share Constant, 233
Wage Stabilization Plan, 268
War
    Deficit Spending and, 145
    Inflation and, 34,126
War Labor Board, 172-73
Wealth and Expenditure, 89

Welfare Cost of Unemployment, 214
Welfare Effects of Inflation, 293
Welfare State
    Inflation and, 130
Widow's Cruse Effect, 29
Whip Inflation Now (WIN) Program 115,171

Worker Mobility
    Inflation Control and, 165
World Inflation
    Domestic Adjustment to, 118-19
World War I, 49,169,172-74
World War II, 140,142,265-66

ABOUT THE EDITORS

James H. Gapinski, Professor of Economics at Florida State University, received his Ph.D. from the State University of New York at Buffalo in 1971. After teaching for several years at Florida State, he was selected as a Brookings Economic Policy Fellow and served in that capacity with the U.S. Department of Commerce in Washington until 1977. Returning to the University, he received a Developing Scholar Award. An active researcher, Dr. Gapinski has published in leading journals such as the *American Economic Review*, the *International Economic Review*, the *Journal of Political Economy*, and the *Review of Economics and Statistics*. Presently he is writing a graduate text entitled *Macroeconomics: Statics, Dynamics, and Policy* for the McGraw-Hill Book Company. Dr. Gapinski, who holds a Phi Beta Kappa key, is a member of the *Southern Economic Journal* editorial board.

Charles E. Rockwood is Professor of Economics at Florida State University. He received the M.B.A. degree from Western Reserve University in 1957 and the Ph.D. degree from Indiana University in 1963. In addition to his academic credentials, Dr. Rockwood has had experience in government, serving most recently as Senior Staff Advisor (Economics) for the National Marine Fisheries Service of the U.S. Department of Commerce in Washington. His research interests include macro-economic theory, problems of inflation, marine resource economics, and social control of business. Dr. Rockwood has written a previous

book on inflation, *National Incomes Policy for Inflation Control*
published in 1970.   He also has written numerous articles
including "National Wage Fixing Arrangements in Australia,"
"What's Wrong with the Wage Guideposts," "National Incomes
Policy in Non-Wage Inflation Situations," and "The Need for
Basic Reform in Federal Income Tax Rates."

About the Contributors

Elizabeth E. Bailey is a member of the Civil Aeronautics Board. She was appointed to that position by President Carter in 1977 and as Commissioner has played an instrumental role in deregulating the U.S. airline industry. A recipient of the Ph.D. from Princeton University in 1972, she was Head of the Economics Research Department of Bell Laboratories and Adjunct Associate Professor of Economics at New York University. Dr. Bailey has also found time to serve on the editorial boards of the *American Economic Review* and the *Journal of Industrial Economics* as well as on the Board of Trustees of Princeton University. Her publications include *Economic Theory of Regulatory Constraint* and "Peak Load Pricing Under Regulatory Constraint," *Journal of Political Economy.* She also co-authored "Regulatory Commission Behavior: Myopic versus Forward Looking," *Economic Inquiry.*

William J. Baumol is Joseph Douglas Green Professor of Economics at Princeton University and Professor of Economics at New York University. He received his Ph.D. from the University of London in 1949. Dr. Baumol has served as the editorial boards of the *American Economic Review*, the *Journal of Economic Literature*, and *Management Science* and as Vice President of the American Economic Association, Vice President of the American Association of University Professors, President of the Eastern Economic Association, President of the Associa-

313

tion of the Environmental and Resource Economists, and currently as President-Elect of the American Economic Association. A member of the American Academy of Arts and Sciences, Professor Baumol has received honorary doctorates from the Stockholm School of Economics, Knox College, and the University of Basel. He holds the John R. Commons Award along with the Townsend Harris Medal. Dr. Baumol's extensive list of publications include *Economic Theory and Operations Analysis*, *Economic Dynamics*, *Portfolio Theory: The Selection of Asset Combinations*, *Performing Arts: The Economic Dilemma*, and numerous journal articles.

Kenneth E. Boulding is Distinguished Professor of Economics at the University of Colorado, Boulder. Born in Liverpool, England, he studied economics at Oxford University graduating in 1939. He has held positions as Professor of Economics at the University of Michigan, Iowa State University, and Fisk University. A recipient of numerous honorary degrees from American universities and a member of the National Academy of Sciences, Professor Boulding has been President of the American Economic Association, the International Peace Research Society, and the International Studies Association. Among his many publications are *Economic Analysis, A Study in the Ethics of Organization, The Image, Economics as a Science, Conflict and Defense, The Meaning of the Twentieth Century, Beyond Economics*, and *The Economy of Love and Fear*.

Martin Bronfenbrenner, who received his Ph.D. from the University of Chicago in 1939, is Kenan Professor of Economics at Duke University, a position which he has held since 1971. Dr. Bronfenbrenner has a diverse professional background. He has been affiliated with the U.S. Treasury and with the Federal Reserve Banks of Chicago and San Francisco. He also has taught at several universities of distinction including Carnegie-Mellon, Minnesota, Michigan State, and Wisconsin at Madison. During 1979 Dr. Bronfenbrenner was President of the Southern Economic Association; earlier he served as Vice President of the American Economic Association and of the Southern Economic Association. His memberships on editorial boards include the *American Economic Review*, the *Journal of Economic Literature*, and the *Southern Economic Journal*. A member of Phi Beta Kappa, Professor Bronfenbrenner is very widely published.

E. Ray Canterbery received the doctorate from Washington University, St. Louis, in 1966. From 1965 to 1969 he held the position of Assistant Professor at the University of Maryland and since then has been on the faculty of Florida State University, where he is now Professor of Economics. A recipient of grants from the Rockefeller Foundation, the National Science Foundation, the Agency for International Development, the Atomic Energy Commission, and the Bureau of Mines among others, Dr. Canterbery has written several books including *The Making of Economics*, and *Economics on a New Frontier*. His numerous journal publications include articles in the *American Economic Review*, the *Quarterly Journal of Economics*, and *Challenge*. A recent paper "A Vita Theory of the Personal Income Distribution" appears in the *Southern Economic Journal*.

David C. Colander currently is Visiting Assistant Professor of Economics at the University of Miami. Previously he had been affiliated with the American Enterprise Institute and, as a visiting scholar, with Nuffield College, Oxford University. He has taught at Columbia University and Vassar College and served as a Brookings Economic Policy Fellow with the U. S. General Accounting Office in Washington, and remains a consultant on tax-based policies for that agency. Professor Colander received the Ph.D. from Columbia University in 1976. His publications include the co-authored works "Towards a New Micro-Macro Synthesis," *Journal of Economic Issues* and "On Price Flexibility," *Journal of Economics*. He also published "Inflation and Inequality: Comments," *Journal of Economic Issues* and edited *Solutions to Inflation: A Reader*, Harcourt Brace Jovanovich, Inc.

Abba P. Lerner currently is Professor of Economics and Policy Sciences at Florida State University. Among his previous professorships are ones at Roosevelt University, Michigan State University, and the University of California, Berkeley. He also was Distinguished Professor of Economics at Queens College in New York. Professor Lerner was awarded the Ph.D. from the London School of Economics in 1943. He has received many honors, including being named Distinguished Fellow of the American Economic Association in 1966. He was elected Vice President of the American Economic Association in 1963. In 1970 he earned the designation of Honorary Fellow by the

London School of Economics, and in 1971 he became a Fellow of the American Academy of Arts and Sciences. In 1978 he was awarded an honorary doctorate by Northwestern University. Currently Dr. Lerner is a member of the prestigious National Academy of Sciences, a position which he has held since 1974. In addition, he serves as President of the Atlantic Economic Society and has been nominated to become Vice President of the Western Economic Association in 1980 and President in 1982. As the dedication page of this volume indicates, Dr. Lerner has given the profession an especially rich collection of lasting contributions.

Mancur Olson is Professor of Economics at the University of Maryland. He has held positions as Deputy Assistant Secretary in the Department of Health, Education and Welfare, as consultant to the Rand Corporation, and as an economist with Resources for the Future. He taught at Princeton University as Lecturer and Assistant Professor, and during the 1976 Presidential campaign served as an economic adviser to Jimmy Carter. His academic training includes an M.A. degree from Oxford University in 1960 and a Ph.D. degree from Harvard University in 1963. Dr. Olson, a Rhodes Scholar, has written *The Economics of the Wartime Shortage* and *The Logic of Collective Action*. His many published articles include "Efficient Production of External Economies," "On Getting Really Full Employment Without Inflation," and "Official Liability and Its Less Legalistic Alternatives."

Don Patinkin is Professor of Economics at the Hebrew University of Jerusalem, a position which he has held since 1949. His previous appointments include a Ford Foundation Visiting Research Professorship at the University of Chicago, Associate Professor at the University of Illinois, and Assistant Professor at the University of Chicago. He earned his doctorate from the University of Chicago in 1947. Dr. Patinkin has published several books and many articles. His volume *Money, Interest, and Prices* is considered a classic in the field of macroeconomics. Other books include *The Israel Economy: The First Decade* and *Studies in Monetary Economics*. Among his most recent journal articles are "The Collected Writings of John Maynard Keynes: From the *Tract* to the *General Theory*," *Economic Journal*; "Keynes and Econometrics: On the Interaction between the Macroeconomic Revolutions of the Interwar Period," *Econo-*

metrica; and "A Study of Keynes' Theory of Effective Demand,"
Economic Inquiry.

Edmund S. Phelps is Professor of Economics at New York
University. He has also taught at Columbia University and the
University of Pennsylvania, and has served on the Brookings
Panel on Economic Activity. Professor Phelps received his Ph.D.
from Yale University in 1959. Four years later he published a
landmark article on the concept of putty-clay capital. Entitled
"Substitution, Fixed Proportions, Growth and Distribution," this
International Economic Review paper stimulated much research
on heterogeneous capital. Another notable effort is his edited
volume *Microeconomic Foundations of Employment and Inflation.* His most recent contributions include "Inflation Planning
Reconsidered," *Economica* and "Transnational Effects of Fiscal
Shocks in a Two-Country Model of Dynamic Equilibrium," *Journal of Monetary Economics.* Dr. Phelps was a member of the
Executive Committee of the American Economic Association
from 1976 to 1978.

Leonard A. Rapping, who received his Ph.D. from the
University of Chicago in 1960, is Professor of Economics at the
University of Massachusetts, Amherst. He has held that position
since 1973. Previously Dr. Rapping was associated with Carnegie-Mellon University and the Rand Corporation. A former
member of the *American Economic Review* editorial board, he
has published numerous works including two co-authored pieces
which incisively consider the theoretical foundation of the
Phillips curve. These papers are "Real Wages, Employment, and
Inflation" in the *Journal of Political Economy* and "Price Expectations and the Phillips Curve," in the *American Economic
Review.* A more recent joint venture in the *Journal of Political
Economy* is "Unemployment in the Great Depression: Is There a
Full Explanation?"

Tibor Scitovsky earned a doctorate from the University of
Budapest in 1932 and a Master's degree from the University of
London in 1938. Currently Professor of Economics at the
University of California, Santa Cruz, Dr. Scitovsky has held the
posts of Eberle Professor of Economics at Stanford University
and J. W. Heinz Professor of Economic Development at Yale
University. A past vice president of the American Economic
Association and a former member of the editorial board of the

Journal of Economic Literature, Dr. Scitovsky was designated a Fellow by the American Academy of Arts and Sciences and a Distinguished Fellow by the American Economic Association. His books include *Welfare and Competition, Papers on Welfare and Growth,* and *Money and Balance of Payments.* Three recent articles are "Market Power and Inflation," *Economica;* "Asymmetries in Economics," *Scottish Journal of Political Economy;* and "Can Changing Consumer's Tastes Save Resources?" *Journal of Cultural Economics.*

Irvin Sobel, Professor of Economics and past department chairman at Florida State University, has held numerous positions of distinction, among them Professor of Economics at Washington University, Ford Foundation Fellow, Fulbright Lectureship, Visiting Professor at the University of Rome, and Katzen Distinguished American Scholar at Hebrew University. In addition to his professorial duties, he has been a consultant for the U.S. Department of Labor and the White House Conference on Equal Employment Opportunity. Professor Sobel earned his Ph.D. from the University of Chicago in 1951. He has published frequently in labor economics and economic history. His most recent paper is "Adam Smith: What Kind of Institutionalist Was He?" *Journal of Economic Issues.* His books include *The Shortage of Skilled and Technical Workers* (co-authored) and *Manpower and the Growth of the Israeli Economy.*

Sidney Weintraub is Professor of Economics at the University of Pennsylvania and an editor of the *Journal of Post-Keynesian Economics.* Previously he taught at St. Johns University in New York and served as an economist for the U.S. Treasury Department. He studied at the London School of Economics and received his Ph.D. from New York University in 1941. Dr. Weintraub is the author of several books including *Price Theory, Theory of Income Distribution, General Theory of Price Levels,* and *Keynes and the Monetarist.* His interest in tax-based incomes policy is reflected in his recent volume *Capitalism's Inflation and Unemployment Crisis: Beyond Monetarism and Keynesianism* and in his Frank M. Engle Lecture "TIP: A Tax-Based Incomes Policy to Stop Stagflation." Dr. Weintraub also recently completed *Keynes, Keynesians, and Monetarists.*